An Alternative Internet

An Alternative Internet

Chris Atton

Edinburgh University Press

© Chris Atton, 2004

Edinburgh University Press Ltd
22 George Square, Edinburgh

Typeset in Ehrhardt
by Hewer Text Ltd, Edinburgh, and
printed and bound in Spain by
GraphyCems

A CIP record for this book is available from the British Library

ISBN 0 7486 1769 8 (hardback)
ISBN 0 7486 1770 1 (paperback)

The right of Chris Atton
to be identified as author of this work
has been asserted in accordance with
the Copyright, Designs and Patents Act 1988.

Contents

Acknowledgements

The opening sections of Chapter 1 have appeared in earlier versions as parts of articles published in the *Journal of Mundane Behavior* and *Southern Review*. Parts of Chapter 2 have appeared in earlier versions as articles in *Ethical Space* and *Social Movement Studies* and in a book chapter for *Studies in Terrorism: Media Scholarship and the Enigma of Terror* (edited by Naren Chitty, Ramona R. Rush and Mehdi Semati). Throughout the writing of this book I have benefited greatly from the generous advice of James Hamilton, Bob Franklin, Mark Deuze, Michael Bromley, Howard Tumber, David Hesmondhalgh and Jason Toynbee. In particular I thank Will Lawson for his insightful comments on how the book might be structured and its place in my work as a whole. I owe much to my parents and, as ever, to Kate, Daniel and Jacob.

Introduction

This book is a study of an 'alternative Internet'. Through a sequence of case studies it explores the use of the Internet as a set of information and communication technologies (ICTs) produced by a range of individuals, groups and organisations whose philosophies and practices I have chosen to term 'alternative'. By this I mean a range of media projects, interventions and networks that work against, or seek to develop different forms of, the dominant, expected (and broadly accepted) ways of 'doing' media. These projects might be explicitly political in intent, such as the media activism of radical, 'amateur' journalists who make up the Indymedia network of Independent Media Centres (IMCs). They might be political in less progressive ways, such as the use of the World Wide Web by political formations on the far right. Some projects deliberately challenge the economic status quo and by so doing seek to overturn received notions of property ownership. This is particularly notable in the anti-copyright and open software movements, where philosophies of communitarianism and usufruct offer alternatives to the political economies of copyright ownership and intellectual property rights. These issues have come to popular attention through the development of file-sharing and peer-to-peer programs such as Napster and Gnutella. The philosophy and practice of the open software and open source movements has led to new ways of thinking about what it means to be a creator. Similarly, the availability of relatively cheap broadcasting technology via the Internet has seen a proliferation of non-professional radio or radio-like projects, which are often used as spaces for experimentation in both the form and content of programmes. These tend to be run by people who are fans first and broadcasters second, whose enthusiasm displaces the dominant profit-driven model of broadcasting.

Already we see that such studies must take us away from an essentialised notion of the Internet. They invite us to consider the Internet as existing in a complex of features and pressures which are at once technological, historical, social, cultural, economic and political. It is tempting – and some researchers and commentators have tried this – to consider the Internet as uni-dimensional. Some might consider it as the study of a recent history of technological arrangements that have greatly expanded what it means to talk about 'the media'. We might, as many have done, consider it as a process through which identity and social relations have been so transformed as to constitute an entirely distinct form of space, a cyberspace populated by 'cyborgs' and 'virtual subjects'. It has been construed by many commentators, particularly journalists, as an economic space that has extended the boundaries and opportunities for wealth creation (the rise of the dot.com companies and online consumption). We might view it as a struggle for a 'new' democratic space, fought over by those wishing to regulate practices occurring there (national and international legislative bodies and multi-national corporations) and by those who consider it as a democratic frontier, a 'digital commons' that must be protected against the predations and limits set on it by the state and its agents. Depending on which side you are on in this struggle, the Internet is either economic opportunity or social utopia – it is rarely conceived as both.

What each of these perspectives risk is the separation of the Internet from its complex, proximate features. This is to essentialise the Internet, whether as political or technological fix (for democracy, for economic downturn), social revolution or social development, or creative or cultural utopia. As in any social-scientific study we need to attend to all these features taken together, the better to understand their relatedness, their contradictions and the richness of the object of study. At the same time we need to understand the Internet in history and in particular in historical relation to the media technologies, products, processes and relations that preceded it and still exist alongside it. As Roger Silverstone has noted, many of the characteristics we consider as unique to the Internet are not new at all: 'digital convergence; many-to-many communication; interactivity; globalisation; virtuality, are arguably, with the possible exception of the specifically technical, not new at all' (Silverstone 1999: 11). We may find these characteristics in modes of communication that precede the Internet: in face-to face communication (which is interactive) and in television and radio (which is globalised and 'virtual'). We must therefore take care not to lionise the Internet as wholly new, nor must we be seduced by its apparent possibilities. Dunaway (2000) argues that it is not enough to identify these characteristics singly; it is in their combination through Internet technology that they suggest transformed ways of communication. For him, the digitisation of sound, when transmitted via the Internet, enables a local broadcaster to 'relocalise' their material, connecting with a global audience which 'can unify small-group interests' (Dunaway 2000: 24). It is doubtful, however, whether such an example on its own justifies his claim that 'the digitisation of sound has opened up a vast range of postmodern possibilities' (2000: 23), whatever we are to understand by 'postmodern' in this context. Yet the distribution and reworking of digitised sound – through peer-to-peer networks – has had implications for creative and economic practices of the maintenance and development of popular culture, as we have briefly noted (and as we shall examine in detail in Chapter 4).

Perhaps it is this emphasis on the network – or, more precisely, what Mark Poster has termed 'a machine apparatus that is networked' (Poster 1999: 15) – that, when combined with other characteristics of the Internet, argues for its uniqueness, at the same time as it connects it with antecedent technologies. Combining a form of many-to-many communication with the 'simultaneous reception, alteration and redistribution of cultural objects' across this network frees both the subject (creator, producer, audience, 'agent') 'from the territorialized spatial relations of modernity' (Poster 1999: 15). It is not simply the capacity of the Internet to globalise the mode of many-to-many communication, it is to consider the place of the subject in a machinic network that enables the creation and recreation of cultural objects through this mechanism. The potential of the Internet thus lies in the capacity of the subject to go beyond the confines of the established few-to-many modes of communication (newspapers, radio, television) and to realise both itself and the cultural objects it encounters through this network. Opportunities thus arise for the 'agent who shapes, controls, and transforms the world of objects' (1999: 18). For Poster this is a powerful form of postmodern communication and suggests a radical transformation of subcultural activity.

The study of subcultures, understood generally, might be said to be the focus of the present book. That is, the notion of a subculture as classically taken as a movement that is at once in opposition to aspects of a dominant culture, is oppressed or marginalised by it and yet is related to it structurally and historically (Hebdige 1979). To study a subculture is to study a transgressive or oppositional cultural formation in respect of its relations with (and within) a dominant culture, a culture from which the subculture proceeds historically and yet is in tension with it. Poster suggests a liberatory impulse at work in the capabilities of subcultural agents as transformed through Internet practices. In observing that the creation of subcultural objects 'emerge in relation to mass cultural objects' he emphasises their marginality in the dominant culture when the means of production and distribution remain determined by dominant, few-to-many modes of transmission. The pirate radio station, the independent record label, the fanzine have all attempted to produce and circulate their cultural objects, yet have remained constrained by access to technology, to capital and to audiences. The economies of scale, to take just one example, have often not been available to such producers, resulting (in the case of fanzines or alternative newspapers) in small-circulation publications whose economic base has been precarious. Whilst many alternative media projects have taken advantage of economic and technological shortcuts (micro-broadcasting makes use of relatively cheap, low-power transmitters, and fanzine producers have used the photocopier as a substitute for professional printing), such attempts have done little to break with this history of marginality. As we already know (Atton 2002a), the history of such alternative media is replete with marginality: economic, cultural and political. The Internet does not, of course, erase such barriers: access to technology is far from evenly distributed and is most often a function of low capital; we must not celebrate the Internet as a panacea for marginality. Throughout this book, however, we encounter examples of media projects that have sought to exceed the limits of marginality through the Internet. This is not simply about economies of scale or even the mass mobilisation of a radical political movement. It is not merely to do with the Internet as a somehow cheaper and faster mode of communication. It is, as Poster argues, to do with the creation, production and dissemination of cultural objects in a machinic network that allows for their reworking. This is where we return to notions of many-to-many communication and interactivity. For, when taken with the placing of the subject and of cultural objects within the machinic network, these modes of communication make possible the recreation of those cultural objects across a globalised space. To this extent, the Internet, by contrast with few-to-many modes of communication, offers an underdetermined space in which both subject and object may be recreated 'as multiple and diffuse' (Poster 1999: 15). The Internet is not simply a more efficient way of maintaining subcultural activity, it is potentially a space for its creation and recreation on a global scale: 'it remains an invitation to a new imaginary' (1999: 17).

SUMMARY OF THE BOOK

In this spirit this book will explore through a set of case studies various aspects of this 'new imaginary'. It will do so, however, with a close eye on the histories of the various cultural, technological, economic and political formations that inform it – what follows, as I have already stressed, will not celebrate the Internet. Nor does it intend to find only benign and original impulses at work. To do so would be to be uncritical, ahistorical and essentialist. Indeed, much of what follows emphasises not a rupture with the past but a continuation, at times a transformation. At times it finds alternative Internet practices to be far less distinct from existing practices of alternative communication and creativity than we might assume. If anything the conclusion arrived at is muted, perhaps even sceptical. This is as it should be; in locating and elaborating an object of study as diffuse as 'an alternative Internet' we cannot hope for completeness. This book must of necessity have focus, and focus means limits. Any claims made for the cases examined must not be taken as representing a totality of an alternative Internet (whatever that is). And in locating and elaborating the study within its necessary contexts of other communication technologies, social relations, cultural production and political economies we not only avoid essentialism, we render its uniqueness problematic.

Chapter 1 explores in detail what I mean by 'alternative media' and also explores how we might conceptualise and identify appropriate methodologies for studying the Internet. Generally the book takes a cultural studies approach to the Internet and to the various media projects under scrutiny in the chapters that follow. The characteristics and forces that underlie all the subsequent case studies are examined here. These include economic and cultural dimensions of globalisation, as well as the legal constraints on communication and freedom of expression. The chapter closes with a discussion of the nature and purpose of the social movements that have arisen to challenge these forces as they are played out on the Internet, and introduces topics such as electronic civil disobedience, and communitarian and libertarian approaches to electronic intellectual property that will be explored in later chapters.

The following two chapters examine two very different forms of media production, both of which have developed within social movement activity. Chapter 2 explores the online journalism of the anti-capitalist movement, in particular that produced under the global media network of Independent Media Centres (Indymedia). This is understood as a radical form of public journalism through which egalitarian modes of address and access to the media produce a journalism that is intimately involved with global struggles against corporate governance. The discourse of far-right media such as that produced by the British National Party (BNP) offers a counterweight to the radical liberalism of Indymedia and is analysed in Chapter 3.

The study of Indymedia examines how grassroots political activism has, through the globalising possibilities of the Internet, enabled the spread of new social and political practices and their integration into other, local struggles. Its focus is on the 'civic journalism' that such practices have developed. Beginning with the Zapatistas' dialogical politics, a strategy publicised through the Internet and one which has been incorporated into many contemporary protest movements, the chapter looks at the horizontal, dialogical methods that inform many of the radical journalism projects on the Internet. It focuses on media projects where 'ordinary people' become reporters of their own lives and struggles such as the Indymedia network, described by one commentator as 'to date the pinnacle model of citizen participation in the media'. The egalitarian ideals of such projects as Indymedia have led to sharing of media platforms by activists and movement intellectuals alike, where the aim is to erode intellectual elitism and division.

The Internet offers the same publicity and access to individuals and groups interested in social responsibility and 'progressive' politics as it offers to what John Downing has termed 'repressive radical media': the media practices of nationalism, fascism, the religious right. Chapter 3 explores how technological and cultural resources are being deployed by the far right, in particular paying attention to how these 'repressive' media are being reconstructed by their producers as forms of progressive politics. The focus of the chapter is an examination of the discourse of the BNP's web site. It explores the site as a form of alternative media, focusing on how it involves members and supporters in its discursive construction of racism, finding that the BNP's site is far from the more open, non-hierarchical practices of 'progressive' alternative media. It reminds us that 'alternative media' need not solely be concerned with struggles for social justice and the liberation of the oppressed. The repressive media of the far right, however, share aspects of their discourse with that of progressive media such as Indymedia. Notions such as post-colonialism, repression and multiculturalism recur throughout both. In the case of the far right these terms are turned on their heads and employed to represent the constituencies of the far right as victims of repression themselves.

The second half of the book moves from politics and the representation of social movements to the study of popular cultural activity on the Internet. The focus on amateur, non-professional media producers is illuminated through a set of studies that examine how audiences for cultural products may become media critics and commentators on those products and thus become creators in their own right. Whether in music file-sharing, radio broadcasting or the writing of fanzines, the amateur media producer is intimately involved in dominant cultural practices, at the same time as they transform those practices through their own 'autonomous' media.

Amongst radical creators and producers the Internet is being employed to foster new forms of social authorship. Known variously as open copyright, anti-copyright and copyleft, such strategies have both an economic impulse and a cultural imperative. Chapter 4 explores how these strategies encourage the circulation of ideas at the same time as they challenge the prevailing, commercially based notions of copyright ownership. The anti-copyright and open publishing movements promote the unlimited reproduction and circulation of ideas and media for non-profit purposes as an attempt to subvert what they consider to be the restrictive practices (commercial and governmental) of intellectual property rights. In the field of music, radical sampling artists such as the Canadian John Oswald and the American group Negativland 'steal' their raw materials from popular culture to construct critical commentaries on that culture. The use by music fans of Napster and subsequent music distribution and downloading software has more than a trivial use; it can serve as a formal protest against a record industry that is seen to be self-serving and rapacious.

Chapter 5 explores a single communication medium of the Internet: sound. It has been argued that the Internet has 'radiogenic' qualities that allow for innovation in the field of radio. True interactivity, the blurring between pirate and 'niche' radio, the fluidity of physical location, all offer significant interventions in an enduring media form. This chapter examines a range of Internet radio projects: for political activism, popular music, development education. It also explores how the Internet might be employed to produce that long-lauded, yet elusive creative form: 'radio art'. We return to the study of fan culture in the final chapter. Fans often resist niche marketing and cultural fragmentation by corporations through the development of an international sharing of information, comment and opinion produced by the fan base. In its printed form, the zine (and the fanzine before it) provides cheap methods of promoting and sustaining identity and community. Despite this, zine culture has tended to elitism. Chapter 6 examines how the use of the Internet to produce zine-like communication opens up and transforms this type of alternative media production to a far wider range of people.

I have chosen to end the book with this examination of cultural practices for two reasons. First, despite the recent flowering of alternative media studies as a distinct branch of media and cultural studies, relatively little attention has been given to alternative media as popular cultural practice. Second, the study of alternative media that depend on dominant cultural practices and products for their existence reminds us that alternative media and their producers, whatever their distinctive characteristics, work in a larger context of political, economic and cultural orthodoxes. Just as the Internet may not be sheared away from its own historical connections and its contemporary context, so we must also consider alternative media as active in and activated by a set of broader and often contradictory forces.

CHAPTER I

The Internet, Power and Transgression

INTRODUCTION

In an insightful essay that argues for the necessity of a cultural studies approach to the Internet, Sterne has pointed to the prevalence within academic studies of considering the Internet as a '*millennial* cultural force' (1999: 258, original emphasis). He finds that the most common approach in these studies is to treat the Internet in terms of binary oppositions, most typically those of revolution/alienation and techno-philia/technophobia. These approaches, he argues, assume the technology is autonomous from other forces (social, political, cultural) and suggest a highly deterministic place for the Internet. Lacking these contexts, such studies fail in their attempts to understand the Internet in two key ways. First, following Bourdieu, Sterne argues that it is the careful construction of the research object that these studies fail to undertake. What, precisely, in other words, does it mean to study the Internet? Is it, for instance, to study a communication tool, an information resource, an electronic network, a mass medium, or even a set of industrial practices? Without clarity on what is being studied we can learn nothing. Too often, it seems, the academic is essaying an investigation that is founded on rhetorical claims ('the information superhighway', for example), rather than critically examining the nature and provenance of such claims and their location within culture. Second, and proceeding from that, there appears a tendency to treat the Internet as a largely autonomous site, for study negates contexts, whether historical, economic, political, social or cultural. To do so is to close off the possibilities of comparison with the histories of other media technologies, with other forms of social interaction, with the complex interactions between various sets of social practices, both online and offline. In short, we need 'to conceptualize the Internet as a modality of cultural transmission . . . [and] as a contextualized social phenomenon' (Slevin 2000: 6).

Perhaps Sterne overstates the case. Certainly his critique has been overtaken by some recent studies that do engage in contextually rich investigations where the object of study is not at all in doubt. Recent work by Hamelink (2000) on the ethics of cyberspace and Preston's (2001) compelling arguments for a 'social information society' are successful in these respects, though neither of them are cultural studies. Nevertheless, Sterne's observations should stimulate cultural studies researchers to attend carefully to their methodological duty. In what follows I shall show how those observations can valuably inform a cultural studies approach to studying alternative media practices on the Internet, and in particular the problems around the identities of audiences for alternative media and the uses to which those audiences put such media.

CULTURAL STUDIES AND ALTERNATIVE MEDIA

The emergence of cultural studies in Britain in the 1950s led to a far more holistic, theoretically complex and situated project of social research into the mass media than those attempted previously. The cultural studies perspective on media research has developed transdisciplinary epistemologies and methodologies (Alasuutari 1995; Kellner 1995) which, in their application to studies of the mass media inhabit the 'borderland' of textual and social research (Jensen and Rosengren 1990: 212). At the heart of the cultural studies approach to media research is the notion of culture as a key to understanding specific features of a particular historical situation; media culture contributes to the constitution of social practice (Dahlgren 1997) and shows how those media 'are embedded, along with audiences, in broad social and cultural practices' (Jensen and Rosengren 1990: 212).

Society, its institutions and the groups and individuals that constitute them came to be seen through this multi-perspectival lens of culture, subculture, ideology and hegemony – relations within society are viewed as constituted by the mass media, at the same time as the media themselves are constituted by those relations. As such, cultural studies appears well placed to examine the situated behaviour of social actors. An understanding of social practices in their situated contexts requires a consideration of the everyday life practices in which media practices are situated and within which they are 'made to mean'. Methodologically this suggests an ethnographic approach that is able to account for the individual's or group's life practices as the cultural context in which their media practices are embedded (David Morley's (1980) study of the 'Nationwide' audience is a key example of this approach).

Alternative media can be understood as those media produced outside the forces of market economics and the state. They can include the media of protest groups, dissidents, 'fringe' political organisations, even fans and hobbyists. It is perhaps in addressing radical questions of citizenship in the public sphere that alternative media are most powerful (what Rodriguez (2000) has termed 'citizens' media'). Perhaps the most powerful application of the cultural studies approach to alternative media on the Internet – powerful in terms of explicit struggles for political aims and for a radically democratic approach to citizenship – is the use of alternative media by new social movements (NSMs). NSMs arguably provide the prime locus for contemporary academic studies of alternative media (for instance, Atton 2002a; Couldry 2000b; Downing 2001; Rodriguez 2000). A study of alternative media in NSMs must examine the production and dissemination of media artefacts, the economics of such activities and the culture within which they are produced and disseminated. It must question how the media are organised, and how its readers – as social movement actors – are involved in those media. Inevitably it will place all these considerations within their proximate socio-historical context as part of NSM activity, as well as within the broader history of the alternative media, drawing on earlier generations of radical publishing. It will also need to take account of the 'political economy of culture' (Kellner 1995: 42) within which the alternative media are embedded and which enable or inhibit certain processes and products of those media. At the heart of the cultural studies approach to media research is the notion of culture as a key to understanding specific features of a particular historical situation. Here it is possible to see a connection between James Carey's 'communication as culture' (1992) and Melucci's argument that NSMs themselves constitute media, that the actors within movements are 'addressing the issues in a pure cultural form, or in purely cultural terms – bringing the issue to the fore, to the public' (Melucci 1996: 36). Just as Carey sees communication as productive of culture, we may understand Melucci's claim and consider NSMs as sites of media cultures produced not simply by, but *through and within*, social movement actors. This has deep implications for how we may consider media cultures.

The media of NSMs also engage in a classic concern of cultural studies, that of resistance. Here I do not refer to the 'oppositional readings' of media texts that have been identified by, amongst others, John Fiske (1992c) as evidence of resistance to cultural hegemony. In this I follow Kellner, who argues convincingly that such readings lack any social responsibility or demand for social change – that they are at best morally agnostic, at worst morally repugnant. I align the resistance within alternative media with those 'channels of resistance' that are deliberately created as ideologically oppositional forms of communication by activists or their spokespeople (for example, those documented in Dowmunt 1993; Downing 2001; and Juhasz 1995). Their power lies in their direct and knowing engagement with political struggle, rather than in a weaker ' "struggle" for meanings and pleasure' (Kellner 1995: 39).

So far, these characteristics are general; they do not apply solely to the use of the Internet. Other characteristics or dimensions of alternative media use by NSMs, however, are highly suggestive of epistemological and methodological approaches that could profitably be applied to Internet research in this area, and which would go some way to satisfying Sterne's recommendations for a cultural studies approach. In what follows I shall present three, related, approaches. First, an acknowledgement of the historical resonances with previous alternative media practices within social movements. Second, a recognition of the banality of Internet practice, that is, of its embedding in everyday life and in pre-existing social practices. Third, the problematisation – rather than either the acceptance or the erosion – of binary oppositions such as alternative/mainstream and producer/consumer. As will be seen, however, the subject matter of the present book is not confined to the use of the Internet by new social movements. Whilst much of it does focus on that (the case studies on Indymedia present the media activities of the anti-capitalist movement; the chapter on peer-to-peer networks examines the Internet as both a conduit and a laboratory for a social movement of sorts, though one rooted in the consumption of popular culture), I shall also apply this analytical approach to alternative media 'projects' that do not sit easily within the notion of social movement (the chapters on ezines and net radio are examples).

In examining these various dimensions of alternative media practice in relation to the Internet I hope to show that a cultural studies approach goes well beyond the epistemologically reductive, methodologically impoverished and millennial claims that their location on the Internet is sufficient to determine them inevitably as 'an autonomous and revolutionary cultural site' (Sterne 1999: 259). Here 'alternative' is employed to denote media practices that 'strengthen democratic culture' (Downing 2001: 95). For Nick Couldry, alternative media are supremely concerned with sustaining a community of citizens engaged in democratic practice, creating a 'community without closure' (Couldry 2000a: 140). Central to such a community is dialogue; independent control over symbolic resources is crucial to enable the 'exchange [of] representations of such "reality" as we share' (Couldry 2002). Studies of the 'progressive', liberal or anarchist media that typify most studies of alternative media are slowly beginning to examine these media formations in terms of how their counter-discourses can be adopted by the mainstream, how their messages can penetrate into the dominant public sphere and how they might make use of mainstream forms of discourse, in terms of technology, rhetoric and 'publicity'. This is to examine alternative media formations not as sets of discrete subcultural practices but as practices that are, as Hebdige (1979) reminds us, challenging the maintenance of hegemony through 'a struggle within signification' (p. 17). Preston persuades us that 'where such Internet applications manage to challenge and resist domination by commercial and other sectional interests, they may also be effective in operating as alternative and/or minority media for the exchanges of news and commentary on political and social developments which are marginalised in mainstream media and debates' (Preston 2001: 209).

HISTORY

First, whilst it is tempting to see in Internet practices only the novel, the undiscovered and what we might call an eternal, millennial present, we should be alert to historical resonances. Kidd has drawn attention to the similarity between contemporary, Internet-based alternative media formations such as Indymedia and its precursors in previous decades of social movement media. These similarities lie not only in their organisation and communication, but in terms of the recurrent issues that arise when radical, networked communications seek to expand, without losing sight of their original, non-hierarchical, 'open' forms of production and distribution. The distributive advantages of the Internet and, in Indymedia's case, the use of open-source programming to enable writer and producers to upload contributions themselves, bypassing the need for an editor or webmaster, offer new forms of media production and distribution. Questions of organisation and production at social and cultural levels, however, remain largely unchanged. Kidd identifies as key issues:

> sustainability; labour and power divisions marked especially by global
> north and south, and by gender; the best use of communications
> technologies, and relations with some of [the] older networks. Some
> of these questions, of who gets supported, to say what, through
> which medium, are achingly familiar. (Kidd 2002)

As it has expanded, Indymedia, far from operating as an egalitarian ideal, has begun to open itself up to conflict. As increasing numbers of individuals and groups wish to open their own, local Indymedia site, issues of centralisation, bureaucracy, 'house style', and even conflict within groups, become acute. The limits of non-hierarchical, horizontal and fully democratic communication become stretched. Addressing these concerns through historical comparison, as Kidd has done, can do much to inform contemporary analyses of organisation and production. We can also use this approach to interrogate the intellectual conflicts and tensions within an ostensibly homogeneous organisation such as Indymedia (Atton 2003).

More generally, James Carey (1998), in analysing the rise of national media, has identified two complementary forces. The first he terms 'a centripetal force in social organization' (Carey 1998: 30) through which the national media controlled space and centralised power and authority. At the same time, and against this, came a centrifugal force, through which 'specialized or minority media indexed the progressive differentiation of social structures' (ibid.). Both processes relied on the transformation of individuals and groups into audiences, but the centrifugal force, through differentiated media, came in turn to reform those audiences back into groups, where we might see (though Carey does not address this) their potential as social movement actors working with 'their' media. Whilst Carey has nothing to say about the blurring of producer and audience, his analysis of national media resonates well – as he intends it to – with the forces shaping the Internet. This time, though, forces and relations are working on a global scale, to produce both a consolidated, centripetal structuring of the Internet and a centrifugal fracturing (accompanied by spasmodic connection and reticulation) of what Carey terms 'the diaspora of the Internet' (1998: 34). We might think of alternative media on the Internet as part of that diaspora, yet one which is intimately linked to – and can only be understood in relation to – the macro-economic and social dimensions of the Internet as a mass medium. Both Carey and Kidd remind us that we must be alert to historical forces (though without implying causation), whether we engage our studies at the macro- or the micro-level.

EVERYDAY LIFE, BANALITY AND AUDIENCES

We can examine radical media practices for examples of how naturalised media frames and ideological codes can be disrupted. This is to suggest the possibility of a counter-hegemony arising from those residual and emergent cultural practices, an oppositional set of practices that, rather than preferring to exist alongside the dominant culture, seek to change society, whether for good or for ill. What is at stake is how differing sets of media practices, each with their own routines, rules and ideological codes, socially construct reality. One of the defining strengths of radical media practices (identified by, for example, Atton 2002a; Downing 2001; Rodriguez 2000) is the possibility they allow for audiences to become producers as a result of democratised media practices. On the one hand, then, market-led technological and economic practices appear to restrict other, decentralised, 'amateur' forms of production; on the other hand we can see how those very restraints may be renegotiated and how the commercial processes they were intended to facilitate may be replaced (or at least challenged) by social practices that re-activate audiences as producers. An understanding of these practices in their situated contexts requires a consideration of the everyday life practices in which media practices are situated and within which they are 'made to mean'.

We must therefore attend to the banality of the Internet and of the everyday practices that construct it and its relations to the wider world. This is not to replace the dominant vision of the Internet within the academy as a millennial cultural force with a banal, 'pop cultural' vision. Meaghan Morris (1988) has rightly criticised a tendency towards the banal in cultural studies which seeks to find subversion in every banal instance of popular culture (she cites Fiske). For Morris banality is an 'irritant' (as is its cognate, triviality) that is harmful when employed as a 'framing concept to discuss mass media' and popular culture (1988: 165). However, Morris's etymological excavation of the term 'banal' ignores its occurrence in medieval French to mean 'communal use'. As I have noted elsewhere (Atton 2001a), we can recover that meaning 'for our objects of study, to refer positively to the productive use of the "common people"' (2001a: 166). The object of this 'banal' cultural study, then, comes to refer to the productivity through which Internet practices – reticulated with everyday practices 'outside' those online – 'signify not the worthless and the worn (the 'trivial') but what we might call the "significant everyday"' (ibid.). A cultural study of Internet practices within alternative media thus comes to examine the congeries of the everyday, what Weigert (1981: 36) has described as 'a taken-for-granted reality which provides the unquestioned background of meaning for each person's life'. The cases discussed in Atton (2001a), which range from fanzines to protest sites and personal web pages, demonstrate this approach.

To recover this communal notion of 'banal' in the context of Internet study is also to suggest a relation between this concept and that of the 'digital commons'. The building of an online civic sector that is to be more than a mere directory of worthy web sites is to advocate a communal approach to the production, development and distribution of ideas that deal directly with the everyday. In other words, an emphasis on the everyday suggests a digital commons that not only addresses people's everyday concerns but is also constructed through them.

Methodologically this suggests an ethnographic approach that is able to account for the individual's or group's life practices as the cultural context in which their media practices are embedded. As Sterne emphasises, 'it is not the ultimate goal of a cultural study to determine what a given event online *means* for its participants (although this may be part of it) but, rather, *how the possibilities for meaning are themselves organized*' (Sterne 1999: 262, original emphases). A hegemonic and materialist approach to radical media practices on the Internet, attending as it must to the evolving relations and identities between producers and audiences, will offer insights into the productive processes of communication (rather than the merely connective) within and across such groups.

BEYOND THE BINARIES:
POWER RELATIONS AND ALTERNATIVE MEDIA

Alternative media have been powerfully characterised by their potential for participation (Atton 2002a; Rodriguez 2000). Rather than media production being the province of elite, centralised organisations and institutions, alternative media offer possibilities for individuals and groups to create their own media 'from the periphery'. Such media formations, through their very practice, will tend to critique notions of truth, reality and objectivity that we find at the heart of mainstream media practices, what Couldry (2002) has termed 'the myth of the mediated centre'. Producers of alternative media can be thought of as re-positioning themselves from a more or less passive audience (*pace* Fiske), consuming the output of mainstream media, to become media producers themselves. Further, the highly democratising practices embedded and developed in alternative media can continually re-create such re-positionings, encouraging more and more people to become media producers, and developing existing producers in different ways.

Turning to the Internet, we may see how the profusion of radical political web sites and discussion lists, net radio sites, fan sites and personal web sites is highly suggestive of these democratising processes in action. But we must be careful not to consider this 'alternative Internet' as if it were entirely separate from the practices and processes that we might term the 'dominant Internet'. Just as Downing (2001: ix) has acknowledged that his earlier binarist approach to alternative radical and mainstream media prevented him from seeing more finely gradated positions, the cultural study of Internet practices within alternative media needs to take account of the relations of power that are continually re-created through the deployment of a market- and engineer-driven technology – that has now come to be seen as a mass medium – for more radically democratic, often subversive ends.

Most accounts of radical media have treated such practices as unique and defining characteristics of radical media. Little attention has been paid to how these practices might be employed by mainstream media, or indeed to how radical media might borrow practices from the mainstream. Gramsci's notion of hegemony is of value here. A hegemonic analysis of radical and mainstream media can encourage us to examine them not as discrete fields of symbolic production, but as inhabiting a shared, negotiated field of relations, subject to 'contradictory pressures and tendencies' (Bennett 1986: 350). The classic features of hegemonic practice – the notion of an unstable, non-unitary field of relations, where ideology is mobile and dynamic and where strategic compromises are continually negotiated (Gramsci 1971) – might thus be applied to a study of the relations between these two media formations. Hegemonic analysis presents these two media formations not as independent, but as articulated in terms of their cultural practices. That is, media practices may be viewed as movable; they may articulate to bourgeois (main-stream) values in one instance, but become joined with radical values in another. A hegemonic approach suggests a complexity of relations between radical and mainstream that previous binary models have not been able to identify.

It follows that whilst we may consider the Internet as both the site and the means for such discussion, we must not ignore the other specifics of the social, the cultural and the economic that together will produce different instances of public spheres. To consider alternative media practices as key elements in developing and maintaining a new, oppositional form of public sphere requires attention. In the light of Habermas's (1992) own acknowledgement of the weaknesses of his original formulation of the public sphere as a bourgeois, male-domi-nated and economically determined site for public debate and opinion formation, we need to recognise that what he was identifying was an historically-based, ideal type of public intervention in the activities of government and state. Since his original formulation, many scholars have offered 'alternative' public spheres of which Nancy Fraser's (1992) notion of a multiplicity of public spheres (working-class, feminist, special and sectional interest groups) is perhaps the most compelling. Her work suggests that it is not enough to consider an ideal single, oppositional public sphere ranged against the dominant, bourgeois formulation, but to explore through empirical investigation the ways in which different groups and movements might see the necessity for – and thus aim to establish – their own particular fora for discussion, opinion-formation and political action. The resulting multiplicity of public spheres will not necessarily be a positive outcome: as Internet public spheres go global, so there is more possibility of a fragmentation of political (and cultural) discourses, with a similar fragmented impact on the possibilities for organising in the real world. Neither should we ignore the inequalities of information access and new media literacy; these too set limits on representation. We also need to consider the Internet as a global capitalist project and explore the ways in which the dominant ideology of capitalism has the power to disarm, prevent, distort or incorporate social practices that attempt resistance within one of its most visible projects.

These resistive, social practices, of course, do not take place in a cultural or a historical vacuum. Terranova (2002) has spoken of the virtual media of virtual social movements, a perilous formulation that tempts comparison with the excesses of a cybercultural postmodernism that has very little to say about people's everyday practices and their historical trajectory. For example, Slevin (2000: 71) identifies Sadie Plant as a prime offender in this, to the extent that she 'treats virtual reality as a zone of unfettered freedom, describing it as "a grid reference for free experimentation, an atmosphere in which there are no barriers, no restrictions on how far it is possible to go" '. The use of the Internet by social movements is inevitably wedded to practices in cultural and social worlds that exist in other discursive arenas beyond the 'virtual': street protests, political lobbying, face-to-face dialogue, community-building. The virtual world of media production equally has its every-day, lived dimension that entails the connection between on-line and off-line relationships, where production that appears to have its outcomes in a virtual world is intimately woven into the fabric of everyday life. Indeed, these 'outcomes' do not properly reside in that virtual world at all; they are sited there temporarily as a function of the carrier medium, but have their origins and their effects (social, cultural, political) in a world that is represented and determined by social forces and practices that cannot be bracketed off from Internet practices.

GLOBALISATION AND THE INTERNET

Robertson (1992/1997) has argued that the concept of globalisation 'is most clearly applicable to a particular series of relatively recent devel-opments concerning *the concrete structuration of the world as a whole*' (p. 4, original emphases). By this we should understand that the deployment of 'globalisation' as a concept is concerned with understanding how a global system of communication 'has been and continues to be *made* (p. 4, original emphasis). Robertson underscores how this system produces and reproduces 'the world'. This is to take globalisation out of the solely philosophical realm, and instead to examine the processes of agency and structuration, the processes of economics, culture and technology ('tech-nologisation'), that is, to examine in what ways and with what results a globalised system of communication 'mediatises' the world. The work of

Anthony Giddens offers a valuable entry into understanding how this might be achieved. He has defined globalisation as 'the intensification of worldwide social relations which link distant localities in such a way that local happenings are shaped by events occurring many miles away and vice versa' (Giddens 1991/1997: 18). The 'time–space distanciation' that Giddens emphasises in his model of 'globalised modernity' involves attending to both the local and 'interaction across distance' (p. 19) and, crucially, the relations between them. He identifies four 'institutional' (what he also terms 'cultural') dimensions through which to understand the processes of globalisation: in addition to the world capitalist economy he classifies the dimensions of globalisation into the nation-state system, the world military order, and the international division of labour.

A focus on economics, coupled with technological developments and their socio-cultural deployment, offers a useful, analytical approach to the study of how new social movements and other alternative media producers have used the globalising technology of the Internet as a media and communication channel, firstly to initiate and intensify worldwide social relations (as Giddens has it) and subsequently to structure the world as a whole (as Robertson has it) and, in so doing, to prompt reflexivity between local and distanciated social relations, which Giddens sees as central to the processes of globalisation.

In his challenging empirical analysis of new communication technologies, Preston (2001) brings many of these concerns together, arguing that 'the new social order and communication order of informational capitalism' (p. 272) is fundamentally unequal and polarised, and that the neoliberal project of a global information society has failed to deliver its promised socio-technical paradigm. Rather than information and communication technologies holding out the possibility of a radical change in the existing social order, instead they reproduce existing social inequalities. Preston emphasises not technological changes but economic, political and social continuities: of persistent imbalances between the information-rich and the information-poor, as well as deep-rooted inequalities of education, employment opportunities, access to health care, ability to participate in democratic government and access to markets. He finds hope not in technological advances, nor in knowledge or information *tout court*, but in 'political will and social mobilisation' (Preston 2001: 272).

At the forefront of this struggle for 'a more egalitarian, inclusive and *social* "information society"' (p. 272, original emphasis) Preston places both the mature and the new social movements. Instead of viewing 'technology as the end of social development' (p. 268) in a competitive, market-driven culture, new social movements – based as they are on notions of equity, inclusivity, social justice and radical notions of democracy – hold out the possibility of transforming the production and consumption capacities of new communication technologies into a new socio-technical paradigm, what Preston terms a 'social holism' (p. 258).

The use of new communication technologies, specifically the Internet, by new social movements can thus be viewed as a double response to international capitalism and neoliberalism. First, the embedding of Internet practices in a wider socio-economic struggle against the internationalisation of capital can be considered as a globalised, radical-democratic struggle against globalised finance. These movements' aims and praxis are fundamentally global in reach, whilst demonstrating the significance of local struggles, not only for those in that locale, but for those who might learn from those struggles, recontextualising the strategies and tactics of others at the same time as drawing moral, economic and political support from them. The notion of 'relocalisation' that we encountered in the introduction to this book is surely related to this (Dunaway 2000: 24). Second, the deployment of new communication technologies offers new social movements prefigurative methods of organising (Downing 2001), in particular through the radicalisation of production to a degree not seen in previous manifestations of social movement media.

Nevertheless, the forces ranged against these interventions represent extremely powerful corporate and governmental elites. Hamelink's (2000) empirical work on the governance of cyberspace endorses this view:

> the fact that the major communication and information corporations provide the essential support structures for commodity and financial markets [means that] the governance of communication issue areas is now largely destined to be subjected to a global trade regime. Global governance of CyberSpace is thus largely committed to minimizing public intervention and maximizing freedom for market forces. (Hamelink 2000: 172)

A market perspective of the Internet privileges consumers over citizens. We can see this at work at a number of specific levels. The Domain

Name System is at the heart of the Internet, regulating the allocation of domain names for countries, sectors and organisations. The privatised, self-regulated nature of the management of this system (by the Internet Corporation for Assigned Names and Numbers – ICANN) presents 'in principle a powerful tool of control' (Hamelink 2000: 145) that has little to do with citizenship and everything to do with consumerism. More specifically, the increasing scarcity of IP addresses, as the number of Internet users increases, has led to engineering decisions being made at the service of the market place. Dynamic IP addresses enable Internet service providers (ISPs) to increase their number of IP addresses to meet user demand. This comes at a cost, however. To become an Internet producer you need a permanent, static IP address. The scarcity of static IP addresses forces up their price, often placing them out of reach to all but large, commercial companies. The idealised view of the Internet as a forum for democratic communication is significantly weakened by such a techno-economic practice (and that is to say nothing about inequality of access in terms of language, skills acquisition, gender, race, class and geography). This dominant practice seems to encourage us – just as we view Internet content as 'always-already "out there"' . . . to impose that identity ourselves [as consumers and audiences] onto a new medium without considering the other possibilities it offers' (Roscoe 1999: 680).

This strategy of 'globalisation from above' (Falk 1993: 39, cited in Hamelink 2000: 172) conducted by multinational corporations and the political elites of the most highly industrialised states suggests, as Papacharissi (2002: 9) argues, that 'internet-based technologies will adapt themselves to the current political culture, rather than create a new one'. The enduring concentration of information technology in the developed countries adds further weight to the continuance of this global capitalist project. The United Nations Development Programme showed that in 1999 '91 per cent of Internet users were found in the OECD countries, which comprise the twenty-nine richest countries in the world and represent 19 per cent of the world's population' (Mattelart 2002: 607). Mattelart also cites a UNESCO report for 2000 that found that over 50 per cent of the world's population do not even have access to electricity, let alone a telephone line. Moreover, there is a significant disparity in connection charges between countries with high and low densities of Internet users: 'the average cost of 20 hours of Internet connection in the United States is $30, it jumps to well over $100 in countries with few Net users' (ibid.). What Mattelart calls this ' "techno-apartheid" global economy' (ibid.) seems to offer little opportunity for the revitalisation or creation of a public sphere such as that hoped for by Preston.

LEGAL CONSTRAINTS

The above appears to confirm the claim made by many critical communication scholars that private, commercial interests and not legislative bodies are the primary determinants of access to and use of the Internet. However, this is to ignore the significant legal constraints that governments across the world have placed on – or attempted to be placed on – the Internet. In some countries access to the Internet is severely curtailed by government legislation. According to a RAND report 'low-tech Leninist techniques' as well as high-tech methods have been employed to curtail dissident use of the system. Dissident is here used to refer to any individual or group deemed to be subversive by the Chinese authorities, and includes not only political activists in China but Tibetan exiles and activists living overseas (Chase and Mulvenon 2002). A fire in a Beijing Internet cafe in June 2002 resulted in the forced closure of thousands of similar cafes throughout the country. Minors have been banned from the cafes, and since November 2002 operators are legally required to keep records of customers and of the information they access. The government routinely arrest users (at least twenty-five people were arrested in 2001–2), effect shutdowns of parts of the infrastructure, and have instituted regular monitoring and filtering of email. In addition, all ISPs in China must register with the police (Hamelink 2000: 141). It has been estimated that up to 30,000 people are employed in digital spying in China (Hennock 2002). Regulation of the Internet in Singapore is effected by a limit on the number of ISPs, by the enforced use of filtering software by all ISPs, and by a licensing system which obliges them to apply the Internet Content Guidelines of the Singapore Broadcasting Authority (Hamelink 2000: 140–1). According to RAND (2002) many Middle Eastern countries enforce similar, strict limits on Internet connectivity through a twin fear of 'the dissemination of Western political thought and the spread of pornography. Many Middle Eastern leaders view the Internet as a Western-based agent of moral and political subversion' (RAND 2002: 6).

Whilst Western governments appear comparatively liberal in their attitudes to the Internet, recent crackdowns on child pornography and concern over the use of the Internet by terrorist groups (particularly since the 11 September 2001 attacks on the World Trade Center and the Pentagon) demonstrate strong government interest. In the US, the USA Patriot Act of 2001, enacted as a part of the country's 'war on terrorism', forced the closure of the web site of a student organisation (the Che Cafe Collective) at the University of California at San Diego, since it provided a link to a site supporting the Revolutionary Armed Forces of Columbia (FARC), listed by the State Department as a terrorist organisation. A clause in the Act outlaws the provision of 'communications equipment' to foreign terrorists, which free speech activists in the US have argued is too broad to be fairly applied. Indeed, the presence of a link on a site to another site that itself supports a 'terrorist' group is not the same as the group which set up the initial site offering direct support to that group. The Homeland Security Act (2002) which, along with the USA Patriot Act of 2001, was enacted as a result of the US government's response to terrorism following September 11, contains within its provisions the suggestions that ISPs read their customers' emails. This has led to a rehearsal of the arguments over encryption in the 1990s when the US government proposed the 'Clipper Chip', decryption software that contained a 'government skeleton key' to decrypt all current forms of encryption. A senior computer analyst has suggested that were such recommendations to be acted upon, users would 'soon realize that sending a plain text email through a commercial ISP is like misplacing a signed confession' (Holtzman 2003).

Internet regulation in the US has a longer history, however. Arguably the milestone piece of legislation was the Communications Decency Act (CDA) of 1996, which sought to impose standards of decency (a notoriously difficult legal area) on the Internet and to make punishable the distribution of texts and images thus deemed offensive. This Act was declared unconstitutional by the US Supreme Court in June 1998, which ruled that its provisions regarding indecent content severely interfered with the constitutional protection of free speech. In 1998 a second Act was proposed, the Child Online Protection Act (COPA), the provisions of which were so similar to the CDA that it was dubbed CDA II by its opponents. This too was struck down, by a federal judge in Philadelphia, as unconstitutional, in that it restricted the free speech of US citizens. The judge noted that there was 'nothing in the text of COPA that limits its applicability to so-called pornographers only' (*Library Association Record* 1999b: 139).

In a separate judgement in 1998, a federal judge in Virginia (former librarian Leonard Brinkema) ruled that Loudoun County Public Library's filtering policy was unconstitutional on the same grounds. The protection of the First Amendment rights of citizens does seem to be the driving force against wholesale censorship of the Internet by the US government and the more piecemeal restrictions on access through filtering software, most prominently in public libraries. As a consequence, legal judgements in the US at least appear to be moving towards a consideration of the Internet as similar to existing print media; that is, judgements are tending to focus on the content of the medium, rather than considering the Internet as a medium requiring special legal consideration (Hamelink 2000: 142). Judge Brinkema ruled in favour of free speech as a result of a case brought by a coalition of civil liberties groups, led by the American Civil Liberties Union. Ironically, as a demonstration of the imperfect 'solution' filtering software offers, other groups at the forefront of campaigns for free speech on the Internet – such as PlanetOut (an online 'community' for gay, lesbian and transgendered people) and the Electronic Frontier Foundation (both plaintiffs in the COPA case) – have found their websites blocked by SurfWatch and Cyber Patrol. The crude methods of filtering software have frequently been shown to be absurd and often humorous; nevertheless such consequences are far from trivial when principles of freedom of speech and access to information are at stake. A British director of leisure services has noted that filtering software that searches for stop words even when they are embedded in longer words and that is unable to distinguish between various semantic contexts can mean that 'you wouldn't be able to get any information relating to Penistone [a town in England], for instance . . . Dick van Dyke would be ruled out on two counts' (*Library Association Record* 1999c: 262).

Professional librarians in the US and the UK have been at the forefront of campaigns supporting the right of individual users – not libraries, and not governments – to control their own access to the Internet (ibid.). In the UK, the incorporation of elements of the European Charter on Human Rights in 1998 has strengthened campaigns against state interference, enshrining the right of freedom of expression and the right 'to receive and impart information and ideas without interference by public authority and regardless of frontiers'. Yet at the same time the European Parliament 'committed 25 million ecus to, amongst other things, developing filtering and rating systems' (*Library Association Record* 1999a: 7). Prior to this amendment to

British law, in 1996 the Metropolitan Police wrote to all ISPs in the UK enclosing a list of Newsgroups believed to contain pornographic material and asking them to 'monitor your Newsgroups identifying and taking necessary action against those others found to contain such material' (Metropolitan Police Service 1996). A year earlier the Dutch ISP XS4ALL had all 6,000 of its web pages blocked by a German academic computer network, apparently because of the presence on XS4ALL of a German left-wing magazine, *Radikal*. More recently in the UK, the Regulation of Investigatory Powers Act 2000 requires ISPs 'to build interception capabilities into their systems and intercept private email on behalf of the police or intelligence services' (*Library Association Record* 2000: 261). The 'RIP Act' includes a crime of 'conduct by a large number of persons in pursuit of a common purpose' (a definition first introduced by the Thatcher government to allow phone-tapping by police during the 1985 miners' strike) and a crime – punishable by a five-year prison sentence – of tipping off someone that their personal email is being intercepted. The fear amongst civil rights groups is that the catch-all nature of such provisions threaten freedom of expression and seek to curtail the human right to 'receive and impart information'. In some cases these provisions fly in the face of international human rights law.

ELECTRONIC CIVIL DISOBEDIENCE AND THE POWER OF 'NAMING'

If, as Mattelart (2002: 603) argues, there has emerged a notion of 'commercial free speech' that, at best, is competing with free speech as a right proceeding from citizenship (and at worst, is seeking to replace the latter entirely), then where and under what conditions does it make sense to imagine – let alone to construct – Preston's 'social information society'? The hope for such a global project appears to lie in the local, in the contestation by groups, movements and individuals of the Internet as a global capitalist project. Slater and Tacchi (2002: 2) have spoken of how local, social projects might 'enlist technologies and their properties within [the] social and biographical projects [of these 'dissidents']' and explore the 'co-configuration of technologies and social forms'. It is useful here to return to Melucci's notion of social movements and in particular their role as contesters. He recognises that as 'mere consumers of information, people are excluded from the logic that organizes this flow of information; they are there to only receive it and have no access to the power that shapes reality through the controlled ebb and flow of information' (Melucci 1996: 180). Whilst we must not ignore issues of access and the control of distribution (which Preston (2001: 203) argues constitute 'the key locus of power' for the forces of 'integration and globalisation' that comprise the global capitalist project of the Internet), Melucci is more interested in what he terms the 'deprivation of control over the construction of meaning' (Melucci 1996: 180). As Vygotksy teaches us, 'talk' (or 'naming' for Melucci) is a set of tools that both transforms and is itself transformed through its use. To recover this power of naming is for Melucci the task of social movements: their 'field of conflict is contemporary societies' unequal distribution of symbolic resources and symbolic power' (Couldry 2003: 137). Symbolic conflict, it may be argued, is at the heart of the struggle over the Internet. As Nick Couldry (2003: 43) has shown, Melucci's emphasis on the contestatory role of social movements against 'the normal concentration of the power of "naming" in governments, corporations and media institutions' offers us a perspective from which to view the Internet as more than a fatalistically, techno-economic determinant of global capitalism. Instead we may see it as a field of conflict, where symbolic resources are fought over, where citizenship and civil engagement may be redefined, where the predations of the asymmetries of symbolic power may be rebalanced. At the same time, as we have already seen, we must not lose sight of the 'social contexts within which, and by virtue of which, information and other symbolic content are produced and received' (Slevin 2000: 55–6).

It is only by attending to the Internet in this way that we can conceive of its capacity to function in support of new forms of public spheres; otherwise we are left only with a public 'space' (Papacharissi 2002). However, it is not necessary to consider all 'alternative' or radical Internet activity as evidence for public spheres. There are many other instances of dissent – cultural and social as well as political – which are worthy of attention. For example, Jason Toynbee's (2001) study of music file sharing on the Internet (through services such as Napster, Gnutella and KaZaa) presents this activity as a social practice that 'makes transparent an established practice: social authorship' (p. 26). His findings critically assess the increasingly contested notion of copyright in a digital age, as well as identifying ways in which musicians are now able to engage in direct promotion of their music through their own web sites, co-operatives and file-sharing services. (The creative, legal and social implications of file sharing are examined in Chapter 4 of the present work.)

Such practices directly challenge established notions of intellectual property and copyright through the medium of the Internet. As such, they may be considered as strategies for recovering the power of naming and placing it in the hands of citizens; in effect, democratising and revolutionising elite business practices, recreating them as elements of a new social praxis. So, whilst there have been significant and successful challenges to Internet regulation through the courts, such actions in the courts are not the only method of challenging what are considered to be illegal restrictions in free speech. Campaigns of 'electronic civil disobedience' have become increasingly common methods of protest. At the milder end of the protests – but no less powerful for that – was the 'Blue Ribbon' campaign launched by the Electronic Frontier Foundation in protest against the CDA, where web site owners who protested against government censorship placed the blue ribbon logo on their home pages. The use of mass emailing by protesters to government departments and their representatives (politicians and civil servants) turns the commercial use of 'spam' into what has been termed 'Internet guerrilla warfare' (RAND 2002). This form of electronic mass protest is also frequently used by protest groups against other, non-governmental targets such as multinational corporations. To term it 'guerrilla warfare' might be exaggerating its nature, yet its impact is undeniably threatening to those receiving it. Mass email campaigns can overload web servers and result in 'denials of service', where the web and email facilities of the victim can be immobilised. In the case of government departments this can seriously disrupt business for as long as the denial of service persists; for commercial organisations such attacks can make trading impossible for a time. Peacefire, the Youth Alliance Against Internet Censorship (www.peacefire.org), offers information about disabling filtering software and has produced free software that enables users to bypass the Cyber Patrol programme.

The notion of electronic civil disobedience sprang from a desire to mobilise international support for the Zapatistas in the Chiapas region of Mexico. In April 1998 a small group of activists calling itself the Electronic Disturbance Theater (EDT) engaged in what has come to be known as a 'virtual sit-in'. Translating the physical tactic of the sit-in as a peaceful, non-violent protest to the Internet, the group encouraged supporters of the Zapatistas to point their web browsers at the web site of the Mexican government and, by repeatedly accessing this link, to slow down the government's server in order to block access to the site. This tactic originated with the Italian Autonomous Digital Coalition as a manual, repetitive procedure (clicking repeatedly on a browser's 'refresh' button). It was soon automated through 'FloodNet' software which, once running, automatically reloaded the web page of the targeted site every few seconds. The EDT claim that for the duration of the protest on the appointed day, over 8,000 activists worldwide participated in the virtual sit-in. Also known as blockading, such tactics have a dual purpose. First, the hope is that the effect of mass blockading will effectively deny other users access to the targeted site through what is known as a Denial of Service attack (DoS). This tactic not only prevents 'legitimate' access to the site (for example, by government agencies), it represents a protest against denials of service effected by governments and ISPs seeking to regulate radical political organising on the Internet. These 'client-side' distributed denials of service aim to reclaim the Internet for civil society. Second, even where such blockades do not disrupt access – as in the case of the EDT's virtual sit-in of the US White House's web site (where the servers are more robust and more easily able to deal with large volumes of Internet traffic) – the protest has a publicity function, drawing attention to the cause being supported, or towards the policies and practices of the owners of the targeted web site (Carstensen 1998). The EDT's sit-in of the Mexican president's web site in 1998 also reveals a creative dimension to their practices of protest: the site's access log was filled with the names of people killed by the Mexican government troops during the Chiapas uprising.

Both aspects of the virtual sit-in were at work in the blockade of the World Trade Organization's (WTO) server during the WTO meeting in Seattle in December 1999. Co-ordinated by another small group of electronic activists, the Electrohippies, this protest (the group's first action) was conceived both tactically and ethically as a direct counterpart to the physical protests taking place on the streets in what has popularly become known as the 'battle for Seattle' (where, in addition to demonstrations and marches, protesters attempted to block physical access to the conference venue). It has been estimated that during the Seattle conference a total of 452,000 protesters succeeded in disrupting the WTO's server for periods of up to five hours, reducing its speed by half (Cassel 2000). The Electrohippies reveal an ethical dimension to their digital activism, arguing that such protests only have legitimacy when they result from mass participation. Whilst it is possible for a single hacker to achieve the same goal of slowing or bringing down a targeted server, the Electrohippies seek to perform mass action 'hacktivism'. To this end they freely distribute blockading software to enable protest groups to set up their own digital resistance projects, such as ClogScript, FloodScript and Web Script. The Electrohippie Collective (2003) emphasises the ethical necessity to configure the software to avoid attacking other organisations using the same network or subnet. (The denial of service attack is not limited to its use by 'progressive' groups. Denning (2001) cites its use by 'anti-terrorist' individuals and groups in the US seeking to disrupt services to countries they deem to be supportive of terrorism against the US, such as Afghanistan. She also notes its employment by groups with links to terrorism, including some militant Palestinians, such as Hezbollah. Despite the rise in number of such attacks in recent years, Denning is careful to separate out acts of sabotage or vandalism from what she terms 'cyber terrorism'. The latter she reserves for attacks that 'generate fear comparable to that from physical acts of terrorism' and those which seek to disrupt 'critical infrastructures such as electric power or emergency services'. However annoying or economically damaging attacks by groups such as Electrohippies might be, they should not be considered cyber terrorism according to Denning's definition.)

Despite this, the Electrohippies' ethos of democratic mandate and careful targeting is not shared by all 'hacktivists' or by other progressive groups. The tactic of the mass email (or 'mail-bomb') was criticised by the Institute for Global Communications when the web site of Basque Euskal Herria Journal (hosted by the Institute) was mail-bombed in 1997. The Institute was forced to close the web site in order to preserve access to other web sites on its server. Oxblood Ruffin of the hacktivist group Cult of the Dead Cow (CDC) has argued for a distinction between 'hacktivism' and what he term '[h]activism' (Cassel 2000). The latter terms he reserves for the tactics of groups such as EDT and the Electrohippies, who consider their methods of protest as extensions of actual, street-based demonstrations. He finds in their praxis two errors. The first is that denial of service attacks attempt to deny the right to free speech (in the US, where Ruffin is based, this is protected by the First Amendment of the US Constitution). He argues that to deny free speech to an opponent is to employ the same tactic against which, amongst others, the activists are protesting. Second, Ruffin places little store by the argument of 'democratic guarantee' advanced by the Electrohippies. The virtual protest is not the same as the physical protest. To transfer the tactics of the latter to the former is to ignore the digital dynamics of inequality of access and the new threats to democracy and human rights that have emerged (and continue to emerge) across the Internet. Instead of looking for a democratic mandate, instead of simplistically overlaying the tactics of the physical protest onto the digital environment ('[h]activism'), CDC aims for 'hacktivism'. This requires both new tactics for protest as well as new targets and, importantly, new modalities for protest in the digital environment. Rather than focusing on methods of protest for social justice that mirror protests on the streets and which reproduce both the nature and the aims of the struggles 'on the ground', CDC works on projects that aim to redress the imbalances of opportunity, access and provision that have come about directly as a result of government regulation or corporate restriction of the Internet. For example, in an attempt to recover the free speech rights of users of the Internet in China, the group has worked on methods to email web pages banned by the Chinese government back to Chinese citizens. CDC is still operating within a social justice framework, of course; the significant difference is that the group's focus is on the technical aspects of the Internet: 'we put the hack into hacktivism' runs their slogan. Ruffin argues that social justice movements that mobilise against multinational corporations have a range of possible tactics at their disposal, some of which may well be more effective than virtual sit-ins at disrupting the business operations of the targeted organisation (such as the mass mail-order return of purchased products) (Cult of the Dead Cow 2000). By contrast, Cult of the Dead Cow focus on injustices that exist solely in the digital realm as a result of technological constraints designed specifically to restrict access and provision. Another CDC slogan – 'programs make a difference, not people' – emphasises this focus, implying that in the digital realm the mass action is an irrelevance; a small group of hackers operating ethically can achieve equivalent, if not more powerful, results. This is not to reduce activism on the Internet to a population of cyborgs: both the Electrohippies and the Cult of the Dead Cow ultimately consider their work as counters to restrictive and repressive political and corporate practices in the 'real' world.

CONCLUSION: THE INTERNET AS 'TRIUMPH'?

'The digital age . . . will result in its ultimate triumph' (Negroponte 1996: 229). This claim from perhaps the foremost champion of the

Internet now appears somewhat naïve. For Negroponte the Internet heralds an 'age of optimism' where digital technologies act 'as a natural force drawing people into greater world harmony', a force that is 'almost genetic' (p. 230). As we have already seen, however, to study the Internet is not to study a natural phenomenon but one that is constructed through human processes. To consider the Internet as an unproblematic force for social change is to ignore the political and economic determinants that shape the technology; it is to pay little attention to how technological 'advances' may be shaped or determined by particular social and cultural elites (corporations, governments); and it is to ignore the obstacles to empowerment that legislation, inequalities of access, limits on media literacy and the real-world situations of disempowerment necessarily place on groups and individuals. Negroponte ignores the differentials of power that exist across the world as a result of differing power structures, knowledge bases, and cultural and social particularities. Where his argument might have some purchase is in his emphasis on decentralisation which, as we have seen, is a defining characteristic of alternative media production and practices.

Yet, whilst it is tempting to map the rhetoric of the decentralised nature of the Internet onto social and cultural practices of digital communication – as if that were to lead unproblematically to some form of digital freedom that is 'natural . . . almost genetic' – to do so is to ignore the barriers and constraints on that freedom that arise as a result of this communication taking place in a commercially and legislatively determined Internet 'market'. It is to bypass the complexities and particularities of global communication as an intersection of various and often conflicting local communication strategies, and to leave aside the divergent political and cultural imperatives of differing Internet 'communities' (if indeed we can talk of communities on the Internet at all). Yet there is clear evidence that projects of resistance are taking place, projects that have their informational and communicational heart in the Internet, whilst their aims and strategies partake of processes and practices in the wider social world. We must proceed with caution here. Preston, for one, is careful to leaven such optimism with the likelihood that 'the extended growth of new decentralised and alternative "mini-public spheres" is likely to remain a fragmented secondary force in comparison to the increasingly centralised, commercially-oriented and global reach of mainstream information and communication systems' (Preston 2001: 209).

CHAPTER 2

Radical Online Journalism

INTRODUCTION

The primary aim of this chapter is to present an overview of the main features that characterise the critical, 'public' journalism that has emerged on the Internet, largely through the media of new social movements and radical political organisations and institutions. It will examine the dialogical and popular methods that inform many of the radical journalism projects on the Internet through a case study of the Indymedia network, described by one commentator as 'to date the pinnacle model of citizen participation in the media' (Giordano 2002). A key feature is the egalitarian mode of address, where intellectuals share media platforms with activists and where it is hoped that elitism is eroded. Here we find the new media used both by grassroots activists and by dissenting academics and other intellectuals participating in a counter public sphere.

This is not to suggest that radical journalism on the Internet has evolved ahistorically and without reference to mainstream journalism practices. As emerging research suggests (Atton 2002b), there are fascinating interrelations between the two types of news cultures (for example, the radical use of tabloid style by alternative journalists, the erosion of expert hierarchy in radical news). Finally, the chapter will critically examine some of the theoretical claims that have been made for this type of online journalism and in particular ask whether it represents as radical a shift in notions of doing journalism as some of its celebrants believe.

The recent book-length studies of alternative media (Atton 2002a;

Downing 2001; Rodriguez 2001) have provided insights into contemporary practices within alternative media that present ways of doing reporting that can be radically different from those of the mainstream. A special of issue of *Journalism: Theory, Practice, Criticism* argued for a philosophy of journalism and a set of practices that are embedded within the everyday lives of citizens, and media content that is both driven and produced by those people. Approached in this way alternative media may be understood as a radical challenge to the professionalised and institutionalised practices of the mainstream media. Alternative media privilege a journalism that is closely wedded to notions of social responsibility, replacing an ideology of 'objectivity' with overt advocacy and oppositional practices. Its practices emphasise first-person, eyewitness accounts by participants; a reworking of the populist approaches of tabloid newspapers to recover a 'radical popular' style of reporting; and collective and anti-hierarchical forms of organisation which eschew demarcation and specialisation – and which importantly suggest an inclusive, radical form of civic journalism.

Such media are radical in the sense that they are opposed to hierarchical, elite-centred notions of journalism as a business – this is an ideology that holds that only through more egalitarian, inclusive media organisations is it possible to even think about a socially responsible journalism. This is to go well beyond the reformist notions of the civic or public journalism movement that has emerged in the US. As recent contributions to journalism studies have suggested, it is this very reformism that has so far prevented the advocates and practitioners of public journalism from making anything but piecemeal interventions in the dominant practices of journalism (Davis 2000; Glasser 2000; Woodstock 2002). Despite its claims, public journalism, working as it does within the market and within long-standing organisational, institutional and professional structures, operates in similar ways to mainstream journalism (of which it is after all, a part): 'traditional and public journalisms adopt similar narrative strategies to effect essentially the same ends: placing the power of telling society's stories in the hands of journalists' (Woodstock 2002: 37). Radical online journalism projects such as Indymedia, on the other hand, attempt to place that power into the hands of those who are more intimately involved in those stories.

'News is no longer the preserve of journalistic organisations,' argues Chalaby (2000: 34) in an exploration of the diversification of news providers through the Internet. Chalaby focuses on content aggregators as news providers, such as Yahoo!, American Online and British Telecom and argues that Internet technology allows 'news sources to communicate directly with audiences' (p. 35). This statement also suggests the leading characteristic of the subject of this chapter, how the media of new social movements and, in particular, how the Indymedia or Independent Media Centre (IMC) network offers news and narratives from the point of view of activists themselves: where activists become journalists. Indymedia is a multi-featured, multi-structured media 'organisation', though its structure is very different from traditional news organisations. It comprises a network of Independent Media Centres, each working independently in its own region, country or city, reporting and commenting on issues that are central to the anticapitalist movement such as third world debt, human rights, the internationalisation of capital, and the political and economic power of transnational corporations.

The use of new communication technologies, specifically the Internet, by new social movements can thus be viewed as a double response to informational capitalism and neoliberalism. First, the embedding of Internet practices in a wider socio-economic struggle against the internationalisation of capital can be considered as a globalised, radical-democratic struggle against globalised finance. The anti-capitalist movement's aims and praxis are fundamentally global in reach, whilst demonstrating the significance of local struggles, not only for those in that locale, but for those who might learn from those struggles, recontextualising the strategies and tactics of others at the same time as drawing moral, economic and political support from them. Second, the deployment of new communication technologies offers new social movements prefigurative methods of organising (Downing 2001), in particular through the radicalisation of production, to a degree not seen in previous manifestations of social movement media.

The rich and diverse history of social movement media practices does not admit of any easy generalisations: particular configurations of political, social, economic and cultural forces at specific historical and geographical junctures make this task theoretically and empirically fraught. Historiographical analyses of some two centuries of social movement media in the US and the UK do reveal, however, some striking common features (Hamilton and Atton 2001). Broadly, the history of social movement media has been one of vanguardism and essentialism. Too often have these media been considered as the political weapons of 'great men', too rarely have they been viewed as the 'voices of the voiceless'. Historical accounts have essentialised these media, divorcing them from historical specificity, seeing them as immanent, structural forces rather than processes of symbolic struggle which are themselves embedded in emerging and continually shifting social and political processes. Such accounts make it difficult to see the realism of social movement media as constellations of symbolic struggle, historically and culturally determined, intimately though not unproblematically connected to the popular forces from which they sprang and which they sought to represent. Rather than accounts of great men, social movement media present the involvement of 'ordinary' people, whose history and aspirations these media seek to reveal and mobilise. This is not to say that these media have been consistently successful, nor that they have not been at times the organs of key individuals.

Whilst internationalism and prefigurative methods of organising are hardly new phenomena within alternative media projects, the earlier dominance of Leninist models of media production has often prevented these features from becoming much more than ideological desiderata. Attempts by various socialist newspapers to have workers write for them – a significant tactic of prefigurative politics – appear to have failed as a result of those papers' reliance on elite groups and hierarchical methods of organising. John Downing notes how the narrow range of people involved in producing working-class papers ('authorities in or close to the Communist Party' in the case of the *Morning Star*, whereas '*Socialist Worker* and *The Militant* . . . tend only to have the faithful open their mouths') stifles controversy and debate, and ensures the marginality of the papers to their readers' everyday struggles (Downing 1980: 198–9). This problem was recognised by the editorial staff of *Socialist Worker* from its earliest days. In his history of the paper, Peter Allen notes that even by the second year of its life, the number of articles written by workers was increasing, but he gives no indication as to the size of the increase or whether it continued (Allen 1985: 211). By the mid-1970s Tony Cliff, the leader of the Socialist Workers' Party, was insisting that '[w]orkers' names will have to appear in the paper . . . more and more often and less and less often the by-lines of the Paul Foots, Laurie Flynns and Tony Cliffs' (cited by Sparks 1985: 145). Allen notes that a general appeal to its worker-readers 'did increase the number of articles written by workers, [but] the increase was neither dramatic nor sustained' (Allen 1985: 220). This clearly caused some anxiety amongst the party's Central Committee, not least to its leader, Tony Cliff. Writing in 1982, he noted that 'to a large extent workers' writing is limited to a small area of the paper'. His solution was to propose that the paper became 'a workers' diary' (Allen 1985: 216), but Allen provides no evidence to show that the paper evolved even partially along the lines that Cliff was demanding.

Yet there is another discernible tradition of social movement media that has focused on projects that radically re-form three key aspects of communication: 'skills, capitalization and controls' (Williams 1980: 54). For the English Radical press (roughly, 1790–1830) this resulted in papers that were characterised by pauper management, where 'journalists saw themselves as activists rather than as professionals' and where there was an interest 'in expos[ing] the dynamics of power and inequality rather than report[ing] "hard news"' (Curran and Seaton 1997: 15). These features reappear at the heart of contemporary social movement media and it is in the continuity of this tradition that we can place the use of new communication technologies by new social movements. Preston's (2001) vision of a social information society offers a useful theoretical framework against which we may test the use of ICTs by new social movements. Where a Leninist paper such as *Socialist Worker* claimed internationalism as part of its ideology and modelled its organisational form on the former Soviet system, ICTs with global reach present the possibility of a more inclusive, networked sociotechnical paradigm. The majority of alternative media examined by Downing (2001) are, at bottom, local interventions, however committed they may be to international perspectives. Preston's social holism suggests not only a global reach in terms of ideology and media content, but one that seeks an inclusivity, an anti-elitist approach to organisation and production that stands in stark contrast to earlier, Leninist forms and to those geographically circumscribed forms of social anarchist media examined by Downing. In this respect at least, the notion of social holism, achievable through the radical deployment of ICTs, suggests a development of Downing's notion of prefigurative politics that potentially has a far greater reach. In terms of Internet use, we can locate the beginnings of this approach as a political strategy in the communication methods of the Zapatistas.

THE INTERNET AND NEW SOCIAL MOVEMENTS

The most widely cited example of radical Internet use by new social movements is that employed by the Zapatistas in their struggle for the

Chiapas region of Mexico. This has been considered the 'radical ideal' by alternative media commentators and social scientists alike. Manuel Castells's (1997: 79) term for their campaign – 'the first informational guerrilla movement'– is arguably over-technologised. After all, their struggle remains at its heart one for land, and for political and cultural recognition, fought in a number of arenas, only one of which is the informational. Yet the significance of the Chiapas movement's deployment of the Internet has had global reverberations as a 'conception of the public sphere as an arena for dialogic praxis . . . an arena for radical inclusivity' (Ford and Gil 2001: 219, 220). The cross-cultural dialogue that the Zapatistas encouraged through the publishing of their communiqués on the Internet, the support they built up across the world, the visibility their message enjoyed in the mainstream media: all grew out of the deployment of an international communications medium for a project of local resistance. In microcosm, the Zapatistas' struggle represented the burgeoning anti-capitalism movement, itself a development of the holistic tendencies of the environmentalist movement, coming together with groups and movements campaigning for Third World debt relief, human rights, employment rights and social justice.

The significance of the Zapatistas' use of the Internet lies in their promotion of dialogical praxis: 'Zapatismo is a living example of how we can open the space, prepare the soil, and through direct democratic dialogue, witness the radical roots going deep' (Jordan 2001: 21). The Internet publicised not only their local struggle but their methods of political communication and organisation as well. Their methods did not proceed from a deployment of the Internet, however. They were embedded in their local struggles. Dialogic praxis effected through the Internet – that is, praxis that sought a 'radical internationalisation' through available technology rather than using the technology to raise awareness of a local praxis – came most significantly from anarchist groups in the West. Inspired by the Zapatistas, hitherto separate groups began not only to act in solidarity with each other, but to act together, publishing and protesting as networked 'affinity groups' (Bookchin 1986), as an anarchist model of organising.

Where early uses of the Internet by anarchist groups had been more or less fragmented assays into small-scale electronic media production, seeing only small increases in the circulation and reach compared to their print precursors and experiencing chronic difficulties in sustaining their media projects economically (Atton 1996a), the development of the McSpotlight web site in 1996 demonstrated a more successful strategy based on international networking, a broadening of the protest agenda and the participation of numerous local groups (Atton 2000). The site provided a non-hierarchic centre for a range of diffuse, only informally connected groups and individuals – Bookchin's affinity groups in action. As the site grew to involve more groups, opportunities arose to expand the interests of the site to cover not only the 'McLibel' trial, but the practices of multinational corporations in all countries, and their links with governments and supra-governmental bodies. Whilst it is not necessary to argue that the current anti-capitalist movement began in McSpotlight, its trajectory may be similarly applied to the development, reach and extent of the latest phase of radical Internet use, the Indymedia network.

THE INDYMEDIA NETWORK

The network of Independent Media Centres has become a highly visible feature of the media landscape of the global anti-capitalism movement at the turn of the millennium. The Independent Media Centres (IMC) or Indymedia network came to prominence during the demonstrations in the American city of Seattle against the World Trade Organisation summit meeting there on 30 November 1999. The Seattle IMC acted as an independent media focus for the broad coalition of social justice groups, trade unions, anarchists, socialist, communists, environmental groups and others – a coalition that has come to be known as the anti-capitalist movement. In Seattle the Centre had both a physical and a virtual presence. Its virtual presence on the Web enabled its small core staff to distribute streaming audio and video footage of the demonstrations, as well as written reports, across the world. Technically this was achieved through the use of open publishing software, where any independent journalist (any activist, for that matter, though the two were often the same) could upload their reports using a pro-forma on the IMC web site. No prior approval was needed from the core group, neither was that group responsible for editing the content of reports in any way. Hundreds of hours of audio and video footage and hundreds of thousands of eyewitness reports, analyses and commentary became available to activists, supporters, detractors – to 'global citizens' at large.

Such independent accounts provide a powerful counter to the enduring frames of social movement coverage in mainstream media.

A study of the framing of the women's movement by US print media (Ashley and Olson 1998) presents what have become standard responses in the mainstream media to social movement actors, their aims and their ideologies. Ashley and Olson found dominant patterns and emphases on surface details, the delegitimisation of feminists and their depiction as disorganised and riven by conflict. Framing devices were used to minimise ideological threats by representing the actors as deviants on the margins of society (a tactic which also exaggerates such threats to the status quo and to 'reasonable' people). These frames are widespread in mainstream coverage of social movements (Gitlin 1980; van Zoonen 1992). The ideologies and practices of social movement actors become simplified and homogenised; rather than exploring the complex, unstable and 'structurally undetermined' components of these protests (K. W. Brand, cited in van Zoonen 1992), mainstream framing devices render deeper explorations of social movement activity unavailable. By homogenising varieties of dissent the mass media reify protest and instantiate the richness of ideologies and actions, often through a crudely simplified single example, such as we saw during the Genoa protests in July 2001, where a photograph of a masked protester, standing defiantly on an overturned car, was reproduced throughout the mainstream media to represent the entire protest movement. By contrast, social movement ideologies and practices are complex and internally contradictory (or so it seems, with socialists working with greens, anarchists with socialists, the different hue of green politics, organised groups working with grassroots individuals). Social movement activity is a process, not simply a series of events – it is 'a network of *active relationships* between actors who interact, communicate, influence each other, negotiate, and make decisions' (Melucci 1996: 75).

Since Seattle, the Indymedia network has expanded. At the time of writing (January 2004) there are over 130 IMCs across the world. The concentration remains greatest in the US (forty-eight) and Europe (forty-two, eleven of which are in the UK). Other regions are far less well represented. There are two IMCs in India and only three in Africa. The Seattle IMC remains as the network's de facto centre, and it is from its collective that the bulk of technical information about uploading comes, as well as proposals for managing the substantial flow of information the network generates. For example, the network now operates a unique form of editorial control. Whilst reports may be uploaded from or by any source, the editorial group reserves the right to remove contributions judged unsuitable. The 'Publish' page of Indymedia (www.indymedia.org/publish.php3) states that 'The Independent Media Center is a collectively run media outlet for the creation of radical, *accurate*, and passionate tellings of the truth' (author's emphasis). Towards this aim the collective state that 'while we struggle to maintain the news wire as a completely open forum we do monitor it and remove posts.' The large majority of these posts are removed for 'being comments, not news, duplicate posts, obviously false or libellous posts, or inappropriate content [such as hate speech].' Indymedia do, however, still make these posts available in a separate page titled 'hidden stories' (www.indymedia.org/search-process.php3?hidden = true). Whilst editing does take place, it does not prevent voices from being heard, nor prevent users from accessing that content. Neither does this quasi-editorial function of the core group extend to the editing of individual pieces of work: if they do not breach the criteria set out above, then pieces will remain on the 'open' pages of the site. These limitations apart, IMC/Indymedia enable any activists to contribute their work. The use of open source software bypasses the need for an editor or webmaster to upload contributions: writer and producers may do this themselves, using the pro-forma on the 'Publish' page.

Each IMC is run by a small collective who know each other well and who tend to share tasks and responsibilities. However, we should not think of this as an elitist group, a command post that directs the work of others. The features of its organisational structure – broadly collective, egalitarian, non-hierarchical – it shares with many alternative and radical media projects. John Downing (2002) locates such features in a continuing tradition of socialist anarchism, finding a tendency to organise on an 'anti-mass' level, privileging local, 'affinity groups' (a commonplace of anarchist organisation; Bookchin 1986) connected informally through international networks of solidarity and resource-sharing. In this respect such media projects share the organisational methods of the new social movements within which they arise (Melucci 1996). As Downing emphasises, they are far removed from both the hierarchical structures of the pluralist media of Western democracies and the centralised, transmission-belt model that characterised the revolutionary, Leninist model of the Soviets. Indymedia connects local work to a global struggle, and it is from within this global context that the movement perceives itself. Despite the presence of some editorial control, open source programming erodes any centralisation of Indymedia that might otherwise occur. From the perspective of both producers and consumers (often the same people when we are talking about activists) Indymedia functions as a content aggregator of independent journalism, organised by country, issue and medium (text, audio, video, multimedia). Not only do journalists place original, previously unpublished work there, IMCs themselves will often link to already-broadcast or published reports. To consider Indymedia as an organisation is to consider a network of independent, collectively-run 'nodes' through which independent journalists may circulate their work, largely unimpeded by the gatekeeping of those collectives.

It is not only the scale (in terms of geographical spread, global reach and volume of material) that makes the Indymedia network an interesting moment for the study of social movement media: it is the most thorough working-out on the Internet of the conditions and processes of radical media projects. The Indymedia network powerfully exemplifies the three core principles of John Downing's (2001) model of radical media organisation. First, there is an emphasis on self-management, resulting in small-scale, collectively-run projects. Second, the project suggests a 'socialist anarchist angle of vision' which, Downing argues, sets contemporary radical media apart from its Leninist precursors (still alive, of course, in some forms). Despite its revolutionary aims and content, Downing finds in the latter an unwelcome emphasis on vanguardism and party 'correctness'. This is not to claim that self-managed media that reject the Leninist, transmission-belt model will easily and unproblematically be freed from concerns over control and correctness. Jo Freeman's (1972) notion of 'the tyranny of structurelessness' reminds us of how even in avowedly non- or anti-hierarchical structures, hierarchies might still develop. Third, and proceeding from this interest in socialist anarchism as an organising principle, the project embodies 'prefigurative politics, the attempt to practice socialist principles in the present, not merely to imagine them for the future' (Downing 2001: 71). Downing's emphasis here on socialism need not prevent us from applying these core principles to an organisation as politically, culturally and geographically diffuse as the Indymedia network. Downing's vision is that of a democratic, non-corporate media network comprising non-hierarchically-run, independent groups and individuals horizontally linked, and where what organisation and control does take place is necessarily light. At this general level at least, the Indymedia network appears to realise his vision.

Indymedia journalists offer news and narratives from the point of view of activists themselves: the journalists are indeed activists themselves. Throughout their history, alternative media have privileged amateur journalists who are writing from a position of engagement with the event or process that is their subject (Hamilton and Atton 2001). 'Amateur' here has everything to say about commitment to radical intellectual and social practices; it has nothing to do with the common notion of the amateur as the ignorant, self-deceived dabbler. These amateur journalists – explicitly partisan – report from the 'front line', from the grassroots, from within the movements and communities they thus come to represent. At this more specific level of journalistic practice, the principles of self-management, organisational and ideological independence, and prefigurative politics are played out in what we can think of as 'native reporting':

> 'Native reporting' can usefully define the activities of alternative
> journalists working within communities of interest to present news
> that is relevant to those communities' interests, presented in a
> manner that is meaningful to them and with their collaboration and
> support. 'Native-reporter' also evokes those local grassroots
> journalists of the South by whom Michael Traber sets so much store,
> whose value lies not in their role of message-creators for a passive
> audience, but as members of a community whose work enables the
> entire community to come together, to 'analyse one's historical
> situation, which transforms consciousness, and leads to the will to
> change a situation' (Traber 1985: 3). (Atton 2002a: 112–13)

The reporters' active, lived presence within events, whilst no guarantor of impartiality, enables the production of news that tells other stories from those reported in the mainstream: 'our news, not theirs'. This is a radical process of reporting where activists become journalists, and where grassroots reporting and analysis takes place within movements and communities. The work of grassroots activists exemplifies the passage of native-reporters from participants in a demonstration to activist-journalists, whilst remaining positioned as 'rank and file' within those movements. The partisan, first-person narratives and commentaries of the native-reporter inhabit an uneasy terrain. The sustained first-person narrative in the mainstream is typically the province of the senior reporter or the columnist; partisan commentary will also come from the columnist or the op-ed writer: these are roles of significant status. The native-reporter, by mainstream criteria, is unauthoritative and marginal, at the bottom of the hierarchy of access. Under the radical conditions of alternative media, these reporters become central:

the role and function of the journalist is transformed and hybridised. Further, the demotic approach of the native reporter, whether evinced by the gritty camcorder footage shot in the heat of protest or by a 'public-colloquial' style of textual discourse (Fairclough 1995: 72), emphasises a radical populism in visual and written language. McLachlan and Golding (2000: 77) have argued that 'the more demotic and convivially casual tone of the popular press [is] rooted in the evolution of a journalism of the market from a more socially anchored journalism of community or movement.' We might consider the radical populism of native reporting as both an acknowledgement of and a return to the roots of popular journalism (say, in the English Radical press), springing from its location and status as a communication technology for communities and protest movements.

The features of Indymedia we have examined so far suggest a rather too comfortable fit with Downing's three principles, offering an almost idealised version of alternative media. To explore Indymedia further, however, is to reveal a more complex and apparently contradictory structure that tests Downing's desiderata and Preston's notion of social holism. To do this we shall focus on Indymedia's reporting in the immediate aftermath of 11 September 2001. Here we will find that Indymedia journalists have had less to do with reporting on the activities of their own social movements; their work has focused more on the selection and editing of the work of others. What role, then, have activist journalists played? How have they reported on events and issues? Importantly, for a web-based independent news service, what sources have they drawn on? Whose writing is represented there and to what purpose? The answers to these questions will increase our understanding of a large-scale, international, alternative media project.

INDYMEDIA AS COMMUNICATIVE DEMOCRACY

A recent contribution from John Hartley to the future of journalism studies (Hartley 2000a) offers a useful way into theorising Indymedia's practices as new ways of rethinking communicative democracy. Hartley develops Chalaby's claim about the Internet affording direct communication from news sources to audiences to argue that the technology of the Internet offers 'a more direct form of communicative democracy' that appears to compete with existing, representative forms (Hartley 2000a: 41). He develops a comment made by Ian Hargreaves (Professor of Journalism at Cardiff University, Wales) to the effect that it is every citizen's right in a democracy to communicate whatever they wish 'however hideous'. The implications of this for professional communicators (especially journalists) and for Hartley are clear. The dominant model of journalistic practice works from within an institutional framework that has established, systemic relationships with other elite groups, organisations and ideological formations. The use of the Internet by citizens has the capacity to transform the practice of journalism, to expand it as a democratic practice where 'everyone is a journalist, and journalism is everywhere' (p. 45). Hartley terms this 'the democratization of public writing' (p. 43), a concept which closely resonates with recent formulations of alternative and radical media practices such as Clemencia Rodriguez's (2001) notion of citizens' media; it has a long history in the tradition of working-class writing (Morley and Worpole 1982). This process of democratisation, made possible most thoroughly in recent years by technological advances and the economic, social and cultural shifts that accompany them, appears to lead to an erosion of the role of the journalism as agenda-setting and decision-making. Instead, Hartley proposes a more inclusive practice, that of redaction, where there is a focus on the processes of reduction, revision, preparation, editing and publishing, and where journalism as original writing is less prominent. Perhaps Hartley exaggerates this shift: he says little about how and where the writing upon which redactional processes rely has its origins. Surely journalism as original writing cannot be dispensed with entirely? Yet the utility of Hartley's argument is clear for the present case: Indymedia practices privilege the democratisation of journalism and the inclusivity that can bring. Indymedia operates outside powerful, elite institutions and contributes to a public sphere where everyone, ideally, can be a journalist. With this ideal comes a radical transformation of the enduring ideological positions and practices of established and professionalised journalism which entails new ways of thinking about received notions of objectivity and impartiality and proposes a new ethical framework on which to base radical community journalism.

THE ETHICS OF ALTERNATIVE JOURNALISM

The professional ideal of objectivity, understood as the separation of 'facts' from 'values', may be considered as the key ethical dimension of journalistic practice. Allan (1999) and Schudson (1978, 2001) locate the emergence of this normative practice in the American press of the 1920s and 1930s. It was due, they argue, to two separate, but linked social forces. The first was rooted in 'popular disillusionment with state propaganda campaigns' and 'a wariness of "official" channels of information' (Allan 1999: 24). If 'reality' could no longer be reliably constructed from officialdom, then a more 'rational' method was needed. This was found in the second social force, that of scientific rationalism. Journalism at this time was aligning itself as a profession alongside science, the law and medicine; thus it appeared 'natural' that it should draw for its rigour on the scientific method employed by those professions. The results, as Allan emphasises, were swift and enduring. Specialised 'beats' emerged, and with them came the expert journalism and the by-lined report. Investigative reporting and interviewing flourished; ' "impersonal", fact-centred techniques of observation' (Allan 1999: 25) informed these practices, with the consequent rise of the columnist whose work was clearly separated from 'the news', and who was allowed the freedom to engage in value-driven writing. Though as Schudson reminds us, the rise of objectivity as an ideology was never a merely technical exercise, not

> just a claim about what kind of knowledge is reliable. It is also a moral philosophy, a declaration of what kind of thinking one should engage in, in making moral decisions. It is, moreover, a political commitment, for it provides a guide to what groups one should acknowledge as relevant audiences for judging one's own thoughts and acts. (Schudson 1978/1999: 294)

Practitioners of alternative journalism have both recognised the moral and political nature of objectivity and have directed their work to revealing its premises in their work, the better through practice to challenge its central assumptions: that it is possible in the first place to separate facts from values and that it is morally and politically preferable to do so. Such challenges are not the sole province of alternative journalists, neither are they new. The Glasgow University Media Group's (GUMG) work stands as a significant project exploring the concatenation of facts and values in television news reporting that still considers itself objective and impartial (Eldridge 2000). Workers within alternative media, however, seek to challenge objectivity and impartiality from both an ethical and a political standpoint in their own journalistic practices. Amongst practitioners in the US and the UK at least, the power to do so in recent decades has come not from the critical media studies of such as GUMG but from American scholars whose prime expertise lies elsewhere. The radical political essays of American dissidents such as Noam Chomsky and Edward Said (especially Chomsky) continue to be cited in alternative media as the major demystifiers of the objectivity of the US corporate media. From these accounts (for example, Chomsky 1989; Said 1981) alternative journalists have begun to finish the story, so to speak. Convinced by and sympathetic to such notions as Chomsky's 'worthy and unworthy victims' and the systematic and longstanding pro-Zionist coverage in the American media at the expense of Arab (specifically Palestinian Arab) voices, these journalists have sought to expose the moral claims of their mainstream counterparts. We may consider this stance as a supremely ethical one, for it seeks to present through radical journalistic practices moral and political correctives to the 'fact-centred techniques' that have been found to be just as value-laden as the 'pre-objective' journalism they sought to replace. But what ethical issues do these radical practices bring with them? What does being an alternative journalist mean in ethical terms? I do not intend to make direct comparisons with mainstream practices here; rather, and in the spirit of my introduction, I will examine the ethics of alternative journalism in terms of its hybridity, how its practices both cleave to and depart from the mainstream.

Alternative media are characterised by their explicitly partisan character. In the language of ethics, they exhibit clear biases, yet they proclaim their selectivity and their bias, and generally have little interest in 'balanced reporting'. What may we find in such practices that makes them different from, say, the tabloid newspaper that exhibits clear and consistent bias against asylum seekers or the gay and lesbian communities, as many British tabloids continue to do? The dominant moral argument within alternative media has two aspects. First, alternative media projects tend to be set up in order to provide a counter to what alternative journalists consider an already biased set of reports. Sceptical of what counts as balance in the mainstream media, they seek to set up their own counter-balance. Hence, the argument runs, the viewpoints already dominant in the mainstream media do not need repeating. What appears as bias and the absence of balance in the alternative media is to be considered not as a set of absolute truths; instead it comprises a set of accounts told from different perspectives. The practice of alternative journalism thus enacts Edgar's (1992: 120) claim that 'journalism cannot be objective, for that presupposes that an inviolable interpretation of the event as action exists prior to the report'. These stories might well use official or semi-official sources in the public domain that have been ignored by mainstream journalism, such as the investigative journalism of *Covert Action Quarterly* in the US and the 'parapolitical' journal *Lobster* in the UK. For example, in 1995 the US journal *Covert Action Quarterly* published an extensive feature on British military tactics to target Republican teenagers in Northern Ireland for harassment and even death. *Lobster* was the first to break the story about Colin Wallace and 'Operation Clockwork Orange', the MI5 plot to destabilise the Wilson government.

Second, alternative journalism seeks to invert the 'hierarchy of access' (Glasgow University Media Group 1976: 245) to the news by explicitly foregrounding the viewpoints of 'ordinary' people (activists, protesters, local residents), citizens whose visibility in the mainstream media tends to be obscured by the presence of elite groups and individuals. Langer (1998) has shown how a limited set of narratives and character-types within mainstream narratives operate forms of cultural closure that prevent other forms of story-telling and other representations (whether oppositional or contradictory) from being essayed. In the case of ordinary people, dominant story-types deal with overturning expectations – there is an emphasis on how the 'unremarkable' individual may be capable of extraordinary achievements (such as through adversity or lack of cultural and material resources). We also encounter ordinary people as subject to the control of external forces ('fate'), in which Langer locates stories of human tragedy (such as accidents, deaths and bereavements). In both cases, such stories and their actors tap into mythic representations of heroes and victims, from which derive their cultural-symbolic power and their resonances with audiences. The representation (and, as we shall see, the self-representation) of ordinary people in alternative journalism seeks not to set them apart as either heroes or victims but as a set of voices which have as equal a right to be heard as do the voices of elite groups. In so doing a further division is erased, that of 'fact-based' reporting and 'value-driven' commentary. As we shall see later, story-telling by those who are normally actors in other people's stories conflates these emblematic types of journalism and challenges the expert culture of both the news journalist and the 'expert' columnist.

The alternative media emphasise a humanistic set of journalistic values that are far removed from either the scientistic attempts at objective reporting or the persistence of the ideological necessity of objectivity. Alternative journalists enact social responsibility journalism with an important difference. Unlike the social responsibility journalism attempted in the US, culminating (for the present) in the public journalism movement, alternative journalists do not inhabit the mainstream – where public journalism seeks to effect change from within current practices and organisational regimes, alternative journalism seeks to do so freed from the constraints that limit the development of social responsibility in mainstream journalism (Davis 2000; Woodstock 2002).

We have already noted that alternative media are not simply about doing journalism differently, they are also about organising differently. This holistic approach to radicalising media practices offers freedom for journalists from many of the constraints that typically face mainstream journalists and that can present an array of often conflicting loyalties which interfere with the daily practices of doing journalism. There is a strong ethical dimension to the organisation and production of alternative media. Advertising is largely rejected, for fear of publications being influenced by external forces (though many publications do take advertising for products and services they approve of, such as those for similar publications and the products of ethically-trading companies). The notion of proprietorial influence is quite foreign to alternative media, given that most are run democratically and co-operatively by the media workers themselves. If the loyalties we find in mainstream media tend to be absent, in their place we find loyalties that centre on 'community', whether a community of interest or an 'actually lived', local community. The journalists place themselves firmly within such communities, espousing a loyalty that proceeds at the same time from specific causes or ideologies and from the particular, activist communities in which they are actors. Such loyalties are increasingly established on a transnational scale (as we find in the global Indymedia network). As Harcup has pointed out in his examination of journalism ethics within the mainstream, this is a significant loyalty that can often be overlooked: 'the journalist as citizen, with a sense of loyalty to other citizens' (Harcup 2002: 103). It is this loyalty, this concern with the citizen and especially with making the voices of those citizens heard that drives much alternative journalism and has resulted in a particular ethics of representation, through the practice of 'native reporting' (Atton 2002a: 112).

NATIVE REPORTING AND ISSUES OF REPRESENTATION

If, as Fursich (2002: 80) argues, 'most reporting is a form of representing the Other', then the most powerful journalistic method employed to
counter Othering within alternative media is surely that of 'native
reporting', where social actors, instead of being subjects of the news,
become their own correspondents, reporting on their own experiences,
struggles and ideas. This has become a common method of alternative
journalism and finds its most developed forms in the 'active witnessing'
(Couldry 2000b: 37) journalism of the new social movements, such as
those produced by the British video magazine *Undercurrents* and the
international, web-based news service Indymedia. Both privilege a
journalism politicised through subjective testimony, through the subjects being represented by themselves: 'native-reporting situates the
activist in both the texts they produce and in the sociopolitical contexts
in which they place them (and are themselves placed)' (Atton 2002a:
113). An illuminating instance of this practice is a video report
produced for *Undercurrents* by 'Jen', an activist for the Campaign
Against Arms Trade (Atton 2002a: 113–14). Her piece presents her as
advocate for arms control, an activist campaigner, a commentator and
an investigative reporter, emphasising the hybrid nature of much
alternative journalism. Here, explicitly partisan accounts are constructed from a personal, ideological commitment that deals with the
emotive and the rational through a radicalisation of journalistic tech-
nique. Bias and selectivity apart, though, what ethical issues does this
approach raise? It is clear from Jen's report that she is not a professional
journalist, nor does she pretend to professionalism. Her interview with
Robin Cook (then Foreign Secretary for the British government) is
opportunistic, unplanned, hurried and brief. I have shown Jen's report
to many postgraduate journalism students and have found a striking
consensus. Whether finding themselves already sympathetic to the
cause being advocated or, if previously ignorant of the issues, finding
themselves satisfactorily informed about those issues, almost all the
students found Jen's lack of conventional journalistic expertise worry-
ing and at times embarrassing. Is this an example of the threat to
professional values that access to technology can bring, where 'anyone
with Internet access [or access to a camcorder or a minidisc recorder]
can, in theory, set up their own media operation' (Keeble 2001: 12)?
Does this threaten standards to such an extent that it undermines trust
in the profession of journalism? Perhaps this is the wrong question to

ask. Fursich (2002) argues that by drawing attention to the practices of journalism within the form of the report itself, we might reveal the constructedness of the reality the journalist seeks to present. Fursich suggests the use of techniques similar to the alienation effects used by the German playwright Bertolt Brecht to discourage audiences from viewing a dramatic performance as 'real', instead encouraging them to attend to the content of the piece. Drawing from the practices of visual anthropology, Fursich recommends a journalistic practice that resists Othering through its presentation of a multi-voiced, unfinished text (she finds instances of these practices in syndicated television travel series such as *Lonely Planet* and the *Rough Guide*). The deployment of a range of voices, she argues, will displace the journalist as colonising expert, just as the narrative without closure challenges the primacy of the omniscient narrator. To essay such journalism is to effect a 'postmodern journalism' that is sensitive to the culture under examination and which presents a space in which representatives of that culture may emerge to challenge the status of the journalist as the sole 'expert' or determiner of 'reality'. Such practices are not intended to weaken or jeopardise the role of the journalist; on the contrary they are to reposition the journalist. No longer on the outside looking in – or rather, on high looking down – nor on the inside pretending to comprehend, Fursich has the journalist occupying a 'liminoid' position on the shared threshold of two cultures: their own and that of the Other. To inhabit such a position is to present an unstable, ever-changing situation, one where histories, relations and cultures are always in tension, always in process. Abandoning the ideologies of objectivity, impartiality and expert culture and critiquing them through postmodern practices becomes the route to understanding, to connection and to knowledge. And knowledge is surely the point. To position oneself on such a threshold is to challenge Derrida's 'violence of the letter'. It is to work against the power/knowledge complex that, as Foucault (1980) has argued, institutes and normalises power relations by presenting certain forms of knowledge as ideologically taken for granted. Without these challenges to our dominant discursive practices we cannot hope to escape the limits they place on us and our representations of the world. (We follow Foucault's arguments in more detail when we turn to examine the discourse of the far right on the Internet. There we shall find the notion of Othering and its resistance to it deployed in very different and far less progressive ways.)

An emphasis on 'standards' might also prevent us from identifying other, more beneficial ethical dimensions. First, such reports are about mobilising public opinion. In this respect, they are no different from the campaigning journalism of the mainstream media. The presence of explicit mobilising information is an enduring characteristic of alternative media, the aim of which is to suggest possibilities for social action to audiences (Bybee 1982; Lemert and Ashman 1983). Second, deprofessionalised approaches to doing journalism have been found to encourage audiences to start their own media projects, to become their own reporters (Atton 2002a: ch. 5). Together these may result in the 'de-naturalisation' of media spaces, encouraging audiences to rebalance the differential power of the media and to consider how 'the media themselves are a social process organised in space' (Couldry 2000b: 25). Media audiences may thus become media activists, having available to them methods for the de-naturalisation of the media, for re-imagining and renaming media power in their own locales, in their own words.

But we must not consider this one example as typical. The value of acquiring conventional training in journalism has been recognised by many alternative media projects and journalists (indeed, some of those who work for the alternative media are 'moonlighting' from day jobs in the mainstream). The writing styles in US publications such as *Covert-Action Quarterly* and *Z Magazine* strongly resemble those found in investigative journalism within the mainstream. *Undercurrents* offered camcorder training to activists and strove to produce broadcast-quality footage. The British alternative political newspaper *Squall* was staffed by activists who had, or were undergoing, journalism training (say, at night classes) and some of their reporters and photographers have produced work that has accorded so well with professional standards that it has been published in more mainstream publications (such as Gibby Zobel's work in the *Big Issue* and *The Guardian*). These differences are simply the result of producing journalism for different audiences. Despite *Undercurrents'* desideratum of broadcast-quality footage, it also celebrated the performativity of 'underproduction': 'turn your weaknesses (few resources, little experience) to an advantage by keeping your feature simple but powerful' (Harding 1997: 149). The primary audience for such work, it was assumed, would be the activist community itself. *Squall*, on the other hand, was more interested in 'talking to the bridge' and celebrated the diversity of their readership (which included British Members of Parliament). The paper operated its own house style in order to preserve its standards. The radical news sheet *SchNEWS*, produced weekly in Bristol, England, also has a house style of its own, yet its espousal of tabloid conventions sets it quite apart from the alternative journalism we have so far considered. In its employment of pun-filled headlines (such as 'Terror Firmer', 'Chinese Horrorscope', 'Water Disgrace!') and its colloquial and irreverent copy style, *SchNEWS* might be considered as the British tabloid of alternative journalism. It takes the ethical stance of native reporting and places it in a framework derived from right-wing newspapers whose ideologies could not be further from its own. In so doing it inverts the hierarchy of access to the media at the same time as it subverts media conventions through which familiar prejudices (racism, homophobia) are communicated.

The representation of, for example, ethnic minorities and of gays and lesbians is rarely an ethical issue for alternative journalists, since they are already operating from within a morally 'progressive' environment where discriminatory practices largely do not arise. Where biased representation may arise is, ironically enough, as a result of a politically progressive notion of free speech. Apparently influenced by Noam Chomsky's dictum that 'if you believe in freedom of speech, you believe in freedom of speech for views you don't like' (cited in Achbar 1994: 184), some alternative media projects have relinquished what has been an abiding ideology of 'no platform for fascists/racists/homophobes' in favour of an 'open platform' approach. This is in part a libertarian impulse, but has also been the result of 'open publishing' software used by Internet-based media such as the Indymedia network.

What began as a technical advance, though, has developed into a political issue. Activist and Indymedia contributor 'ChuckO' (2002) has called for 'aggressive action against racist and anti-semitic posts [which have] damaged Indymedia's reputation with Jewish people and people of color'. The loyalty to communities is once again present, though here it is part of a dilemma: to support free speech but to denounce hate speech. The issue is complicated further by the independence of Indymedia sites. Each of the seventy-odd sites that comprise its international network is editorially independent from the rest. As Sara Platon (2002) notes in a response to ChuckO, 'each one of them has its own editorial policy and its own way of dealing with racism or other "unwanted" articles and comments in the main newswire. Some are more pro free speech, and some are more restricted in what they "allow" on the website.' Just as we find a range of hybridised approaches to doing alternative journalism, we also find an array of ethical responses, often apparently in conflict with those prevalent across mainstream media. Whilst alternative journalism has no written code of ethics (nor is it likely to, given its heterogeneous and libertarian nature), its ethical practices are explicit. Platon argues that 'unlike as in more traditional forms of mass media, disagreements within the Indymedia news network are often out in the public domain'. However alien the ethical practices of alternative journalism might appear from within the mainstream media, the various methods and techniques it has developed to address bias, impartiality, representation and professionalism are similarly out in the open. At the very least we may attend to them. We may find in them a range of practices and also challenges to those practices. We may also find in them challenges to dominant journalistic practices that, some might argue, are long overdue.

INDYMEDIA, 9/11 AND BEYOND

From this we should expect radical online journalists, in their role as native reporters, to write from their own experience on events and issues with which they are involved as protesters and demonstrators, as political activists and dissidents. This has been their dominant *modus operandi* during, for instance, the protests against the WTO in Seattle and against the G8 summit in Genoa in 2001. The reporters' active, lived presence within the event, whilst no guarantor of impartiality, enabled the production of news that told other stories from those reported in the mainstream: 'our news, not theirs'. The events of 9/11 in 2001 and their aftermath have, however, presented a very different context. Indymedia journalists have been no less active, though their role has been less to do with reporting on the activities of their own social movements.

A study of Indymedia's '9/11: Peace and Justice' pages (Atton 2003) has shown a distinct move away from Indymedia's practice of 'open publishing' – these pages offered articles, interviews and broadcasts dealing with 11 September and its consequences that were *selected* by the Indymedia collective in Seattle from various sources: other IMC sites, alternative media sources, even mainstream and official sources on occasion. This approach to world events sees a distinct shift from an open access policy towards a more 'controlling', redactional function. What are absent are any contributions by self-identified Indymedia reporters, those who were prominent in Indymedia's coverage of the anti-capitalist protests in Seattle, Gothenburg and Genoa. There is little of the 'active witnessing' (Couldry 2000b) we find in such accounts. We do find practical proposals for activism and examples of mobilising information, though these account for only two postings. The majority of the pieces presented are written by those we might consider as movement intellectuals, of whom Noam Chomsky is pre-eminent, having the greatest number of contributions in the 9/11 pages (others include Edward Said, Howard Zinn, Michael Albert and George Monbiot). Despite its international network and international reach, Indymedia's choice of intellectuals is firmly US-centred.

This emphasis has to do with Chomsky's continuing currency within a wide range of both politically aligned and non-aligned radical move-ments, both in the US and across the world. In both the radical socialist and anarchist communities, for instance, Chomsky is a highly favoured author, contributing articles to the socialist and anarchist press (even on occasion to the European liberal press, though not in his home country). His work is used frequently as the intellectual bedrock for critiques of US foreign policy (for example, Chomsky 1992 and 1993) and critiques of the mass media (Chomsky 1989; Herman and Chomsky 1994). Chomsky's position on the US as a foreign aggressor is consistent and long-standing. The fundamentals of his work have remained essentially unchanged in their theoretical framework – the details of newly emerging cases (whether they be Vietnam, Nicaragua, East Timor, Iraq, Yugoslavia or Afghanistan) simply provide more weight of evidence to confirm the theory. Whilst, then, Chomsky's contribu-tions to Indymedia provide a mass of detail about the historico-political context for America's attack on Afghanistan (the history of US funding of Osama Bin Laden; the US's tolerance of Afghanistan when it was attempting to repel a Soviet invasion, for example), his conclusions are 'more of the same' – the US has shown itself once again the major aggressor in geopolitics, whilst attempting to pass itself off as the injured party.

We find the Chomskyan perspective underlying the range of intellectuals' contributions. Writers such as George Monbiot and Robert Fisk may be considered as 'mainstream radicals', professional writers and journalists, usually working within the liberal mainstream press (Monbiot in *The Guardian* in the UK, Fisk in the *Independent*) who are able to present radical ideas within the standard frames of mainstream media practices. In their chosen channels their voices are not necessarily prominent, nor inevitably acceptable to all their readers, viewers or listeners. Whilst they may offer a radical corrective to dominant mainstream media ideologies, their work may also be read as an enactment of pluralistic news values. This pluralism is developed further in what for the radical media is a surprising use of mainstream sources such as the BBC, CNN and the *Los Angeles Times*. These items appear to have been chosen either as evidence of dissent within official political discourse (such as the piece from the *LA Times* on Democrat Barbara Lee's lone dissenting voice in the House of Representatives' vote for 'all necessary and appropriate force' against the perpetrators of the 9/11 attacks), or to offer news that can contribute to a critique of the US position towards Afghanistan, such as the BBC report that the US was planning its attack on the Taliban well in advance of 11 September. The presence of mainstream sources might come as a surprise, given Indymedia's status as an activist-run news 'agency' staffed by activist or amateur journalists, until we recognise the pluralism that Indymedia is developing in its 9/11 pages. Unlike more radical media practices (such as elements of the anarchist press), Indymedia is not pursuing an ideological purity in the nature of its sources; the highly selective procedure it operates does, however, strongly suggest an ideological focus for the content of the 9/11 pages: the selections from the *LA Times*, for example, are in line with the arguments made by movement intellectuals such as Chomsky and Albert; the analysis of US support for the Taliban prior to 9/11 is used to argue for the US's hypocrisy in its foreign policy and for the historic predictability of its actions.

By contrast, there are relatively few contributions by what we have termed native reporters. Of the six that can be clearly identified, four are brief written pieces by individual activists. For example, Edward Aruna draws parallels with the attacks on the World Trade Center from experiences of state terror in his native Latin America. Tamim Ansary (described as an Afghani ex-patriot on the ezine *The Oracular Tree*, where her piece was first published) argues emotively for the innocence of the Afghan people and for Bin Laden to be treated as a war criminal, at the same time as she denounces US foreign policy towards Afghanistan, as does Saifedean Ammous in his 'letter from a Palestinian', where he offers a personal condemnation of the September 11 attacks, placing them in the context of his experience of Israeli aggression towards his homeland. All of these contributions appear to develop their ideology from the Chomskyan theory of US foreign policy. Whilst we should not ignore such 'intellectual contributions' as examples of activism – after all, these demonstrate dissident writing as activist intervention (and Albert and Shalom's 'Five Arguments' piece is located within the 'Action' section of Indymedia's 9/11 coverage) – what are absent are any contributions by any self-identified Indymedia reporters, who were prominent in Indymedia's coverage of the anti-capitalist protests in Seattle, Gothenburg and Genoa. There is little of the 'active witnessing' we find in such accounts. We do find practical proposals for activism and examples of mobilising information in the 'Action' section, though these account for only two postings. These are posted by activist collectives to promote the mobilisation of protests against Operation Enduring Freedom and comprise an 'Activist Calendar' of anti-war protests (posted by peace.protest.net) and a 'Hate-free Zone' organised by globalexchange.org that offers features, ideas and tactics for orga-nising against the war in Afghanistan and includes poster designs to publicise local actions for circulation and copying.

These are the only examples in the 9/11 pages of grassroots organis-ing across the spectrum of the anti-war coalition that was at this time being mobilised across the world. The remaining examples of organis-ing against the American campaign against the Taliban operate on a sectional, interest-group level only: the Mexico Solidarity Network's polemic in the 'News' section draws attention to Republican Congress-man Bill Thomas's attempt to push the Free Trade Area of the Americas bill through Congress, allegedly under cover of the 9/11 events (this bill, the piece argues, will impact deleteriously on the political and economic freedoms of Mexico). A statement from the Black Radical Congress argues for the necessity of solidarity across the African American community in the US in the anti-war protests. Arguably, the two selected communiques from the Revolutionary Association for the Women of Afghanistan (RAWA) might be con-sidered as types of native reporting – they engage from first-hand experience with the repressive aspects of the Taliban at the same time as they condemn US military intervention.

Apart from these few exceptions, the contributions on the Indymedia 9/11 pages we have examined (and which account for almost two-thirds of the contributions) are driven by US-based, movement-intellectual concerns: explications and analyses of US foreign policy, anti-war arguments, economic and political analyses. From this perspective, Indymedia's 9/11 coverage resembles more the coverage we would expect to find in radical political journals such as *Z Magazine* (a number of the contributions by Albert and Chomsky, for instance, are taken from that magazine's online version, ZNet). Thus far, Indymedia coverage hardly depends at all on its international network of native reporters – on the few occasions where it does draw on 'native voices' these tend to be drawn from radical groups and collectives, either based in North American or Afghanistan. There is only a partial, limited sense of the globalised reach of the Indymedia network.

Turning to the five radio contributions in the Selected Radio News section of the 9/11 pages we find hybridity that is less to do with hybrid writers; it has more to do with the general nature of the news source seen as an institutionalised medium. The choice of radio stations and radio web feeds presented under 'Selected Radio News' are firmly independent, though the professional make-up of their staff and their production values set them apart from the more rough-and-ready, de-professionalised media formations we have considered as native report-ing. Whilst the section highlights specific broadcasts, it also emphasises the ongoing coverage, analysis and commentary provided by the five (US) stations selected here. These include two stations 'in exile': Free Speech Radio News, a production of Pacifica Reporters Against Censorship, made up of reporters boycotting the independent Pacifica Radio for alleged censorship; and the web-based WBIX ('WBAI Radio in Exile'), comprising production and reporting staff fired from New York City's WBAI Radio. From the 'in-depth daily newscasts' from KFPA (Berkeley, California) Indymedia selected a single interview with Noam Chomsky.

The micro-independent Shortwave Report is produced by one person (Dan Roberts) and is a weekly, thirty-minute compilation of news broadcasts and interviews culled from shortwave broadcasts in English (such as those by the Voice of Russia, Radio China Interna-tional and Radio Havana Cuba). Shortwave Report demonstrates an interesting hybrid – the editing of a range of official, professionalised international radio stations is performed to highlight 'activist' issues: protests against the G8, Western-led political repression, stories from the 'other side' (positive news, for example, from Cuba, about literacy and human rights). We might construe Roberts as a 'native editor' whose personal editing decisions, whilst they may not indicate any representative or thoroughgoing presentation of the output of the stations he monitors, do at least – in the context of Indymedia's 9/11 pages – present a wider, international scope (in terms of sources) than is generally found elsewhere in the pages. The radio sources demonstrate the inadequacy of the fourfold writer-type model in accounting for alternative voices in Indymedia. Instead we can consider these sources as hybrid forms of alternative media – Shortwave Report offers a radio-based version of an alternative news clippings service; the established stations present the marriage of radical content and news values with mainstream production values, institutional frameworks and professionalised reporting.

There are six other alternative sources across the remaining sections of the 9/11 pages, three of which come from titled publications: an essay on 'the containment myth' in US Middle East policy, written by Stephen Hubbell, an editor of the independent *Middle East Report* (Hubbell is the *Nation*'s former Cairo correspondent); a 'think piece' from Bruce Shapiro, contributing editor to the *Nation*; and an anonymous article from Fairness & Accuracy In Reporting's (FAIR) web site, examining the overwhelming support for the 'war on terrorism' in the US media. The remaining three items all come from independent, web-based journalists. Two of these also deal with the US media's support for the 'war' and come from the web sites of John Tarleton and Pat Holt. Both Tarleton and Holt have histories as professional journalists: Tarleton as a former news and sports reporter, Holt as former book reviews editor for the *San Francisco Chronicle*. Both appear to have become radicalised (Holt describes himself on his site as a human rights activist) and to publish exclusively from their own web sites. Frances M. Beal, a political columnist for the *San Francisco Bayview* newspaper, posts a personal commentary directly to the 9/11 pages that takes the same political argument as that of the Black Radical Congress, for African Americans to organise against the US president's 'complete contempt for the global justice movement' (Beal is the National Secretary of the Black Radical Congress).

MAKING SENSE TO READERS

How are readers (perhaps more properly, visitors) to make sense of this range of contributions? They are left to understand or critique the sources and content of the material presented to them: are mainstream sources acceptable on a radical media site? How do we understand the presence of these mainstream sources? Are the political analyses rigorous and defining? What action should be taken against the US? Readers are left to perform their own critiques, based on the implicit selection decisions made by Indymedia as a set of redactional practices.

In its coverage of 9/11 the site has expanded significantly from its original role as a supplier of alternative news. The shift to commentary and analysis, coupled with a wider range of sources, suggests a media intervention that is confident that its assumed readers will find value and purpose in such pieces. Indymedia appears to be assuming that its activist audience is interested in understanding as well as action. To judge from their minimal coverage of activism, the 9/11 pages privilege analysis and discussion the better to engage readers in informed praxis. Mobilisation, whilst it is hardly ever suggested explicitly, will therefore come from reflection on the lessons of history. Whilst this emphasis on knowledge production in new social movement media is not unique (a study of Earth First!'s UK publication *Do or Die* has found a similar impetus at work; Atton 2002a: 121–6), such a complete giving-over of activist-led accounts to movement-intellectual discussion is new. With this comes an opening-up of Indymedia to those beyond the faithful. John Downing (2003) has drawn attention to the 'locked circuit' of alternative media participation, in which activists 'colonise' the alternative media, closing off access to both non-activist sources and non-activist audiences. In the present case, Indymedia's practices suggest a widening of access to sources.

In terms of audiences, the site is also available to those beyond the faithful. Readers are encouraged to append their own comments, and many do. As Platon and Deuze (2003: 349) note, '[c]ontrol of quality and "truth" stays in the hands of the reader . . . since every news item can be commented upon and argued about.' Whilst the majority of these 'meta-commentaries' supports the critical and analytical work presented on the pages, and adds little to it in terms of content, there is a large number of posts that are extremely critical of the contributions, some virulently so. In response to Saifedean Ammous's 'Letter from a Palestinian', 'GP' appends the following comment: 'I should expect no less from a murdering Palestinian . . . When you can admit your own faults Jew killer, come back and rant some more, until then do us all a favor and shut up with your propaganda bull' (GP, 'What a moron'). This outburst demonstrates that Indymedia is not preaching entirely to the converted and that along with other web-based radical media sites, the 'publicity' of the site enables critics, detractors and denunciators, as well as supporters and more neutral searchers for information, to interact with its contents (Atton 2000). The nature and impact of the use to which the site is put, whether by activists or others, remains open to question; Downing (2003: 625) has noted the 'disturbing gulf between . . . the mass of descriptions and theorisations of alternative media' and a general lack of information concerning the uses of such media. Here is yet another pressing case for audience research, one which, to judge from the preceding, would yield especially complex results.

The 9/11 pages emphasise not direct-action news, nor even hard news about what came to be known as Operation Enduring Freedom, but largely present in-depth, discursive features that seek to understand the wellsprings of the attacks of 11 September and the US government's responses to them. Alternative understandings and explanations are preferred over alternative news reports. These are presented from a much wider array of sources than we would expect from previous studies of alternative media: mainstream sources are more prominent than in most grassroots media projects. It appears that Indymedia's argument is that their readers may obtain 'the news' anywhere – what is more difficult is to see beyond the daily news cycle of events to the various histories of politics and policy that inform these events. The selections on the 9/11 pages provide what Indymedia believe are the appropriate analyses, commentaries and background. They may also be seen as implicit media critiques, presenting information and opinion that Indymedia's readers are unlikely to find easily. We might consider these interventions as a type of 'meta-journalism', in which the opinion pieces and commentaries implicitly critique what their authors – and Indymedia's editors – consider to be the shortcomings of the mainstream media. To this degree at least, the 9/11 pages are concordant with one of Indymedia's primary aims, to function as a critical repository for the re-telling of global news. In addition, despite the lack of native reporting, the site does offer materials intended to provoke discussion and debate amongst its publics, and to this degree presents itself as 'dialogical journalism' (Deuze 2003).

THE POSSIBILITIES OF RADICAL ONLINE JOURNALISM

Deuze (2003) proposes three characteristics of Internet technology that are useful in understanding the communicative dimensions of online journalism: interactivity, hypertextuality and multimediality. Interactivity he understands as the possibility for Internet publics (audiences) to respond to, interact with or even customise the content presented to them. As we have seen, the Indymedia project privileges the accounts of non-professional writers (activists), whom we might consider also as constituting a major part of Indymedia's audience. Even in the edited 9/11 pages, however, there is opportunity for interactivity – readers are able to post their responses to them (as they can to any Indymedia news item or commentary) and many do. Indymedia is heavily dependent on hypertextuality, both to link the central site in Seattle to its many global 'partners' in its network, and to provide access to other, original sources of its news and commentary. Finally, whilst the examples drawn on so far refer to text-based items, there is a wide array of media formats available through Indymedia (streaming and archived audio and video, photo archives and music).

Deuze goes on to explore these three broad characteristics in relation to four types of online journalism: 'mainstream' news sites; 'index and category' sites; 'meta and comment' sites; and 'share and discussion' sites. When these are applied to Indymedia it is apparent that the network's methods of doing journalism are extremely hybridised. Whilst his examination of mainstream news sites focuses on commercial news organisations, Deuze also places dedicated 'alternative' news sites such as Alternet and Indymedia in this category, as a subset he terms 'net-native' sites (a term which recalls our earlier characterisation of radical journalism as 'native reporting'). Indymedia also appears in his exploration of 'meta and comment' sites and 'share and discussion' sites – we have already seen how Indymedia's 9/11 pages present discussion and critical commentary on world affairs and the reporting of commercial news organisations and how the site offers the possibility for the exchange of ideas and opinions by its readers. Already, then, despite the (temporary?) shift in the nature of content in its 9/11 pages, Indymedia retains its broader remit of enabling criticism, discussion and 'sharing' amongst its writers and readers.

Deuze's careful and considered analysis of the possibilities of radical online journalism is in sharp contrast to the more celebratory claims of many commentators and analysts. In her historical account of Indymedia, Kidd (2003) employs hyperbole familiar to us from earlier, utopian accounts of electronic communication, claiming 'an extraordinary bounty of news reports and commentaries' that 'circulate almost instantly with a global reach', without any consideration of the nature and quality of such content, nor any sustained exploration of how it is used by audiences (nor, indeed, of who these audiences might be). Whilst more theoretically nuanced, Kahn and Kellner's (2003) account of Internet 'post-subcultures' engaged in a 'postmodern adventure' characterised by a technologically-saturated media environment, makes perhaps some of the grandest claims for radical online journalism. For them, the very characteristics that Deuze finds – in particular, inter-activity – are sufficient to argue that radical journalistic practices on the Internet enable 'the revolutionary circulation and democratisation of information and culture'. They focus less on communitarian, net-worked projects such as Indymedia, finding their 'revolution in journal-ism' located within the 'subculture' of bloggers, that is, of individuals and groups who have established their own web logs (or blogs) as extensions of personal web pages. These they use to post commentaries on mainstream news, to enable discussion with and amongst visitors to their sites and, on occasion, to originate their own news. Blogging is, if you like, a less reticulated and less social-movement minded version of the global network of Indymedia, applying similar principles of native reporting, media critique, discussion and dialogue amongst its writers and readers.

The blog has become a focal point for much mainstream media attention. This is perhaps due to its personal roots, which enable mainstream journalism to develop human-interest stories around its creators rather more easily than it can explore the more abstract, political goals of networks such as Indymedia. Trent Lott's resignation as the US Senate's majority leader in December 2002 followed his comments expressing 'indulgence towards the racist policies of the Old South' (Burkeman 2002). These comments, Burkeman notes, were first picked up and commented on by bloggers some days before the mainstream media ran the story. More recently, during the Gulf War of 2003, mainstream media attention was drawn to bloggers posting from within Iraq during the conflict. 'Smash', the pseudonym of an American military officer serving in Iraq, posted chronicles of his experiences – along with critiques of the conflict – on his web site (Kurtz 2003). Professional reporters used blogs to post commentaries that their employers would not be prepared to publish. Kurtz also cites a CNN correspondent based in the Kurdish section of Iraq, whose audio-visual journal caused enough concern with his employer that the reporter was forced to suspend his blog. Blogs run by professional journalists were also used in Indymedia's 9/11 pages. Two of these presented critiques of the US media's support for the invasion of Afghanistan (John Tarleton and Pat Holt).

It would be mistaken, however, to consider the blog as a homo-geneous phenomenon. As Matheson and Allan (2003) have shown, bloggers hardly constitute a discrete set of native reporters as we have explored that term here. Instead, they represent a wide range of backgrounds. During the Gulf War of 2003 blogs were posted from professional journalists 'moonlighting' from their day jobs. These included BBC reporters such as Stuart Hughes. The BBC and the British newspaper *The Guardian* established 'warblog' sites during the conflict. Blogs were also employed by NGOs such as Greenpeace as well as by US military officers posted in Iraq such as 'L. T. Smash' and 'Will'. A blog run by 'Salam Pax' claimed to be written by a Baghdad resident; the US journal *New Republic* ran an online diary by Kanan Makiya, a leading Iraqi dissident. Despite this range of voices Matheson and Allan find common features. They note that even the professional reporters tended to eschew the established standards of objectivity and impartiality, preferring instead a style of address that has more in common with what we have termed native reporting. That is to say, they wrote from direct, personal experience about those experiences, and emphasised their independence from organisational or administrative constraints. From their interviews with professional journalists who maintained blogs during the war Matheson and Allan find that it is these aspects of their writing that the reporters believe resonated with their readers: it was the direct, 'authentic' account of personal experience that counted in the midst of mainstream coverage that was dominated by the carefully controlled output of 'embedded' journalists. It is, they argue, the transparency of such methods (just as we have seen in other examples of native reporting) that establishes trust between writer and reader – it is this relationship, developed from subjective modes of address, coupled with disillusionment and scepticism towards the mass media, that make the blog a valuable site for re-imagining news practices. For the weblog, trustworthiness springs from the setting-up of a subjective position from which to write about one's own experiences – it is less to do with the facticity of the reporting. It is, as Matheson and Allan show, the connectedness that a sharing of personal experience between writer and reader can bring that is emblematic of this 'new' journalism. This journalism is less focused on the journalist as expert and the report as a commodity produced by a news agent; instead it proposes a relationship between writer and reader where epistemological claims may be made about the status of journalism and its practitioners. This has less to do with the novelty of the knowledge being produced (a focus on uncovering 'hidden' stories); instead it suggests new ways of thinking about and producing journalism (a focus on what kinds of knowledge are produced and how readers and writers may come together to make sense of them). Arguably such practices are not new – writers such as Jack London and George Orwell had performed similar styles of native reporting in their literary journalism (Atton 2002b). What distinguishes the present examples is the space in which they take place; the medium of the Internet enables publication of such reports outside the industrial arrangements of the publishing industry or media corporations. It is arguable, though, that the work of the Iraq warbloggers came to public attention precisely through these arrangements and thus came to be considered within the established techniques of media framing as 'celebrities'. This only remains a problem, however, if we insist on some kind of 'purity' (isolationism) for a field of alternative journalism. If the most powerful outcome of these new practices is to challenge an existing epistemology of news production, then it is of less significance how we come to learn about such challenges; whilst the structural modes of publicising such reports might endure, there is little reason to believe that those structures will have any influence on the modes of knowledge being produced. Indeed they may even contribute to a normalisation of such practices through their power as publicisers.

The Gulf War of 2003 found Indymedia sites, in similar fashion to the warbloggers, returning to their earlier practices of native reporting, in addition to offering critiques and commentaries. In part this was due to the presence of 'human shields' in Iraq, peace campaigners who, independently of governments and NGOs, had chosen to place themselves at strategic public utilities (such as water purification plants) in the hope that a human presence would dissuade combatants from attacking such facilities. The human shields were drawn largely from the European peace movement, and their access to Internet technology (laptops, satellite phones) enabled them to post accounts of their experiences to their 'home' Indymedia sites. In some cases, an individual acted as a conduit for reports from human shields and independent reporters. For example, 'Robdinz' posted such accounts on the IMC Italian site (italy.indymedia.org). As a demonstration of the international, co-operative nature of the Indymedia network, IMC Switzerland (www.indymedia.ch) undertook to translate these into French and English on its site. Indymedia was not unique in this. During the conflict many other peace movements adopted similar strategies. The Belgium peacerace site (www.peacerace.be) ran many stories from human shields in Iraq.

Such practices of native reporting, then, are not simply the domain of the unprofessionalised, grassroots journalists. Just as we may locate a species of native reporting in the work of writers such as London and Orwell, we may find versions of these practices in the commercialised and professionalised cultures of online journalism. In their study of online journalists in the Netherlands, Deuze and Dimoudi (2002) find a 'new profession' emerging that is less interested in reproducing the agenda-setting and advocacy roles of the professional journalist. Instead we see at work journalists whose reporting springs from the discussions and deliberations of the online communities that comprise the audiences for commercial, online newspaper sites. The autonomy and independence from their offline colleagues that journalists find in their online newsrooms have produced, it seems, journalists 'with a powerful sense of the public's wants and needs as reflected in the desire to provide the widest possible audience with new ideas, a platform for discussion and a more or less pluralistic analysis of the issues in the news' (Deuze and Dimoudi 2002: 93–4). These ideas, platforms and analyses spring not from the maintenance of journalism's historical role as watchdog, surveying the social and political landscape from above, but from active negotiation with the audience. Working with audiences to produce the news in this way is to position the journalist as a type of native reporter. It is possible to see in this productive conjunction of professional journalist and audience a future for the development of public journalism and with that an opening-up of further possibilities for a journalism that promotes and is intimately part of a communicative democracy.

CONCLUSION

Reports of events such as those at Seattle were considered newsworthy by independent journalists to the degree that they were able to counter the dominant mainstream coverage. Such accounts attempted to take back 'our news' with accounts of peaceful protests, of discussion and debate, analyses of the complexity and heterogeneity of the various protest groups. The native reporter typically reports from within the context of their own active, lived presence at an event, as was the case in Seattle. In the 9/11 pages we found not direct-action news but in-depth, discursive features and commentaries.

The dominance of the Chomskyan model throughout the analytical, background and commentary pieces in the 9/11 pages renders the majority of their content timeless in terms of the analyses they undertake. This resembles Braudel's (1980) notion of *longue durée*, where issues and rationales are presented as largely fixed, motionless. The static nature of the 9/11 pages suggest this structurally, too. Emerging issues, the timeliness and dailiness we might expect from such contributions as part of an Internet media project is eroded the longer the pages remain static – the twenty-four-hour news cycle (Braudel's *histoire événementielle*) is absent. The major features that typify Indymedia's non-hierarchical, collective approach to web-based reporting and discussion – timeliness; a diversity of voices that emphasises native reporters; the scope for unlimited postings; a wide range of international sources – are all rendered problematic by an analysis of the 9/11 pages. We find much hybridity that draws equally from alternative and mainstream sources, that includes highly selective polemics from special and sectional interest groups and individuals. This hybridity is underscored by a shared radical-intellectual foundation for its analysis and commentary.

The emergence of blogs offers individuals the opportunity to create their own news sites, though in the main these tend to personal commentary and opinion. However, in times of crisis – and as circumstances permit – we have seen how some bloggers are able to offer us eye-witness accounts that their professional work both enables and inhibits; their profession has provided them access to experiences, whilst their professional duty constrains them from communicating these experiences save through a personal, non-professional channel. We have also seen how specific geopolitical situations prompt action from particular members of social movements. In the case of 9/11 and the war in Afghanistan, limited access to that country reduced the possibility of native reporting – hence, arguably, Indymedia's reliance on commentary and opinion. During the Gulf War of 2003, whilst such writing was also being done, the European peace movement's presence as human shields saw a return to extensive native reporting. We see here a deployment of various radical journalism methods, encompassing first-person native reports; radical critiques of government policies, government actions and the mass media; the occasional use of mainstream and 'radical mainstream' sources; and the creation of spaces for discussion and debate. The picture of radical online journalism thus presented is one that is heterogeneous, flexible and responsive. What its various practices share, to be found equally in Indymedia as well as in the variety of warblogs, though, is a critique of dominant news values and practices that is effected through the performance of this 'new' journalism. This is perhaps its most significant feature, one which has the capacity to transform dominant practices of journalism, not through the numbers of journalists practising radical online journalism, nor indeed through the size of its audience. In short, such new practices signal a challenge to the epistemological basis of mainstream news production. In its place we see enacted a socially situated and self-reflexive form of journalism, one which reveals the constructedness of journalism through its emphasis on subjective experience and its knowledge claims: '[t]ruth is not seen as an absolute but as an infinite sampling of perspectives of a given situation' (Platon and Deuze 2003: 345). We see a move away from journalism as expert culture and commodity; readers are invited to approach the knowledge presented here not as the product of an elite authority but as the result of a process that comes about through the impersonal connectedness of journalist and reader. This is to move away from the essentialisation of alternative media as explained only by reference to its novel coverage or of under-reported events, situations and perspectives. Instead it is to posit these various forms of alternative journalism as epistemological processes which call into question the accepted and taken-for-granted forms of doing journalism.

CHAPTER 3

Far-right Media on the Internet: Culture, Discourse and Power

INTRODUCTION

The 1990s saw a dramatic movement of the European far right towards the centre of national politics, through a series of attempts to establish 'respectable' electoral parties. Right-wing parties with policies based primarily on nationalism and immigration (such as Joerg Haider's Austrian Freedom Party and Jean-Marie Le Pen's Front National in France) resonated with publics increasingly disillusioned with what they saw as centralist policies of the European Union, of a liberalism that to them appeared to favour the rights of 'aliens' above native-born citizens, and a globalisation that seemed to ignore domestic issues such as law and order, housing and employment. Such parties sought, with some success, to normalise a racial nationalism based on 'whiteness as an essentialised social identity which they say is under threat' (Back 2002b), a strategy also followed by the British National Party.

We might think of these developments in mainstream political culture as the penetration into a dominant, Habermasian public sphere of debate and opinion-formation (assisted in no small way by the mass media's coverage of these popular right-wing parties) of hitherto marginalised political groups. Parallel to this normalisation of right-wing discourse in the public sphere we find an increasing use of the Internet by fractions of the far right which essay more extremist versions of the populist rhetoric of such as Haider and Le Pen, which resonated so deeply with significant sections of their respective countries' electorates. In effect, we witness the emergence of their 'publicity' (in Habermas's sense of the term) into the public sphere at the same time as these fractions are developing their own cyber-subcultures or alternative public spheres on the Internet. It is these latter that I wish to explore here, for the following reasons.

First, little attention has been paid to right-wing media as alternative media. At the first international meeting for alternative media scholars ('Our Media, Not Theirs', Washington, DC, May 2001) there was much debate over the morality of studying such media. Even amongst those who recognise the area of interest, there is concern that the extremely hierarchical methods of organisation and production within the groups promoting such media work against consideration of far-right media as 'alternative'. Here 'alternative' is employed to denote media practices that 'strengthen democratic culture' (Downing 2001: 95); the desideratum of 'self-governing media is simply not imaginable' (p. 94) for what Downing terms the 'repressive radical media' of the far right. Nick Couldry has nuanced this problem in terms of citizenship practices. As we saw in Chapter 1, Couldry emphasises the place of alternative media in creating and sustaining a 'community without closure' (Couldry 2000a: 140). Central to such a community is dialogue; independent control over symbolic resources is crucial to enable the 'exchange [of] representations of such "reality" as we share' (Couldry 2002). For Couldry, 'one of the central values of, say, neo-Nazi media is to *close off* certain others' abilities to speak of their experience, as part of constructing or sustaining a community *with* closure' (ibid., original emphases). Compelling though Couldry's argument might be from an ethical perspective, his argument does not rest on any empirical investigation. What is clearly needed is research to investigate this claim and, indeed, to compare the findings of such research with his idealised, 'pure' form of alternative media practices that apparently operate without such closure. There is, for instance, evidence to suggest that there is a distinct ideological framework within which certain of Indymedia's media practices operate. In Indymedia's coverage of 9/11 and its aftermath a distinctive, 'Chomskian' version of events is significantly privileged, leaving little room for other, even sympathetic counter-discourses (Atton 2003). A hierarchical control over symbolic resources is therefore apparent even in this highly democratised communication process. Whilst Couldry is right to argue that the media of the far right are just as interested as Indymedia in 'contest[ing] the concentration of symbolic power in media institutions' (Couldry 2002), any hostility to the values expressed through such media should not be sufficient to close off empirical work.

Second, and following from this, studies of the 'progressive', liberal or anarchist media that typify most studies of alternative media are slowly beginning to examine these media formations in terms of how their counter-discourses can be adopted by the mainstream, how their messages can penetrate into the dominant public sphere and how they themselves might make use of mainstream forms of discourse, in terms of technology, rhetoric and 'publicity'. This is to examine alternative media formations not as sets of discrete subcultural practices but as practices that are, as Hebdige (1979) reminds us, challenging the maintenance of hegemony through 'a struggle within signification' (p. 17). For some researchers of alternative media, the media of the far right seek to merely maintain that hegemony. However, a study of far-right media practices could reveal other dimensions of ideological struggle.

Participatory communication and radicalised professional practices of journalism are considered to lie at the heart of alternative media. Might such practices also be features of far-right radical media, and thus just as worthy of being considered as 'citizens' media' (Rodriguez 2000)? In terms of graphic design and typography, at least, racist skinhead music fanzines such as *Blood and Honour* drew explicitly from the same subcultural rupturing of dominant codes that Hebdige (1979) found in the punk fanzine. More recently, in the far right's use of the Internet we find some intriguing, if not disturbing, modalities for transforming elements of dominant, 'normalised' discourses into racist media practices. Les Back has found that far-right media in the UK have recently assimilated the language of multiculturalist discourse through their adoption of terms such as 'equality', 'fairness' and 'rights' – significantly he notes that the British National Party's 'house pub-lication' has been relaunched as 'Identity': 'their dominant motif is that whites are now the victims' (Back 2002b). He has also noted the attempts on a White Power web site to co-opt the writings of Adorno on the culture industry into the canon of extreme racist literature: 'Adorno's work is *used* to criticize the involvement of cultural entre-preneurs and then organized into a conspiratorial anti-Semitic view' (Back 2002a: 637, original emphasis). Back explains these attempts at co-optation and assimilation as a consequence of a contemporary destabilisation of political languages; 'increasingly, liquid ideologies are capable of assimilating elements that on the face of it seem incompatible' (Back 2002a).

A THEORETICAL PERSPECTIVE

Back's emphasis on 'liquid ideologies' suggests a theoretical perspective for this study that can draw on a hegemonic framework that appears well suited for such an analysis. A hegemonic analysis of radical (in the present case, far-right) media should encourage us to examine it not as a discrete field of symbolic production, but as inhabiting a shared, negotiated field of relations, subject to 'contradictory pressures and tendencies' (Bennett 1986: 350). The classic features of hegemonic practice – the notion of an unstable, non-unitary field of relations, where ideology is mobile and dynamic and where strategic compromises are continually negotiated (Gramsci 1971) – might thus be applied to a study of these relations. That is, media practices may be viewed as movable; they may articulate to bourgeois (mainstream) values in one instance, but become joined with radical values in another.

The present analysis is not about to reveal a benign transfer of practices between two sets of equally matched media practices; it is about struggle, the aim of which (in Gramsci's terms) from the point of view of the bourgeoisie, is to contain and to incorporate dissident values of subordinate groups within an ideological space (Hebdige 1979: 16). This ideological space must then appear permanent, natural and commonsensical, even as it is continually contested. We can examine radical media practices for examples of how naturalised media frames and ideological codes can be disrupted. This is to suggest the possibility of a counter-hegemony arising from those residual and emergent cultural practices, an oppositional set of practices that, rather than preferring to exist alongside the dominant culture, seek to change society, whether for good or for ill. What is at stake is how differing sets of media practices, each with their own routines, rules and ideological codes, socially construct reality.

If Couldry and Downing are right in their assertions that the radical media of the far right represent a community with closure, where the principles of authoritarian populism prevent any meaningful debate and work against any notion of democratic communication, insisting instead on hierarchical control, then we would expect to find more or less distinct divisions between producers and audiences, and with them a relative absence of creativity, freedom and exploration of ideas and arguments, along with similarly curtailed forms and styles of presentation and structure.

Hamilton and Couch (2002) have recently proposed a move away from the study of the linear relationships between producers and audiences through revisiting Marx's exploration of the relations between production and consumption. They argue for a decentring of the concern 'with individuals, their intentions, their individual actions, and the effects of specific messages', to be replaced by 'a focus on the making and maintenance of forms and relationships which prescribe, encourage, and delimit certain kinds of social action and processes'. In the case of the media of the far right, such a decentring, according to Couldry and Downing, would hardly appear necessary. The extent to which this is or is not the case would be a further element to the present study.

Methodologically this suggests an ethnographic approach that is able to account for the individual's or group's life practices as the cultural context in which their media practices are embedded. As Sterne emphasises, 'it is not the ultimate goal of a cultural study to determine what a given event online *means* for its participants (although this may be part of it) but, rather, *how the possibilities for meaning are themselves organized*' (Sterne 1999: 262, original emphases). A hegemonic and materialist approach to the media practices of the far right on the Internet, attending as it must to the evolving relations and identities between producers and audiences, will offer insights into the productive processes of communication (rather than the merely connective) within and across such groups.

EXAMINING THE DISCOURSE OF FAR-RIGHT MEDIA

The present study will need to examine two aspects of the radical Internet media of the far right. First, it must analyse the texts themselves in order to reveal the extent to which they are constructed hegemonically, to assess the presence of 'liquid ideologies' that are mobile enough to borrow from a variety of discourses in order to present their arguments. The text therefore becomes central. Second, it must be capable of examining the social and cultural relationships that form and re-form around the text, as a way of critically exploring the producer–audience nexus. These aims suggest a twofold approach to the study that comprises: first, an analysis of content that goes well beyond the reductionism of quantitative methods and that examines the interrelation between texts in the same document, texts across documents, and the cultural and social import of these texts; second, an examination of the cultural status of the texts, in relation to its writers and readers as well as according to the wider economic, political and social forces that shape it. This is to examine these texts as cultural objects in relation to the social institutions and actors (editors, writers, readers) that make meaning and transform the content of such objects through and into their daily experience, their hopes and fears – and, it might be said, 'culturally activate' them, to borrow Tony Bennett's (1983) useful concept.

Given that discursive practices both convey and construct meaning (Van Dijk 1997), then a suitable method would be that of discourse analysis. Discourse analysis typically adopts a social constructionist view in which it is accepted that language is not simply reflective of reality, but is significant in constituting reality. In this sense discourse is viewed not only as a form of language use (text) or discursive practice, but also regarded as a form of *social practice* – the arena within which social life is produced, be it economic, political, cultural, or everyday life (Fairclough 2001). Fairclough (1995) presents a three-dimensional framework for analysing discourse from a critical perspective. This reflects the interdependencies between language use (text), discursive practice (processes by which texts are produced and interpreted), and social practice (the institutional, material and organisational factors surrounding text production and interpretation).

Text is a product rather than a process. Analysis is concerned with the formal content in terms of vocabulary, grammar and textual structures. The set of features we find in a specific text can be regarded as specific choices from among the positions available in the discourse types. Discursive practice refers to the process of production, of which text is a part, and the process of interpretation, for which text is a resource. Here the analyst focuses on how the text was produced and interpreted within the social situation under study. Fairclough stresses the need for analysts to be aware that practices which underlie texts are based in particular social relations, and particular relations of power. An account of the processes of production and interpretation is not complete without an analysis of ways in which they are socially determined. Texts and the processes by which they are produced and interpreted have social origins – they are socially generated, dependent on the social relations and struggles out of which they are generated.

THE TWO–WAY PLAY OF DISCOURSE

Valuable though such an approach may be, the notion of text as product determined by external forces and relations limits our understanding of discourse; viewed in this light, discourse is the result of ideological production. This approach forces us to examine only how ideology constructs discourse, and with it forms of identity, subject position and social groups (Wetherell and Potter 1992: 61). At the heart of this approach is the Marxist notion of 'historical accounting', where we seek the roots and causes of particular social actions (in this case, discursive and textual constructions). This approach assumes that through a 'non-ideological understanding' we can reach a 'veridical understanding' (p. 62) of the forces at work. This ideological approach is an important element in discourse analysis, since it entails an examination of the 'established' (p. 86) aspects of discourse. It suggests analyses that seek to identify the historical resources upon and through which discourses are constructed, and how those discourses are mobilised to construct new social formations and identities. However, in their study of Pakeha ('white') racism in New Zealand, Wetherell and Potter (1992) argue that this is only one aspect of discourse analysis. They argue for a 'double movement' of discourse analysis (p. 86) which comprises an interplay between the 'established' aspect of discourse and a 'genealogical' or constitutive aspect. Following Foucault (1980), they argue that discourse is not only constituted by existing social formations and historical accounts, but is itself constitutive of social groups, subject positions and identities. That is to say, discourse is not only produced, it is productive: productive of agents and subjects, of material interests. To consider it as little more than reflecting existing class positions or material interests is to ignore the role of discourse in producing power. For Foucault (1980), power is not merely played out or exhibited in discourse, it is produced through discourse. Knowledge is constituted through discursive formations and through that knowledge is constituted power. This generation of power is capable of forming agents and subjects. In contrast with the 'established' approach, a constitutive understanding of discursive formations emphasises how discourse can produce forms of social action, not merely reflect them ideologically. In Foucaultian terms, we might consider these discursive formations as 'rituals of power' and look for the effects such rituals have on agents and subjects. Power becomes the central term, and it is through discourse (knowledge production) that power is created and dispersed:

Power must be analysed as something which circulates . . . Power is employed and exercised through a net-like organisation. And not only do individuals circulate between its threads; they are always in the position of simultaneously undergoing and exercising its power . . . The individual which power has constituted is at the same time its vehicle. (Foucault 1980: 98)

The double movement proposed by Wetherell and Potter seeks to combine the established and the constitutive notions of discourse analysis in a continual interplay: 'a double movement between styles of reading that emphasize the constitution of subjects and objects and those that emphasize the ideological work of discourse' (Wetherell and Potter 1992: 93). For the present study this approach has distinct advantages. First, it enables the analyst to explore how existing knowledge and structures (particularly, in the case of racist practices, socio-economic determinants, the history of immigration, the colonial legacy) have constituted the power relations within racist discourse. Second, it encourages an analysis that examines that discourse in terms of the power it has produced: what new forms of identity or social action have been constituted? Third, this double movement suggests next a return to the established form of analysis, in order to explore how, for instance, the social action produced by discourse might itself be re-formed by subsequent knowledge formations, for example, in the deployment of the discourse of multiculturalism in contemporary racist discourse (Back 2002b). How might that new discursive formation then be productive of new, or altered, subject positions and identities within racist groups? There is further value in this approach. One of the aims of this study is to examine the extent to which racist discourse on the Internet might be considered a species of 'alternative media'. The double-movement approach can also be applied to the abiding structures, power relationships and social formations typically found in 'progressive' alternative media projects. How do these structuring aspects of media formations determine the formation of far-right media? Are they transposed, reconstituted or ignored? And how does the discourse of the media practices of the far right produce subjects and identities amongst those involved in it, whether as writers or readers? In short, following Foucault, this study will not attempt to discover 'truth' (understood ideologically as a version of events, social practices and knowledge) – instead it tries to discover 'how truth is formed' (Wetherell and Potter 1992: 81).

The present study will put this double-movement approach into practice in a text-based setting. It will focus primarily on 'fixed' texts, that is, on writings rather than conversations. It will also engage in the structuring of those texts with each other, both rhetorically (intertextually) and technologically (for example, through hyperlinking). It will emphasise discourse as social practice. The previous section has emphasised the socially productive nature of discourse. The location of discourse within history, economics and culture, the ways in which discourse produces through those contexts elaborated forms of those contexts, and how that discourse produces social action all suggest a method that is concerned with the mobilisation of concepts (rhetorically and discursively) and their situated use, rather than with any abstracted or reductively quantitative approach (Wetherell and Potter 1992: 93). This is not to say that elements of Fairclough's critical discourse analysis will not be of use. In particular, his three broad areas of discourse analysis (the text, the discursive practices through which the text is developed, and the wider social practices that determine those discursive practices) will all be useful entry points (Fairclough 1995). Through these three levels we can examine how the text is designed, why it is designed in this way, and how else it could have been designed. We can explore what discourses are drawn upon, and how they are articulated together in the text (for example, what discourses do the writers draw upon to legitimise their arguments and de-legitimise opposing arguments?). An analysis of discursive practices can examine how texts of this sort are produced, and in what ways they are likely to be interpreted and used.

Finally, an analysis of wider social practices brings into the picture the wider conditions (including economic and political ones) which constrain texts, in terms of systems of knowledge and beliefs (and ideologies), social relations of power and the positioning of people as social subjects. Together, these three levels will be employed to examine the use of language, not merely to focus on stylistic and grammatical elements. And whilst Fairclough's approach sits squarely in the 'established' notion of discourse analysis, his methods may be used reflexively to explore the constitutive aspect of discourse: what social relations are produced through discourse? How is power created and enacted through discourse? Fairclough's method seeks to examine social conditions and practices and knowledge systems as the foundations of discourse; we might also examine discursive practices from the other way round, to explore how they transform social practices and construct knowledge, through which new social practices and dimensions of power operate. This attention to the contours and contexts of discourse analysis, rather than a microscopic focus on the grammatical or the syntactical, should enable the methods of critical discourse analysis to be applied to the double-movement approach outlined above.

It is, however, Wetherell and Potter's notion of mobilisation that is most suggestive of the actual, analytic practices that might be employed. As examples, they suggest 'the way concepts of "race", "culture" and "nation" are mobilized, paying close attention to their specific construction, to their placement in a sequence of discourse, and to their rhetorical organization' (Wetherell and Potter 1992: 93). To understand these in their situated contexts, Wetherell and Potter draw on the work of John Thompson (1984) who recommends that ideological analyses must not only deal with the analysis of discourse; they should also examine the social relations and histories relevant to that discourse and, finally, bring the two together in an 'interpretative or hermeneutic act' (Wetherell and Potter 1992: 105).

What, though, should be our objects of study? That is, how shall we select far-right Internet sites for this analysis? Stempel and Stewart (2000) have drawn attention to the difficulties in the sampling of Internet sites: 'Suppose the researcher wanted to do an analysis of hate sites? Is there a list? How did the list maker define hate groups? . . . The question is whether the group of sites identified is really representative of the category' (p. 345). There are two methodological questions here. First, how do we identify the population of far-right Internet media from which we shall sample? Second, how do we ensure the representativeness of that sample? Both assume a quantitative approach to Internet research ('Is there a list?' '. . . really representative') that sits uneasily with the critical, qualitative dimensions of the double-movement approach to discourse analysis. This study does not pretend to statistically significant representativeness. Instead it will present an analytical and interpretative account of far-right discourse that does not seek to be definitive. It will emphasise historical contingency and shifting social and cultural conditions; other accounts may arise that are equally valid. The validity of the account thus shifts away from statistical representativeness towards the construction of a (provisional) system or holistic model of the phenomena under consideration. Nevertheless the question of how to identify and choose sites for analysis remains. Here the study will be guided by the definitional work of others as well as by their analytical foci.

On the matter of defining the activities and ideologies of far-right groups on the Internet, Brophy, Craven and Fisher (1999) identify a range of ideological positions, amongst them racist, homophobic, fascist, right-wing, ultraconservative, social Darwinist and supremacist. They note both the historical linkages that many far-right groups make through their use of such ideologies (fascism and Nazism are the most salient) and the transformations that this terminology has undergone in recent years, as far-right groups aim for 'respectability' (emphasising 'community' and 'identity' over more explicitly separatist and inflammatory terms). In selecting sites for analysis, then, it will be important to choose sites that suggest both aspects of these ideological positions: one that has drawn on emerging discourses in its efforts to re-position itself within a discursive world that is far more multicultural than that found in previous histories of far-right activity, and one which has undertaken no such discursive transformation, which deals in explicit hate speech. Back's (2002b: 1) observation that 'the language of hate is increasingly being articulated through invocations of love' suggests a detailed discursive examination of these practices. Whilst Back does not attempt this, his emphasis on the British National Party (BNP) as one site for such practices suggests that the Internet media produced by the BNP will be an appropriate subject for the present study.

This study will therefore focus on far-right Internet media in the UK, though the local nature of this choice will be enhanced by attending to the international networks within which these media might be embedded. Taking the BNP's site as a foundation, the study will also attend to other sites as they present themselves through the reticulated nature of the Internet, intending to embed the discursive practices of the British sites within the international context of far-right activity. The decision to begin with a narrow, local focus and to use the resources of that focus to broaden the investigation is based primarily on a desire to locate the study within a coherent framework and thus to avoid imprecision. As Brophy, Craven and Fisher's (1999) discussion of terminology suggests, the variety of far-right activity on the Internet, its aims, methods and ideologies, coupled with its international nature (which exhibits hybrid forms of ideologies), make any comprehensive analysis impossible. To begin somewhere is enough. A UK focus makes the analytic task more straightforward, whilst not precluding further analyses across national and ideological boundaries.

THE POLICIES OF THE BNP

Under its first leader and founder, John Tyndall, the BNP had been notorious for promoting forced repatriation and racial violence. In 1995, party activist Nick Griffin wrote in the extremist publication *The Rune* that the defence of 'rights for whites' could only come from 'well-directed boots and fists. When the crunch comes, power is the product of force and will, not of rational debate' (cited in *Searchlight*, 1999). Since becoming chairman of the party in 1999 Griffin has sought to distance himself from such rhetoric and to reposition the BNP as a party of 'racial nationalism and social justice', to build a 'responsible' movement that 'becomes the focus of the hopes not just of the neglected and oppressed white working class, but also of the frustrated and disorientated traditional middle class' (cited in *Searchlight*, 1999). Despite this shift in rhetoric (and some dilution of its earlier policies) towards a 'new nationalism', the BNP's policies remain founded on racism. Its primary policy is that of immigration, and from this all its other policies proceed:

> On current demographic trends, we, the native British people, will be
> an ethnic minority in our own country within sixty years. To ensure
> that this does not happen, and that the British people retain their
> homeland and identity, we call for an immediate halt to all further
> immigration, the immediate deportation of criminal and illegal
> immigrants, and the introduction of a system of voluntary
> resettlement whereby those immigrants who are legally here will be
> afforded the opportunity to return to their lands of ethnic origin
> assisted by generous financial incentives both for individuals and for
> the countries in question. We will abolish the 'positive
> discrimination' schemes that have made white Britons second-class
> citizens. We will also clamp down on the flood of 'asylum seekers',
> all of whom are either bogus or can find refuge much nearer their
> home countries. ('Immigration – Time to say NO!', www.bnp.org.uk/
> policies.html#immigration)

The BNP's other policies – on Europe (it seeks 'independence' from the EU), on the economy and employment ('British workers first!'), on education (the party is against 'politically incorrect indoctrination', and for 'knowledge of and pride in the history, cultures and heritage of the native peoples of Britain') – all assume a white racism based implicitly on a racially pure, historically embedded notion of 'British' culture. Nevertheless the party is emphatic that it is not racist, only interested in the preservation of British culture:

Q: The politicians and the media call the BNP 'racist'? Is this true? A: No. 'Racism' is when you 'hate' another ethnic group. We don't 'hate' black people, we don't 'hate' Asians, we don't oppose any ethnic group for what God made them, they have a right to their own identity as much as we do, all we want to do is to preserve the ethnic and cultural identity of the British people. We want the same human rights as everyone else, a right to a homeland, security, identity, democracy and freedom. We are not against immigrants as *individuals*. We are against a *system* which imports cheap labour regardless of the wishes of the host population. The British people were never asked if they wanted a multi-cultural society, immigration was forced on us undemocratically and against the clear wishes of the majority. (www.bnp.org.uk/faq.html, original emphases)

Our interest is less in these policies and in the BNP's limited success in a number of local council elections in the UK, and more in how these explicitly racist policies (which is what they are, despite the party's denials) are being presented on the BNP's site and how the party actively constructs its cultural identity.

CONSTRUCTING CULTURAL HISTORY

The introduction to the 'Heritage and Culture' section of the BNP's web site emphasises the BNP's political end as 'the long term survival of our people and our nations in this island group in the North Atlantic which happens to be our homeland' (www.bnp.org.uk/culture/poetry/ 2003_apr.htm). The plea is not for the alienation, repatriation or (as in much supremacist discourse) destruction of immigrant populations and communities, nor even for the defence of whites against an immigration 'onslaught'. It is both much simpler and much more invidious than either of these. The section seeks to isolate the defining characteristics of British culture, the better to 'preserve all the positive aspects of our culture' (ibid.). This culture is emphatically pan-British, emphasising Celtic and Anglo-Saxon influences. It draws on both the mythic and the literary-canonical for its explanatory power – an explanatory power, though, that is left unstated, as if already understood. The works of Shakespeare (voted 'Fifth Greatest Briton' by BNP members in a 2003 poll) are prominent here, available online (with a link to MIT's Shakespeare site) as a corrective to the 'onslaught of "politically correct" reworkings' of his plays. Each month a poem by a British writer is presented in this section, along with a brief critical appraisal of its significance. Poets are chosen from across the British Isles and are generally in the canon: G. K. Chesterton, Sir Walter Scott, W. B. Yeats. A poem from Scott's novel *Ivanhoe* is made to represent both the ancient roots of Britain and the present necessity to fight against Britain's 'disappearance' into the EU. The reasons for choosing Auden's 'Night Mail' are less clear, unless it is to stand for the security that might come from nostalgia, as might the emphatically non-canonical choice of 'Albert and the Lion'. Similarly, the anonymous folk lyric 'John Barleycorn' celebrates a timeless past through its depiction of brewing ('a very key aspect of British society'). The selection points to a past of innocent pride – even Scott's martial poem is set in myth – there is no engagement here with an actual history of power. The culture portrayed is benign and worthy of preservation; by implication, 'our' British present is likewise benign and in need of defence, for it is under cultural attack. The discursive space established by these choices (it is unclear who is making the choices but, given the hierarchical nature of the party – a feature it shares with mainstream British political parties – we can assume that the choices are approved by its chairman and chief spokesman, Nick Griffin) is one occupied at once by racial purity (we shall find no works here by authors whose origins or influences are admitted to lie outside the British Isles) and by a (limited) inclusiveness that brings together the English, Irish, the Welsh and the Scots (and sub-groups such as the Cornish) as a coherent nation whose cultural history needs to be maintained against the 'politically correct' incursions of the Other. The Other, it is suggested, might not only be the 'immigrant'; it might easily be other 'British' people, most obviously 'liberals' and 'the left'. The Other is constructed as the threat of multiculturalism, against which the BNP's discursive construction of its cultural heritage presents itself paradoxically as a monoculture that draws on a variety of cultural histories.

Two issues emerge from this construction. The first is to do with how these discursive resources construct white identity as othered (seen as repressed and in need of defence), and yet perceive that identity as under threat by cultures which themselves are subject to othering.

Stuart Hall's work on cultural identity offers a dialectical approach to understanding this apparently contradictory and specious mechanism of cultural defence. In his critical essay on Caribbean cinema and cultural identity, Hall (1990) identifies three 'presences' through which we can consider Caribbean cultural identity: *présence Africaine*, *présence Européenne* and *présence Américaine*. It is the first two that are most useful to the present argument. *Présence Africaine*, he argues, represents that 'imagined community' (he cites Benedict Anderson) to which the Caribbean people can never return. 'Africa' becomes the '*origin* of our identities, unchanged by four hundred years of displacement' (Hall 1990: 231, original emphasis). The Britain constructed through the BNP's 'culture and heritage' resources, with its melange of Shakespeare, Yeats, King Arthur and Odin is similarly imaginary. The point is that we constitute ourselves through representation and, as the forms and means available to that representation develop as a consequence of other 'presences', so does our identity change, positioned as it is historically. Cultural identity is not simply about a shared culture, it is also about how these presences – and our interactions with them – produce difference, and with that difference a cultural identity that is 'subject to the continuous "play" of history, culture and power' (p. 225). *Présence Européenne* represents the play of power in the cultural history of the other, a presence that is 'endlessly speaking – and endlessly speaking *us*' (p. 232, original emphasis). Here the subject is positioned within the frames of representation that proceed from the experience of colonialism.

The cultural discourse of the BNP appears to proceed precisely from the dialectic of these two presences. The imaginary of white cultural history is here presented as immutable; a collective history that produces identity to the degree that its fixity assures and asserts its normalisation. This imaginary is confronted, according to the BNP, by a colonising power that seeks to speak for 'us', indeed to 'speak us' (in Hall's term), thus to reduce 'our' capacity for self-determination. This is sophistry of a particularly pernicious type – we need only to look at the continuing struggles in the UK for the human rights of asylum seekers, the identification of institutional racism in the police force and other public services, the persistence of racial discrimination in employment and education. For the historical colonisers – the oppressors – to construct themselves as the Other, as both repressed (*présence Africaine*) and silenced (*présence Européenne*) is shocking. However repugnant or irrational such construction is, we must attend not only to the materials through which it is achieved but also to on whose behalf it is achieved.

From this emerges our second issue. The selection of cultural resources presented on the site tells us little about how we are meant to understand them or deploy them. Some, such as the poster of Odin riding Sleipnir offered for sale by the Excalibur 'heritage store', appear as symbols of racial pride. There is, though, little evidence, outside white racist practices, of a strong cultural identification with Norse mythology; its signification can be little more than a token for some unexpressed 'heritage'. Whilst Shakespeare has much more widespread cultural currency in the UK than Norse mythology, his works too appear shorn of their meaning – again, he appears to stand in for some timeless, abstracted notion of 'Britain', left as yet undefined. This timelessness of signification – what is at once always-already under-stood yet underdetermined in the meanings of significatory practices – recalls Hall's *présence Africaine* as an imaginary space: 'the original "Africa" is no longer there. It . . . has been transformed' (Hall 1990: 231). Of course, there was never an original Africa, only ever an idea. Yet that 'absent Africa' served to form community and cultural identity. However, to look back at that Africa as an immanent and replete cultural signifier is, warns Hall, to 'collude with the West which, precisely, normalizes and appropriates Africa by freezing it in some timeless zone of the primitive, unchanging past' (p. 231). The cultural-historical constructions of the BNP work in similar fashion, though under conditions of extreme contradiction. First, they freeze British culture through a melange of cultural symbols. Second, through this freezing they seek to normalise British cultural identity. An array of symbols alone cannot, however, 'achieve' identity; they must be activated through cultural practices. Third, we must note that this 'freezing' is not the result of an oppressive force or any collusion with it – the BNP is its sole agent, through which it essentialises its cultural-historical position. Fourth, and apparently contradictorily, the BNP does appear to collude with the Other, at least to the degree that it confirms the notion (held by the Other) that its membership is racist, primitive and retrogressive. Fifth, there is no inevitability at work here – the BNP's self-construction is self-willed and willing.

What is most shocking is that this ensuing 'powerlessness' is not, to use Hall's phrase, the historical outcome of 'the old, the imperialising, the hegemonising, form of "ethnicity" ' (p. 235). The cultural discourse of the BNP suggests a choice – they have chosen to place power in the hands of the Other; this is not a structured, historical condition. Of course, there is no actual transfer of power here – the objects of the BNP's racism are hardly empowered by this 'act' – it is a purely rhetorical act that seeks to represent the BNP itself as repressed, as Other. Thus the rhetoric of ceded power is perversely and speciously deployed as evidence for an actual ceding of power. This subject-constructed fantasy of powerlessness is, then, to be countered through a subject-constructed, pseudo-historical continuum of 'British' cultural identity. What, though, underlies and 'justifies' this desire for constructing the Other as the dominant cultural force in British society? To call it 'racism' is accurate, but that is to essentialise – and close off any examination – of the cultural-discursive practices (the 'voices') that generate such a desire. For, just as the BNP's discourse of cultural heritage seeks to normalise a 'positive' racism through a set of cultural-historical symbols that are (obscurely) intended to fully explain and establish white British identity, so the 'new nationalism' of the BNP entails a normalisation of the individuals who constitute it and who must therefore be similarly constructed as othered by the Other. It is to the discourse surrounding these individuals – that both constitutes them and is constituted by them – that we now turn. In particular, we shall examine the extent to which the BNP's promotion of white cultural identity has usurped the 'old racism' and how social and cultural relations are presented by and through the rank and file members of the BNP through their letters and personal profiles on the web site, 'the ways in which whiteness is brought into being as a normative structure, a discourse of power, and a form of identity' (Ware and Back 2002: 13).

WHO ARE THE BNP? RACISM AND THE EVERYDAY

As part of its 'Resources' section the BNP's web site features 'Meet the Real BNP', which profiles four 'ordinary people just like you' who have joined the BNP to 'stand-up [sic] and do something positive to change this country for the better'. Beneath a photograph, each member has contributed a couple of sentences summarising their reasons for joining the party. Below each text is a longer paragraph written by, we can assume, a BNP press officer or other party official, arguing the reasons for joining the party. Though brief, the contributions by the four 'ordinary' members emphasise unspecific statements of problems ('the changes in this country which are threatening our way of life'; 'I want to help make Britain great again'), the maintenance of value systems ('traditional and Christian') and the hope for a 'British future for my children'. Explicitly racist views only appear once, in a declaration by 'Mr Nick Cass' that his concern for the future of his 'two small children' proceeds from 'a country which gives preferential treatment to ethnic minorities and asylum seekers'. This view is reinforced by an editorial commentary that asserts 'that life is hell for young white mothers in todays [sic] inner cities. They have to face the risk of assault, racial abuse, see the graffiti, the litter, the vandalism.' It is understood that the sole cause of these social problems stems from 'immigrant' communities. Once more the repressed Other is cast as the oppressor; the normative notion that racism is generally that suffered by ethnic minority groups is turned on its head – 'racial abuse' is suffered by whites, in part through their exposure to anti-'white', racist graffiti. Even those who drop litter are non-whites, exhibiting oppressive behaviour. There is a reflexive discourse at work here that renders white racism as an everyday, non-extreme practice (these are mothers and fathers worried about their children, not skinhead gangs or KKK members). Racism is presented as a reasonable reaction to the imputed racism of the Other. The only explicit mentions of racialised actions are attributed to non-whites. It is 'asylum seekers' who inflict 'racial abuse'; the implicit racism of the BNP is born out of suffering and repression, not hatred. This 'strong current of victimology in far-right discourse' (Ware and Back 2002: 50) is played out in the everyday lives of the BNP members depicted here – and what could be more everyday than a 'retired vet', a 'businessman' and a 'customer services adviser and mother' (we have only a name for the fourth)?

History, culture and 'heritage' are again to the fore, particularly in the BNP's own editorialising in this section. Here, though, the mythic is rehearsed through actual historical events: 'one thousand years [during which Britain] stood proud against the foreign invader'. The Battle of Trafalgar is invoked, as are the two world wars. The cultural history and identity thus invoked are to be defended against the 'threat' to 'our heritage and the birthright of our children'. Here the twin discourses of the coloniser and the colonised are again conflated. The racism of the BNP is occluded, presented through a twin lens of history and future prospects. This casts the BNP's ideology in romantic and emotive rhetoric. The appeal to a highly selective history that assumes racial purity is rationalised through an appeal to a powerless section of society:

children. The editorialising of the BNP emphasises an unspecific 'threat to their [BNP members'] children's future'. If a triumphalist, imperialist history (from which the discourse of a multicultural history is entirely absent) is the cultural bedrock of the BNP's racism, its social imperative for the future rests on a racist construction of white children and young people. Here we see enacted, as Deleuze and Guattari (1988) understand it, a 'fascism [that] is manifest in the micro-organization of everyday life' (Ware and Back 2002: 96). At the time of writing (September 2003) the headline banner on the BNP site advertises 'Camp Excalibur: The Young BNP Event of the Year'. An appeal to a mythical history is conjoined with the everyday: an 'annual activity-packed getaway' for BNP families. Activities include 'paintballing, five-a-side football, archery, water-sports, Saturday night social and a full English breakfast'.

The photo galleries that document the BNP's Red, White and Blue festival of 2003 similarly demonstrate the everyday normalisation of racist politics as harmless social activities (www.bnp.org.uk/rwb2003/gallery1.htm). Whilst we do find there displays of the Union Jack, BNP leafletters and a portrait of a distinguished visitor, an unnamed representative of the 'FN' (Front National), there is an abundance of photographs showing the banalities of an outdoor, family festival: a bouncy castle (captioned 'Safe Fun'), people wandering around the site ('Finding Family and Friends') and buying ice-cream ('Keeping One's Cool'). A shot of children is captioned 'Our Bright Future'. It was at this festival in 2001 that Nick Griffin, the BNP's chairman, declared that 'his party was not the mouthpiece of racial hatred. On the contrary, the BNP, he said, was "the party of love"' (Back 2002b: 1). If the visual discourse of the 2003 festival does not explicitly espouse 'love', it certainly seeks to annul the notion of the BNP as a party of racial hatred, even as its very appeal to ordinariness, reasonableness and respectability is founded on prejudice, separatism and oppression.

LETTERS OF LOCAL RACISM

The racists of the BNP are thus constituted by a discourse that represents them as victims of racism and as oppressed by those who previously had been the victims of the party's racism (and as if they are no longer subject to that racism). Members and supporters of the BNP are encouraged to see themselves as fighting to regain (another paradox) a colonial past that has been (or is in imminent danger of being) erased by a new colonising force – those very colonial subjects of the empire the BNP seeks to recover. So far we have considered examples of constituting discourse. If we consider this discourse as producing a 'new' subject position for white racists, what are the consequences? Do these racists then go on to employ a discourse that proceeds from this subject position? The fragments we have already examined from rank and file members are too brief to answer these questions with confidence, though they do, as we have seen, contain within them the seeds of this 'new' discourse. The 'Letters' section (www.bnp.org.uk/letters/current.htm) of the site does, however, offer a richer base from which to examine the movement from constituted to constitutive.

There is a significant concordance between the 'official' discourse of the BNP and that of its members' letters, the majority of which are anonymous, or have been anonymised (the exceptions being letters from BNP local councillors). Once again, editorial commentary has been added which reinforces the official discourse. An 'alarming report from Cardiff' comments on the 'success' of protests against converting a disused hospital into a centre for asylum seekers, but notes that 'the latest plan' for the hospital is to convert it into a 'residential college for Islamic studies'. The author's reaction brings together what are now familiar features of racist discourse: the local community will be 'over-run' by '1,000 students studying Islam', 'a recipe for youth boredom, which so often leads to crime, as well as a potential hotbed of racial tension'. The assumptions that the students of the proposed college will not be 'British' and that they will be responsible for destructive, racist practices against the local, 'white' community, 'many of whom are elderly', concord with the perverse discourse of Othering we have already encountered. The threat to tradition is signified, rather subtly, by the writer's observation that this college will be founded on a 'listed hospital building'. In its editorial response, the BNP makes the author's argument explicitly confrontational: 'it is down to the work of the local [white, racist] community to stop such destruction of their local living and working space'. A proposal to develop an educational institution for the study of a world religion is thus rendered as an act of racist destruction, more evidence of colonisation by the colonised. Elsewhere, response to a brief note complaining about the absence of a BNP councillor from the web site of Kirklees local council is editorially transformed into an example of the ideological work of the supporters of multiculturalism. Once again, it is the BNP who are the victims; they (the other members of the local council) 'treat BNP members like dirt' through their 'warped ideologically correct ideology' which 'condemns the indigenous population to the status of second-class citizens in their own homeland'. The BNP's rank and file must fight against such marginalisation, as another correspondent emphasises:

> Our victories in the Black Country, and all over the country, in addition to the excellent and many, second and third places, could never have been achieved without the seriousness of determined, and very ordinary people, who helped not only leaflet, but canvassed with a passion and good manners to boot. (www.bnp.org.uk/letters/current.htm)

The extremism of hatred comes not from the BNP, but from its opponents, who include the Anti Nazi League ('inciting people to riot and break the law') and 'the media': 'All this in the face of the kind of media hatred that seems sometimes to come from a totally foreign, ideologically perverse set of spoilt elites, whose evil plan has been ruined' (ibid.). Finally, repeatedly, the plea for solidarity and activism in the face of ideological and cultural 'invasion' comes at once from imperialist history and an innocent future: 'You all have under a year to make it happen, and please don't just rely on others – your children, and the history books will never forgive you.'

THE BNP IN CYBERSPACE

So far we have examined the discourses on the BNP site without attending to their 'technosocial' aspects. Our analysis so far might easily have been of reports, manifestos and contributions in a printed document. We need to ask, then, to what extent does the BNP position itself in cyberspace, what use does it make of the technologies of the Internet and the World Wide Web, and how does this use impact on its discursive resources? The BNP makes use of the expected technologies of web site construction and presentation, such as internal hyperlinks, PDF downloads, online shopping, email links, mailing list, Realplayer audio and video extracts from public and commercial broadcast media. Whilst it presents email links through which members and supporters might contact head office and their local branch officers, there is little evidence of a reticulated site through which its members may communicate with one another. There is, for example, no forum for the interactive exchange of views, no chat room or discussion board. There is the 'Policy Forum' (www.bnp.org.uk/policy/policy_forum.htm), which offers a limited opportunity for members to present sustained arguments about policy issues they believe the BNP should address. The BNP is careful, however, to point out that 'all articles contained in this section [and there are only seven there at the time of writing] are not official policy and are solely the work and thoughts of the individual authors concerned'. Some of these demonstrate a significant departure from the twin, racist discourse of victimology and the struggle for nationalism we have already encountered. Instead, they emphasise a libertarian philosophy towards such issues as transport, education and economic policy. Here too, though, we encounter traces of that twin discourse. On these occasions the dialectic of powerlessness/struggle is applied to motorists ('Criminalise Criminals – NOT motorists!') and those who champion streaming in education ('We need an educational elite . . . so why did the government close the Grammar schools?').

Whilst the 'Policy Forum' section appears to broaden the political interests of the BNP and to position it as much more than a single-issue party, its fundamental policy of a racism that is to be mobilised throughout society and its institutions is never far from these contributions. Despite the 'environmentally-friendly' proposals for transport reform, which include the promotion of cleaner fuels and car-sharing (now part of every political party's environmental policy in the UK), the BNP's solution rests not on such reformist measures but on immigration control:

> We regard the road congestion crisis as not the fault of 'selfish'
> British car owners, but as yet one more symptom of the chronic
> over-population of our country – a situation caused to a large extent
> by the effective surrender of our borders, and several decades of
> virtually uncontrolled immigration to our shores. (www.bnp.org.uk/
> policy/motorists_transport.htm)

If anyone is any doubt that the status of this document as a Policy Forum contribution renders it 'not official policy', we need only note its concordance with the analyses of the BNP's discourse (as well as noting that this piece is unattributed, and written in a collective style of address ('we regard', 'we will eliminate', 'we will promote') that is entirely harmonious with other 'official policy' statements. The by-now predictable confluence of a discourse that represents whites as victims oppressed by the Other with that of a discourse of regaining imperial pride and power recurs:

> In the Town Halls we will expose and oppose the left-wing Marxist councils who waste hardworking Council Tax payers' money providing FREE driving lessons and FREE cars (brand new in some cases) for 'Asylum seekers', and who then blame and penalise local motorists for congestion problems!! [Our policies] will both reduce traffic and fuel consumption, and help return Britain to the country our Grandparents told us about – a place where neighbours are also friends. (www.bnp.org.uk/policy/motorists_transport.htm, original emphases and capitalisation)

The presence of such explicitly 'party-line' documents in what is presented as an 'unofficial' space for discussion confirms a notion of right-wing media as 'constructing or sustaining a community with closure' (Couldry 2002). In the present case, this may be understood as the functioning of a web site of a political party, where the question of which voices get to be heard is closely controlled by the party's hierarchy, yet it appears odd that a party that places such an apparent premium on the voices of an 'oppressed' culture speaks so much on their behalf. One convincing explanation is the reported unpopularity of the BNP leadership amongst its local activists. Many consider Griffin's disavowal of the party's espousal of racial violence under its previous leadership as a betrayal of their cause. In 2003 two prominent Scottish members 'resigned in disgust over the party's adoption of candidates with Black relatives' (*Searchlight*, 2003).

The BNP also adopts the language of progressive Internet media, claiming that its 'Resources' section is 'to cater for "cyber-activism"'. What it proposes, though, is very different from the cyber-activism we find within the progressive new social movements. The activism promoted by the BNP is centralised and party-based. It does not encourage its members to use the Internet as a tool for protest, to make direct contact with its opponents (whether construed as the 'politically correct' ideologues of New Labour, or the othered ethnic minorities against which the BNP see itself as struggling). By contrast with the reticulated and independent grassroots activism of, for example, the anti-capitalist movement, its notion of cyber-activism is quite attenuated. It amounts to providing PDF leaflets 'which people at home can download' in order to distribute by the traditional means of doorstep circulation: 'put on some comfortable shoes and get out into your neighbourhood!' (www.bnp.org.uk/resources.html). Its 'Campaign' section, in which, at the time of writing, the party was running three campaigns, once more offers leaflets in PDF (for its 'Campaign against Crime'). Its 'Campaign to Stop BBC Bias', however, resembles a more engaged form of cyber-activism. Amongst its materials it offers a pro-forma which members are encouraged to complete and submit to the BNP, detailing the 'bias' they have experienced on BBC radio and television programmes. 'Bias', in this case, means primarily bias against the BNP, as well as 'examples of anti-white racism' and 'examples of distortion of the historical facts regarding Empire, British history and our nation's finest heroes' (www.bnp.org.uk/campaigns/bbc_bias_feed back.htm). The 'Campaign for Freedom of Internet Access' explicitly encourages members to take action in their public libraries, by attempting to access the BNP's site. Should access be blocked, they are encouraged to complain directly as well as to complete a pro-forma for the BNP's campaign. The BBC and the Internet campaigns once again demonstrate in their protest activities the familiar discourse of marginalisation, where a majority population is constructed as a minority, oppressed not only by a numerical ('immigrant') minority but by a state apparatus (public broadcasting, libraries) that 'should' be supporting it.

Ware and Back (2002: 98) have argued that 'the rhetoric of whiteness becomes the means to combine profoundly local grammars of racial exclusion within a translocal and international reach, which is made viable through digital technology'. How, then, does the BNP's localised discourse of racial exclusion combine with other racial discourses through the technologies and social networks that characterise cyberspace? Beyond its own pages, how does the BNP connect with other groups and organisations, what is the nature of those groups and the nature of those connections? The external links on the BNP's web site fall into two broad categories: affiliated and support groups (mostly in the UK), and a comprehensive set of links to other, 'white nationalist' parties. The latter include all the major European nationalist parties, such as the Austrian Freedom Party, France's Front National, the Danish People's Party and the Italian Northern League. Whilst we do not know how these 'local grammars of racial exclusion' are relevant to or employed by the rank and file (how many of the party's members, for example, would be able to understand the various languages of these sites?), it is reasonable to assume that such links at least symbolically demonstrate the international reach of the new nationalist movement, and function as offering solidarity to what is objectively a minority political party as well as one which casts itself in a minoritarian light. The UK-based groups affiliated to and/or supportive of the BNP function as special interest groups, offering services to specific sectors of the British nationalist movement. The relationship between these groups and the BNP is unclear in some cases (for example, the Association of British Ex-Servicemen); the discourse of others, though, is in line with the twin discourses of othered and othering we have already met, such as the 'white victims' support group' Families Against Immigrant Racism. There is little evidence here of any significant social networks in the cyberspace of British nationalism, even less of any global reach or reticulation. A number of the associations and groups listed have only post office box addresses (which is a feature of many extremist organisations across the political spectrum) – very few have web sites.

Despite the general absence of interactivity or of a discussion space for rank and file activists, we do find one space where an attentuated form for such communication does take place. This is on the site of the BNP's Directory of White British Businesses (www.whitedirectory.tk). The link takes the viewer not to the promised 'fledgling project to encourage Britons to use local small businesses in their area', but to a discussion page which begins with a handful of enquiries about the absence of the directory. The posts then broaden to include messages of support for the party, criticism of its leadership, and justifications (apparently born of personal experience) for being opposed to immigration. The occasional interpolation by the list owner (we assume a BNP official) chides posters to 'keep on topic' – though in the absence of the business database itself, it is difficult to see what the topic would be. Here is the only space available through the BNP in which its members (and others) may post their unmediated opinions and communicate with one another. The fortuitous absence of a resource has resulted in an opportunistic move by BNP members. The frustration of the list owner at this is palpable; returning to the discussion list only two days after first viewing it, we find the link broken, the page unavailable. In a double irony the rank and file members have colonised a space in which to establish their own discourse, using the resources of the powerful (the party) through which to express themselves. That party has responded by dispossessing those members of that space, placing it off-limits, effectively erasing it. Perhaps this is a suitable point to close this analysis, with the discourse of coloniser and colonised played out within the structure of the BNP itself, turning its complex of minoritarianism and imperialism in on itself, to render its cyberspace closed and constricted.

The discourse of the BNP on its web site constructs a minority community under supposed attack from 'immigrant racists' who are supported by the British government and a dominant discourse of 'multiculturalism'. As such, the BNP represents a closed community that seeks to protect 'those betrayed and beleaguered Britons' (www. bnp.org.uk/letters/current.htm). Whilst it draws on the imperial past of the United Kingdom, and talks of recovering power, pride and patriotism, this is largely achieved through a minoritarian, victim-based discourse. Paradoxically, though, the site offers little opportunity for its members to construct their own discourses, and through those to construct their own identities. It is as if the BNP's 'protectionism' extends to closing off its own constituency (an actual, lived community) from the discursive community the party has constructed. To do so is to essentialise even further the already-essentialised accounts of 'race', 'identity', 'power' and 'culture' on its web site. Ware and Back argue that 'cyberspace illustrates the contemporary resonance of poststructuralist philosophy, which emphasises *becoming* over *being* and *performance* over *essence*' (Ware and Back 2002: 95, original emphases). How might we consider the BNP's presence in cyberspace along these lines? Its site is profoundly essentialist in the sense that it generates closure upon a contemporary discourse of racism, a discourse that is not available for transformation by the party's members and supporters (or indeed its detractors – the BNP's site is hermetic to that extent). Instead, members and supporters are constructed discursively as elements of that discourse and their constructions employed selectively to portray the BNP's racism essentially. The discourses of the rank and file are largely absent and with them are absent the everyday, contradictory and 'messy' social practices that constitute such discourses. The absence of the quotidian contradictions, illogicalities and inconsistencies of white racism leaves a presence of an apparently conflict-free, consensual and consistent discourse. Yet at the same time this apparently static and essentialist discourse is historically concerned with 'becoming': the discourse performs racism, it is not simply emblematic of it. It is about white racism becoming something other than the predictable 'essential racism' of the white supremacists and neo-Nazis.

Neither does the site exhibit the 'arborescent quality of net-Nazi activism' that Ware and Back (2002: 95) find in their examination of fascism in cyberspace. That is to say, if we understand 'arborescent' as a process of international reticulation, then the position of the BNP in cyberspace hardly goes beyond the local; it exhibits little of the 'translocal and international reach' of the cyberfascism encountered by Ware and Back, 'a white rhizome of translocal interconnections' (Ware and Back 2002: 109).

The BNP's connections are ostensibly to strengthen its grassroots (national and local support groups) and to connect it (at least symbolically for its members, though politically for its leadership) internationally with similar parties. The 'old racism' of the white separatists, white supremacists, neo-Nazis and skinheads does not operate with such administrative and organisational precision; neither does it seek political power through democratic means. Its need for cyberspace is thus quite different from that of the BNP – it is about mobilising fragments and globalising tactics, sharing its racist culture in an effort to maintain its cohesion as a movement, not as a party. Racist political parties such as the BNP use cyberspace very differently – whilst it might share the old racism's use of the Internet for recruitment and publicity, its hierarchical organisation and its cleaving to the persistent political tactics of British party-political culture (door-to-door canvassing, public meetings, face-to-face mobilisation at local level) would render a site that was 'arborescent' in cyberspace potentially liable to fragmentation, dispute and (with no irony intended) a loss of identity. The international sites to which the BNP connects are 'mirrors' of itself: hierarchical, closed communities, generally lacking the personal, discursive possibilities of sites where 'people can *participate* in an *interactive* way in a largely autonomous, although not hermetic, racist Networld' (Ware and Back 2002: 122, original emphases). The 'social networks and aspects of the everyday life of racists' (ibid.) that are constructed online through the discursive practices of racists operating globally are quite absent from the BNP's web site. Or more precisely, it is not that they are absent, but that they are constructed by the leadership of the BNP on behalf of its members and supporters from the very discursive materials of its (actual and ideal) members and supporters. The everyday social practices of racists are essentialised as surely as are the objects of their racism. This is not to say that such discursive constructions do not accurately reflect those practices (it is not the aim of this study to either confirm or disconfirm the 'reality' of such discourses – as noted earlier, we have followed a Foucaultian path of looking at how 'truth' is formed), nor that they might not resonate with those whose lives are discursively constructed on their behalf – it is to emphasise the absence of any shared space in which those 'ordinary racists' might construct, reconstruct, reflect or resist their own discursive formations. This is the contradiction at the heart of the web site, that the populism of the BNP – its appeal to the everyday, lived experiences of a white, 'othered' class – appears at odds with an inclusive populism of grassroots activism, of a multiplicity of local, contesting values. The populism of the BNP, its discourse suggests, is one of control and determinism, not one of reticulation and contention.

CONCLUSION

We began this chapter with a consideration of far-right media as a species of alternative media. We sought to provide empirical materials with which to examine Couldry's assertion that far-right media, unlike more 'progressive' alternative media, sought to construct a 'community with closure' in which an explicit ideological framework not only prevented counter-discourses from arising in those media, but curtailed a multi-voiced discourse from developing even amongst sympathisers and supporters through its hierarchical control of symbolic resources. Following Downing, Couldry asserted that the opportunity for media audiences to become media producers or, at least, active discussants through those media, would be absent from far-right media. Whilst the work of Ware and Back contradicts this assertion to some extent, the findings of the present study confirm Couldry's position. The BNP's web site maintains a hegemony of ideas, of how 'new nationalism' is to be discursively understood. The authoritarian populism of the BNP is enacted discursively through its deployment of populist symbols (a mythic past, a repressed present and a secure future for the innocent) and draws on the everyday experiences, identities and social processes of its members' lived experiences. Yet it does so on their behalf, giving those individuals little opportunity to construct themselves discursively on the web site. As Couldry predicts, there is little evidence here of that 'democratised creativity' we find in other alternative media formations, little space for the sharing or exploration of ideas and arguments.

Yet the study has done more than merely confirm an assertion. Underlying Couldry's assertion is surely a dismissal – that the media of the far-right need not concern us as a form of alternative media. Whilst its form, its processes and practices might be quite apart from the progressive alternative media, to attend to its discursive strategies is itself revealing. What this study has shown is the extent to which an ideology founded on racism, hate, separatism and exclusion might re-form itself discursively by making use of the very discourses to which it has historically been opposed, and which we will find in progressive alternative media. The deployment of post-colonial notions such as the Other; of the discourse of a struggle to maintain and develop a cultural identity in an oppressive present; of the hope for a future free from fear: all these are powerful features of the discourse of multiculturalism. For the BNP, though, they are deployed in order to critique – indeed to reject – their original site of production. The BNP is anti-multicultural, anti-equality and anti-freedom, yet its discourse uses the tropes of multiculturalism, equality and freedom to maintain an ideological space where racism and repression may appear natural and commonsensical. Its authoritarian populism ensures that this view, within the space of the BNP's web site at least, will remain uncontested.

This new discursive formation and the contradictory notions of power that are constituted through it (multiculturalism as racism, freedom as repression) reveal themselves through the interplay of various symbolic resources. The 'truth' of new nationalism is formed through a threefold historical continuum: past, present and future. Each movement in this continuum draws on a specific set of discourses. We have seen how the BNP constructs a mythic history that draws on Norse and British myths, but which also finds historical power from actual, more recent events, such as the Battle of Trafalgar and the First World War. It presents these as essays in defence, not as acts of aggression or domination – the colonial history of Britain, its status as a world power and its history of immigration are quite absent from this discourse, an absence which can be understood as seeding the next movement of the continuum. The present state of Britain ('white' Britain) can then be represented as a response to attack from the Other, an attack that threatens historical pride and seeks to repress a belea-guered 'island race'. The historical defence of traditional values is played out in contemporary society as a reasonable response to a multiculturalist, 'politically correct' discourse that is imposed on white Britain by both a political elite (the present government) and the Other (ethnic minority groups). From this develops the strong, minoritarian discourse of the BNP, the construction of a 'New Minority' (Back

2002a: 639). Finally, the establishment of a defensive, unracialised discourse in the present (for that is what is presented here) becomes the wellspring for an innocent, idealised future, where (white) children may grow up in a culture that is secure from the predations of a repressive ideology of multiculturalism.

Together, these three movements are employed to construct 'new nationalist' subjects that are – in ideal-discursive terms – quite unlike the old racists of the National Front (or the BNP before its present leadership). In this manner, the two-way play of discourse is productive of an altered subject position. The social action produced by the discourse of old racism (physical violence, hate speech, calls for forced repatriation) has been found, by the BNP at least, to be politically counter-productive. This knowledge has prompted a new discursive formation of racism (rendered as the new nationalism) which, as we have seen, draws on the very discourse it rejects in order to normalise its political agenda. Power is thus created through the transmutation (however perverse or untenable that transmutation may be) of a minoritarian discourse that is mapped on to racist subject identities in order to reconstruct them as oppressed and thus unthreatening, reasonable and 'ordinary' people. The extent to which this discursive transformation of white identity is played in the social action of the BNP's members remains to be seen. The 'community' established by the BNP in cyberspace is replete with closure: organisationally, dialogically, discursively. The very subjects of its identity formation (its members) play only a liminal part in their own construction. The exclusive nature of the discursive practices of the BNP prevents its members from active participation in the transformation of 'their' identity on the BNP's web site. Paradoxically (and dangerously) this is to render the enduring, 'banal' racism of the BNP's members invisible.

CHAPTER 4

Radical Creativity and Distribution: Sampling, Copyright and P2P

INTRODUCTION

As we saw in Chapter 1, the progress of digital technology in recent years has hastened legislators and commentators alike to suggest methods by which the electronic transmission of information and ideas might be monitored, some would say policed. We have already met arguments based on national security, morality and economics. This chapter explores the last two of these in relation to intellectual property rights on the Internet, and does so through an examination of the implications of the exercise of those rights for creative practices and in particular the legal and commercial threats to 'social authorship' (Toynbee 2001). Finally, it examines peer-to-peer file-sharing networks (such as Napster and Gnutella) from this perspective. It considers such practices as aspects of social creativity, not simply as intellectual property theft. Yet such practices have not emerged from nowhere. They are the outcome of at least three major intersections of cultural practice: the recent history of illicit reproduction of artists' performances by audiences (home taping and bootlegging) and the social networks that grew alongside these practices (tape swapping constitutes peer-to-peer (P2P) networks before the fact, as it were); the various movements (such as shareware, the Electronic Frontier Foundation, interventions such as open copyright and open publishing) that have developed on the Internet, but which also have pre-digital antecedents; and the history of creative appropriation across numerous artistic movements, including high art and the demotic (visual and aural collage, folk song, the many syntheses of popular music styles into 'new' genres). In current language it is convenient – and, I intend to argue, revealing – to consider this last cultural practice as 'sampling' (this is to greatly extend this term from its most visible use in genres of 'dance' music). This cultural practice will be examined first, before we move on to applying its theoretical and conceptual insights to contemporary Internet practices of P2P and other movements against intellectual propertarianism.

SAMPLING THE GOODS, SAMPLING THE COMMONS

Since the establishment of musical sampling in the 1980s as a common element in much popular music (and not just in rap music and the hip-hop culture where it first came to prominence in popular music production), many musicians and their publishers have taken great pains to establish their rights over the use of even the briefest extract of their music by other musicians. There have been many successful prosecutions for unauthorised sampling in rap music (such as those recounted in Korn 1992 and Schumacher 1995). We must also consider the large-scale borrowings that appear in the musical transformations of the Canadian composer John Oswald and the more explicitly politicised, media-critical appropriations of the American group Negativland. The manipulation of samples by these two artists emphasises arguments over 'social authorship' and creativity that have urgent impact on the use of the Internet both by creators and audiences, at times blurring the lines between them. Their work may also act as a framing device from which to explore the continuing legalistic and economic struggles over intellectual property rights. This is not to place such work as a beginning or as a summation, but as a moment in creative-intellectual history that reaches back as easily as the early twentieth century, arguably even further (as Hamilton 2003 convincingly argues). Such a focus also contributes to the problematisation of the separation between 'high' and 'low' cultural practices. To examine such work is to consider musical sampling beyond what many audiences might conventionally understand it. Whilst this chapter is less interested in musical sampling as it is generally understood, it is appropriate that we begin there, if only to begin on familiar territory, the better to locate historical antecedents and subsequent developments. To begin with sampling as part of rap and hip-hop is also to present a core of theoretical arguments about the legal, cultural, economic and social dimensions of musical creativity which impact on latter-day Internet practices.

Citing Walter Benjamin's 1936 essay 'The Work of Art in the Age of Mechanical Reproduction' (Benjamin 1936/1982), Schumacher (1995) follows Benjamin's argument that reproduction entails the loss by the art object of its 'aura of authenticity' and its gaining of 'a foundation in relations of power' (p. 260). Yet the notion of intellectual property rights is based on the older concept of the art object that has its aura intact, and this despite technological mediation. As many authors have emphasised, however, technological mediation (particularly in popular music) not only jeopardises this notion of authenticity, the deployment of technology in the production of popular music has established new routes to musical creativity. Schumacher notes correctly that 'techno-logized music is the product of not just auteur-musicians but of the work of musicians and engineers alike' (p. 261). Musician and music theorist Chris Cutler has taken this position further. He traces the history of studio-based experimental and avant-garde 'serious' music through such figures as John Cage, Karlheinz Stockhausen, Pierre Schaeffer and James Tenney, and in the studio work of rock groups such as Faust and the Residents. Here he finds musics developing that only have an existence within the studio, where the roles of musician and engineer are combined in an individual or group. Pierre Schaeffer, for example, was a sound engineer working at ORTF in Paris, who became a composer when exposed to the possibilities of sonic manip-ulation in the studio, developing what has become known as 'musique concrète'. Composers such as John Cage became technicians, if you will – his 'Williams Mix' (1952) is a four-and-a-half minute collage of existing sounds edited together laboriously by Cage and his colleagues over nine months in the studio. Through these processes, Cutler notes, '*composers* had become *performers*' (Cutler 1985: 141, original emphases) – at the same time, these composer-performers were now working with technologised music where the fixing of a composition on manuscript paper was being replaced by the fixing – the constructing – of the sounds themselves (not merely their representation in notation) onto magnetic tape.

For our present purpose we might consider such compositions as proto-sampling. Cage's 'Williams Mix' employs hundreds of sound sources, many taken from copyrighted recordings, as does Stockhau-sen's 'Opus 1970', which played back existing recordings of Beetho-ven's music to musicians who would develop what they heard in performance. Sampling closer to how we understand it today was employed in high art by James Tenney and Richard Trythall. Both constructed their pieces out of recordings of popular recording artists: Tenney from Elvis Presley's 'Blue Suede Shoes' ('Collage No. 1', 1961); Trythall from Jerry Lee Lewis's 'Whole Lotta Shaking Going On' ('Omaggio a Jerry Lee Lewis', 1975). Within rock music such experiments were less frequent, in part through limited access to technology, in part through the difficulty and complexity of realising such compositions. Only the American group the Residents, in such work as *Third Reich and Roll* (1975) and their Beatles tape collage 'Beyond the Valley of a Day in the Life' (1977), came closest to realising this hybrid, technologised form of composer/performer/engineer in their manipulation and rearrangement of existing sounds. None of these works attracted any attention from copyright holders or their agents, perhaps due to their marginal status in their own music worlds. The commitment required to learn complex recording and sound-manipulation techniques, allied to the time and expense such processes consumed, also determined that such compositions would remain rare. The development of scratching, 'mastermixing' and rap music, which developed out of American disco culture in the 1970s, would not only offer a cheaper and faster method of sonic manipulation, through its collaging and transforming of popular music from within popular music itself, it would also attract the attention of legislators and copyright holders. Records were used as rhythm tracks, to add drum fills (breakbeats), instrumental breaks and even vocal and instrumental solos. As Cutler (1994) points out, the digital sampler, first launched by Ensoniq in the mid-1980s, expanded the opportunities for sonic manipulation. Not only was it quicker and easier, the sampling keyboard offered more precise sampling and a far wider range of effects that could be achieved either by the splicing of magnetic tape or the real-time manipulation of records. Whilst Ensoniq's Mirage sampler and its more sophisticated offspring such as the Emulator, the Fairlight and the Synclavier became studio fixtures for all manner of popular music recordings, digital sampling became inserted into the existing scratching techniques of rap music: '[s]ampling, far from destroying disc manipulation, seems to have breathed new life into it . . . It is almost as if sampling had recreated the gramophone record as a craft instrument, an analogue, expressive voice, made authentic by nostalgia' (Cutler 1994).

That the manipulation of pre-recorded sounds constitutes a form of creativity and a mode of expression, and that the technology used to effect this might be considered akin to received notions of instrumental virtuosity, remain at the heart of the conflict between these 'new' creators and the established notions of the legal representatives of the music industry. We return to Schumacher's reading of Benjamin, where outmoded, auratic notions of authorship are in conflict with technologised, mediated and hybridised notions of creativity. The normalisation of these practices, which draw on an historical stock of available materials for transformation, takes place within what Schumacher terms an 'aural commons' (1995: 265). This social dimension of creativity presents a fundamental challenge to the Romantic notion of the singular artist, of the 'genius' as the sole wellspring of the creative work. In so doing it also challenges the legal edifice upon which copyright law is constructed. For, as Schumacher points out, 'copyright is still influenced by the ideological construct of the "author" as a singular "origin" of artistic works' (1995: 259). The commercial exercise of copyright (which goes beyond the moral claims to a copyright) also entails the argument that only authors and their agents (including the corporations that exercise and very often own an author's copyright 'on their behalf') should benefit financially from the author's works. 'Creative theft', artistic appropriation and sampling threaten this status quo and tend to be seen as threats to the livelihoods of creators. They might also be considered as types of defamation, for it might be argued that the use of the sample or fragment is used in a context which might affect the original artist's reputation – again, though, a commercial imperative is at work here. From the perspective of industrial capitalism the music created by such social practices has no legal or moral right to exist, unless its creators seek permission from copyright holders for the use of their music and, inevitably, pay for its use. All such art should properly be impossible under present copyright laws, it is argued, since its practices are no more than examples of plagiarism. Yet the music does exist, and its creators have been forced to argue from within the discourse of the commercial world to justify its existence. Their arguments have taken various forms, of which the most common is the legal doctrine of 'fair use' but, as we shall see, some artists have taken more radical positions.

'TAKING SAMPLING FIFTY TIMES BEYOND THE EXPECTED'[1]

In 1991 the American group Negativland were sued by Island Records and Warner-Chappell Music for sampling about thirty seconds of a song by the Irish band U2 without permission, along with fragments of a broadcast by Casey Kasem, an American radio presenter. The piece created from these (titled 'U2') – and other unidentified samples, as well as original music by the group itself, was intended as both cultural commentary on the music industry and a form of satire. The terms of the settlement included the destruction of all unsold copies of the record, along with all mechanical parts used to manufacture the record. All copyrights were assigned to the plaintiffs. In addition, Negativland paid out a total of $70,000 in settlement, legal fees and lost revenue – 'more money than we've made in our ten years of existence,' declared the group. Island and Warner-Chappell both reasoned that Negativland's actions were denying the members of U2 (and their publishers) income that was rightfully theirs as owners of the song. Yet there is no evidence that such sampling reduces an artist's revenue, only the economic argument that since the artist owns their original work, any part of it (however small) may only be used with their permission and by paying (often very sizeable) permission fees. A group such as Negativland, whose collage approach can entail hundreds of samples in a single piece, would find it impossible to create their music if they were to adhere to such an imperative.

In common with many dance and rap musicians, Negativland incorporate samples of radio and television programmes – as well as music – into their musical collages. They do this in order to produce sonic commentaries, critiques and satires on aspects of the mass media. In this respect their work might be considered as media criticism, differing only from that published in articles and books in terms of the nature of the quotations they employ. Whereas as a writer may legitimately quote a section of another's written work for the purposes of review or criticism, such a privilege is not granted to commentators working in a sonic medium. Indeed the law does not recognise sonic commentaries such as Negativland's as anything but copyright in-fringement – effectively, theft. Most discussion centres on the protec-tion of copyright in electronic forms for the commercial benefit of the

---

1. The quote is the title of Oswald (1990).

copyright owner. Yet one might consider sampling as 'fair use' when used to create a work of art that seeks to comment critically on another's creation, in much the same way that quotation from printed sources is permitted for a similar purpose. This was precisely the argument made by Negativland, who cited the 'fair use' principles operating in US copyright law. The defence of fair use in US law covers uses for pedagogical, illustrative, critical and parodic purposes, and in all cases must emphasise the not-for-profit use of the material, particularly in its use for educational purposes. The use of another's work needs also to be considered in terms of the amount and 'substantiality' of the extract of the work used. Finally, consideration needs to be taken of the impact on the continued market value of the original work (Schumacher 1995: 256). The classic case of the fair-use defence in popular music is the sampling of Roy Orbison's hit song 'Oh, Pretty Woman' by the rap group 2 Live Crew in 1991. Whilst this recording was for profit and was not intended at all for educational purposes, it was successfully defended as parody, a purpose of fair use that is established in US law. The case became complex, with various appeals overturning the initial decision that the defence of fair use was acceptable due to the use of the sample for purposes of parody. Ultimately the case was found against 2 Live Crew because of the for-profit nature of the recording. It is at this point that sampling by rap and other artists becomes self-regulated. Though there remain many exceptions to this state of affairs (usually residing in small, independent productions), the use of samples by artists signed to large record labels is subject to meticulous checking. Copyright permissions are sought and paid for – if they are not forthcoming or if the fees asked are deemed to be too high, then the entire nature of a work might have to be altered for legal and commercial reasons. De La Soul's debut album, *Three Feet High and Rising* (1989), sampled dozens of artists without permission, yet the success of this record and the attendant visibility of the group persuaded their record company that for their second album all samples had to be sourced, permission sought and fees paid. The release of that record was delayed by a year as a result, and much of the sampled material had to be jettisoned (yet it remained a record heavily constructed by samples). The legal status of Negativland's 'U2' was settled out of court and so their position was never properly tested legally. Their unsuccessful defence rested not only on fair use (interpreted as criticism), it also argued that the limited distribution of the record through small, independent record shops and the small (if any) profit that might accrue to the group (they had – and continue to have – only a minority audience, with distribution and sales in the low thousands) weakened the argument that their work was significantly for-profit.

The Canadian composer John Oswald took the not-for-profit argument further at the same time as he took sampling 'fifty times beyond the expected'. Since the 1970s Oswald has been creating pieces made entirely out of other artists' work. In 1989 he released a CD (*Plunderphonic*) on which each piece was constructed from the work of a single artist or group. Oswald has termed his compositional procedures 'electroquoting' and 'macrosampling'. His aim is to bring out aspects of the work of others that lie hidden in the originals, aspects that were unknown and unintended to the original creators or to their audiences. Oswald distributed 1,000 copies of this recording as part of his *Plunderphonic* CD on an explicitly not-for-profit basis to radio stations, libraries, the press and to each of the artists (or their representatives) sampled on the recordings. None was available for sale. By January 1990 all extant copies and the masters of the *Plunderphonic* CD had been destroyed following the Canadian Recording Industry Association's pursuit of Oswald on behalf of Michael Jackson, whose song 'Bad' is reworked by Oswald as the first piece on the CD. Since that time, however, these pieces have circulated on CD and cassette – without the involvement of Oswald – through radical 'anti-copyright' networks such as the Copyright Violation Squad (who have also distributed copies of Negativland's 'U2' single). Oswald has continued his work, at times at the request of copyright holders themselves. The Grateful Dead invited him to 'plunder' their concert archives for the double CD *Grayfolded*, which samples dozens of Dead concerts from three decades, at times overlaying guitar solos and vocals years apart to effect an orchestral approach to the group's music. He has also continued his unauthorised sampling, the zenith of which is *Plexure*, made up of thousands of samples of Top 40 hits, each one lasting less (sometimes substantially less) than a second. Oswald is not passing off other's work as his own; neither, in the case of the *Plunderphonic* CD, did he make money from his work. It is also doubtful that his work detracts from the original; as Cutler suggests, Oswald's work does not replace the original, it encourages us to hear it anew. Oswald's work is highly creative, yet it remains irredeemably illegal within existing copyright law. It 'radically undermines three of the central pillars of the art music paradigm: originality – it deals only with copies; individuality – it speaks only with the voice of others; and copyright – the breaching of which is a condition of its very existence' (Cutler 1994).

Oswald's work is at once a radical creative process and a radically social process. His oft-quoted dictum 'if creativity is a field, copyright is the fence' not only unconsciously echoes Bourdieu's concept of the field of production, it resonates with Schumacher's notion of the 'aural commons' and earlier artistic movements that have considered popular culture and its signs as the raw material for creation. In terms of sonic art, an aural commons can be thought of as the space 'where listening and production, criticism and creation elide' (Cutler 1994). We might find similar features in the 'digital commons' of the Internet, a space characterised, as John Perry Barlow has argued, by processes and relations, not property: 'the economy of the future will be based on relationship rather than possession. It will be continuous rather than sequential' (Barlow 1993: 250). In 1990 Barlow co-founded the Electronic Frontier Foundation, 'a nonprofit Internet advocacy group to combat the enacting of what he considered unfair and uninformed laws to regulate the Internet' (Alderman 2002: 19). The Electronic Frontier Foundation was established to argue for and promote the notion of a digital commons, a space where processes and relations based on social authorship and 'non-propertarianism' might be performed in ways similar to the creative activities of Negativland, Oswald and their artistic precursors. The next section will examine these processes and relations through Internet practices, in particular focusing on the open software and file-sharing 'movements'.

TOWARDS SOCIAL AUTHORSHIP: 'ELECTRONIC NON–PROPERTARIANISM'

I have previously suggested (Atton 2002a: 30) that Bourdieu's notion of a 'demotic restricted field' of cultural production (Bourdieu 1993: 128) offers potential for us to break down the binary opposition of restricted field production and large-scale, mass production. In the case of the avant-garde (for want of a better term) creative applications of plagiarism we have found in the work of Negativland and John Oswald, this helps us to consider their activities as at once taking place within the avant-garde of a high-culture tradition (Negativland cite the DaDa movement, amongst high-art movements, as precursors) and within popular cultural activity (the folk song as an example of how texts may be reworked in the public domain). We might also see a further breakdown of the binary in the appropriation and deployment of the technological tools of the dominant culture by such artists. The use of digital media, both as a resource for cultural raw materials and as a means of distribution afforded by the Internet, render the notion of an elitist, underground avant-garde problematic. The 'cultural collisions' that follow from Negativland's sonic collages and cultural critiques, or from Oswald's cultural repositionings of popular artists, exemplify 'a demotic avant-garde that appropriates and repositions capital and authority' (Atton 2002a: 30). Yet for all their radicality, there is, in the case of Negativland at least, a surprising tameness towards the key aspect of the political economy of cultural production: copyright. In arguing for the principles of 'fair use' to be applied to their work as equally as it does to the use of quotation for educational or scholarly work, they appear to retreat from the radical consequences their work suggests. In any case, we already know, even in scholarly work, that the quotation of musical examples (including lyrics, perhaps especially lyrics) is subject to much greater restraint than quotation from prose works. Copyright permission needs to be sought and successfully obtained for even the briefest quotation from a song lyric. To claim 'fair use' under this regime is to be naïve at best, uninformed at worst. Negativland's special pleading thus operates firmly within the existing political economy of the recording and music publishing industries. What is absent is any radical argument to challenge the regimes of those industries, to suggest ways of rethinking socio-economic practices that might be placed alongside the already-practised cultural activities. To do so requires nothing less than rethinking the ideological practices of copyright, and in particular the contests over copyright that continue to be played out over (and through the medium of) the Internet.

The sonic art of Negativland and John Oswald, as we have seen, can be understood through the work of earlier radical art movements such as DaDa and Surrealism and in particular through the work of the French Situationists. The Situationist notion of *détournement* acts as a template for the creative plagiarism of artists such as Negativland. Guy Debord's (1967/1983) theory of the 'society of the spectacle' engaged him and other Situationists to 'see modern life for the detached spectacle it was, to steal ideas from the old world, and so create a new more engaging reality' (Clement and Oppenheim 2002: 42). Situationist strategies of plagiarism have nothing to do with the generally accepted notion of intellectual 'theft' that seeks to pass off others' ideas or expressions as one's own; instead they subvert those existing ideas and expressions in order to create combative and critical work that seeks to expose the ideological bases of the 'reality' expressed by the original work, at the same time as they create alternative forms of that 'reality'. *Détournement* consequently creates anew, cutting through and across societal and cultural norms. Working with familiar materials (a cartoon strip, a political speech), it renders the familiar unfamiliar and hopes to subject it to radical critique.

To attend to such practices is to problematise what it means to be creative and the place creative practices have in the cultural-economic contexts of intellectual property rights. As the Internet has become an increasingly contested site for the creation and distribution of intellectual property, so governments and corporations (in particular, media conglomerates and their agents) have sought to enact stricter regulation over how their property is used. Frequent calls for stricter regulatory frameworks and the use of 'secure technologies' such as Digital Rights Management Systems have developed alongside a culture of litigation that seeks to prevent unauthorised use of copyrighted materials. Against this we can place the sonic art of Negativland, the prevalence of sampling in hip-hop music culture and the appropriation and reproduction of entire creative works (songs, albums) by music fans through P2P networks such as Napster, Gnutella and Freenet. Radical art, popular music and file sharing on the Internet all invite us to rethink and reframe our accepted notions of copyright and intellectual property.

I do not propose to provide a history of copyright and intellectual property rights here (for a useful overview, see Toynbee 2001). Instead, and in the spirit of this book, I want to present alternative frames for considering intellectual property. A useful starting point is in the political philosophy of anarchism and Proudhon's well known formulation, 'all property is theft'. But even if we accept this axiom, with what might we replace it? Murray Bookchin (1991: 50) has proposed that we consider 'usufruct' as a counter to property rights. As Clement and Oppenheim note (2002: 42), this concept does not solely reside in anarchist thought; it is part of the legal structure of Canada, for instance. Usufruct should be contrasted with property. Where the latter implies the permanent ownership of resources, usufruct is 'a temporary property relationship based on utility or need which meets the demands of communality' (Clement and Oppenheim 2002: 42). It is not, though, communal property, neither is it based on reciprocity; according to Bookchin there is no necessity to tie usufruct in with obligations of exchange. Indeed, to do so is to risk a project of self-interest that itself might be deleterious and that might, at worst, lead to such temporary property relationships approaching a permanence of ownership that the practice of usufruct seeks to avoid, even to replace. Clement and Oppenheim (2002: 43) argue persuasively that, despite existing copyright legislation that forbids the copying of a work without permission, 'usufruct is the norm' on the Web. This they term 'electronic non-propertarianism' (p. 47). Their arguments reveal, however, two distinct sets of practices based on usufruct. The first concerns the use of copyrighted materials (texts, music, images), whether for personal enjoyment (the file-sharing practices that define P2P technologies) or for *détournement*. The second are concerned with the 'bottom-up production of difference' (Fiske 1992b: 165). Instead of appropriating existing cultural products from the dominant culture they seek to create products – or perhaps more accurately 'process-products'. A well known example of this is the operating system Linux, whose very origins proceed from considering usufruct as a communal, creative process that is paradigmatic of social authorship. Linux was established under the notion of 'copyleft' (GNU Project 1999). Copyleft, as the word suggests, was intended as a non-propertarian rejoinder to copyright, and implies intellectual practices that encourage software developers to adapt the Linux system as they see fit, as long as they do not establish it as proprietary. Consequently, Linux has been developed by many hands on a social basis, each improvement being made available to developers and users without cost and without permission needing to be sought. The continuing history of Linux is a significant working model of usufruct, and of Clement and Oppenheim's 'electronic non-propertarianism'. It is anarchism in action. (The notion of copyleft has also been borrowed by commercial publishing. In 2002, the popular science magazine *New Scientist* published an article simultaneously in print and electronically which its editor declared as 'copyleft' (www.newscientist.com/hottopics/copyleft). This, though, was a very different reading of copyleft, closer in intent to the anti-copyright projects of many anarchist publishers (Atton 2002a: 42–5), where the aim is to encourage unlimited distribution of a particular text without distributors – mostly readers of the text – having to seek permission from the copyright holder. *New Scientist*'s copyleft project had nothing to do with social authorship understood as a creative and communal process. We might also consider the adoption of the term by a professional publisher as a somewhat cynical exercise, limited in its impact, though it did at least inform its readers of a radical notion that many might have been unlikely to encounter.)

As a social electronic process Linux demonstrates the possibilities of the Internet to be employed for the purposes of social authorship, as it eschews the limits of private intellectual property and the restrictions on creativity that the established legal frameworks of copyright entail. The enactment of such possibilities takes place within what we have already referred to as a species of Bourdieu's 'demotic restricted field'. Despite their significance, their success and their liberatory power, such practices inhabit a field that is quite separate from the legal-commercial field within which intellectual property rights remain strongly protected. For whilst Linux might be a threat to commercially developed operating systems, it does not threaten the integrity and the ownership rights of its commercial rivals. Other forms of social authorship do threaten the intellectual property rights of commercial organisations and in these cases we are presented with an Internet culture (arguably what has come to be its dominant culture) where these rights are jealously guarded and fought over. Nowhere is this struggle more conspicuous than in the legal and commercial struggles that have been taking place over the development of P2P (file-sharing) systems, such as Napster, Gnutella and Freenet.

SOCIAL AUTHORSHIP AND P2P NETWORKS

Jason Toynbee's deliberately ambiguous phrase 'creating problems' (Toynbee 2001) points up the dialectic of the desideratum of creative freedom and the constraints of economic and legal frameworks. The threats faced by those creating on the Internet according to principles of usufruct and social authorship are themselves problematised by those creators; the history of capital faces the history of cultural production, and this confrontation forces us to re-evaluate the relationship between capital and culture and our place in it. Toynbee's analysis provides us with an extremely productive and challenging perspective on what has become a central question in the cultural and commercial uses of new technology. Toynbee also draws on Bourdieu's field of cultural production as a theoretical model from which to understand the cultural practices that constitute social authorship. For him, though, this is to examine a field of popular cultural production that is far wider and far less restricted in terms of its creators, their creative acts and its audiences than we have already encountered. Toynbee's task is no less than to explore the creative practices of the history of popular music production.

Toynbee's conception of social authorship proceeds from his locating authors in a field of cultural production within which they 'work by recombining symbolic materials from a historically deposited common stock, and [who] must negotiate with audiences which have a powerful influence through the market over which texts are selected' (Toynbee 2001: 2). This formulation goes well beyond the elite notions of plagiarism, appropriation and *détournement* that we found in the avant-garde practices of Negativland, John Oswald and the artistic-political movements that preceded them. It is to recognise a shared creative history which not only determines the artistic choices that may be made within a particular field, but which also functions as a depository of formal and content-based resources from which authors choose, combining, realigning and reinterpreting them to create their 'own' work. In these terms social authorship is concerned with the creative collisions between the author as a contemporary creator, as a historical component within cultural production and previous authors; all combine in the field of cultural production. But Toynbee goes further, adding to this mix the crucial function performed by audiences in selectively valorising the texts thus produced; understood as active players in the markets for creative products, the audiences themselves become social authors.

Before we follow Toynbee in his application of social authorship to P2P networks on the Internet, we need to clarify the relationships that are taking place within the field of cultural production. Toynbee identifies in Bourdieu (particularly, Bourdieu 1984 and 1993) three 'structuring structures' (Toynbee 2001: 8) which together clarify how authors create in this social manner. These are: the 'field of works'; the 'field of cultural production' itself; and the 'habitus' of the individual author. The field of works comprises the store of 'historically accumulated symbolic resources' from which creators within a particular genre (the field of cultural production) draw to produce their work. The choices they make and what they do with those resources – the ways in which they combine and adapt them (or privilege some over others) – is explained by the artist's habitus, the personal social history and context of each artist (such as class, educational background, professional values, training). Bourdieu examines these in the context of 'high art', specifically in French literature, but in applying them to the creative possibilities of popular music as a field of cultural production

Toynbee argues that there is a 'greater openness of the field of production to variations in the habitus of producers, plus the range and diversity of the field works [which lead to] greater instability than in consecrated art and a less clear-cut distinction between heretical and orthodox positions' (Toynbee 2001: 9). Cultural production must therefore be considered as a set of social processes, one which in the case of popular music is at once determined by these 'structuring structures' at the same time as those structures are contested and struggled over. In short, 'creativity actually depends on the recycling and synthesis of musical resources produced by previous creative action' (Toynbee 2001: 12).

This argument has deep implications for copyright and intellectual property, for it suggests that, as Toynbee states, 'a good part of creativity belongs in the public domain' (2001: 12). We have seen throughout the twentieth century what Toynbee terms increases in 'bandwidth', a continual increase in the carrying capacity of media (radio, records, film, the Internet). This increase expands the field of works available for creators as well as facilitating the means through which those works are accessed. This expansion of 'phonographic orality' (Toynbee 2001: 14) on the Internet has been accompanied by a networked, peer-to-peer logic of distribution that challenges the prevailing industrial logic of distribution – a one-to-many process that privileges a central node from which cultural products, highly regulated, are distributed to audiences. The network logic is not new, of course. Music sharing amongst enthusiasts has been practised for decades: in the form of tape swapping (whether of long-deleted recordings or bootlegged studio or live performances) and, more recently, CD burning. This is not simply a technological advance on earlier taping practices, it has also impacted on creators – the distribution of on-demand or small-run CD-Rs by musicians (whose projects we might term 'micro-independents') has increased the number and availability of the field of works. What is new is the extent, the thoroughness and the normative status that music sharing (as file sharing) has achieved amongst Internet users. It is no longer restricted to a relatively small number of obsessive fans of particular artists (though they still remain) – file sharing is now a normative practice on the Internet. What I have elsewhere referred to as 'little worlds of publishing' (Atton 2001b: 30) can be used here to delineate a field of cultural production that is at once populated by creators and fans, and is in some way also an industry (Fiske's 'shadow cultural economy'; Fiske

1992a: 30). The 'market' that this 'shadow cultural economy' implies is both separate from and deeply implicated in the dominant market practices of the record industry. It can be considered as 'a sort of "moonlighting" in the cultural rather than the economic sphere, a form of cultural labor to fill the gaps by legitimate culture' (Fiske 1992a: 33).

It is through this 'social nature of musical creativity' (Toynbee 2001: 26) that social authorship on the Internet is most powerfully realised. A nexus of artists and fans has developed where the creative work is developed socially – through collaborative creation, circulation, commentary and consumption. The Internet has facilitated collaborative creation to a great degree. Though collaboration between artists working at a distance from one another is not new – before the Internet, recordings could be exchanged through the mail, for example, for others to work on – the use of email and broadband lines, along with digital editing and processing software available on the Internet (often as shareware), enables collaborators to work in real time and in creative spaces that do not require elaborate and expensive studio facilities. The use of the laptop computer in many forms of electronic avant-garde, dance and rock music has expanded the notion of the 'bedroom' musician and opened up possibilities of collaboration across the Internet to such an extent that, at least in terms of the sophistication and availability of recording and processing equipment, we are seeing an erasing of the boundaries between amateur and professional creative practices. The Internet is also increasingly being used for promotional purposes. We are all familiar with the use of brief audio samples that act as publicity for complete commercial recordings, but in less commercial fields of music-making we will find entire compositions and performances available, at times even entire 'albums'. Many of these, unlike the forays into album-selling by the large record companies and some of the larger independent labels, are available free of charge, often with no copyright restrictions upon them. At one level this can be understood as an extension of the radical notions of copyright we found in the work of Negativland and John Oswald, simply extended to one's own work. At another, it suggests that the desire to have one's music heard is greater than the desire for commercial success. In part this reflects the marginal status of much of the work undertaken by such artists (many of whom might well be unknown even to afficionados of the field); in part it demonstrates again a non-propertarian notion of creativity, where the norm is to create within a digital commons, the upshot of which is to distribute one's work in that digital commons according to the same, non-propertarian principles. Even established artists will make use of this method, though not to the exclusion of more conventional, commercial means. Robert Fripp, for example, whilst continuing to sell the bulk of his work on CD through his own Discipline Global Mobile record label and distribution company (and artist-run labels whose primary presence is on the Internet are another feature of this aspect of creativity), has made available single works as MP3s for downloading from his web site. These function as occasional 'gifts' to the digital commons.

It is perhaps what fans do with these creations once they are digitally available that provides the greatest moral impetus to the notions of non-propertarianism, radical copyright and digital commons. Despite the varying approaches of artists towards the Internet as a distribution and promotional tool, the circulation of their material by fans flattens out these approaches and presents further ones. The trading and swapping of tapes recorded by fans (whether of commercially available material or of bootlegged material from broadcasts, concerts or unreleased studio recordings) has been an important aspect of fans' contribution to social creativity for decades. It has also been illegal, of course, and – or so the record industry has consistently argued – a grave threat both to profit-making and to artistic creativity. There have been no detailed studies of tape networks to my knowledge. Heylin's (1994) account of the history of the bootleg record industry emphasises not the social nature of the enterprise; rather it finds in it practices similar to those of the main-stream (centralised, competitive, profit-making). By contrast, and based on my own experiences as a member of various tape networks in the 1970s and 1980s (though that is perhaps to render the experience more formal than it ever was), tape networks were only occasionally based on finance – the norm was to exchange tapes, not to pay for them. However, in order to exchange tapes each member had to have material that was desired by the other – the cultural capital thus available would make one a valued member of the network and would in itself attract other members, offering their material in the hope of obtaining yours. The multiple, and often only marginally overlapping, nature of these networks enabled a member to use material gained in one to demonstrate cultural capital in another. A recording I obtained from a friend in Germany as part of an 'avant rock' network featured a famous British jazz musician. Its rarity gave me an entry into a network of jazz tape swapping which I had long sought. 'Friend' is significant here, for friendships did develop, through writing to each other not only for requests but to evaluate the qualities (recording and aesthetic) of material being exchanged. In my experience, the networks were compact, no more than a dozen people. But they were the 'right' people, those with the highest cultural capital and those with whom one could build a friendship. Our membership of other networks meant that we would acquire material from other sources, but we tended to deal with a far smaller number of people than the sum of all members in all networks.

Do we find similar structures in today's Internet-based peer-to-peer networks? Whilst the networks in which I participated were entirely concerned with making available rare, unreleased recordings, the ease with which digitally produced material can be duplicated and transmitted greatly expands the available repertoire of material. For example, the music on a commercially available CD that has been deleted may be copied easily, as might that expensive boxed set of studio outtakes by your favourite artists, released by a major label belatedly alerted to the commercial value of such work. The transfer of vinyl and cassette recordings to a digital format enables their circulation on a far wider scale than the tape network, for which a new copy had to be made for each request (and in real time, except for the few who could afford a high-speed copying machine). The notion of scarcity begins to disappear. Whilst Internet-based music-sharing networks had been in existence before (conducted through newsgroups and message boards), it was the launch of Napster in 1999 that began the current species of P2P networking of recorded music. Alderman (2002: 169) refers to Napster as 'merely a vessel' and cites a number of commentators who argue that Napster's founder, Shaun Fanning, developed the software 'because he could', with none of the 'ideological passions' (p. 177) for a digital commons that we find explicit in the GNU manifesto or in the work of the Electronic Frontier Foundation, or indeed in the more hidden (though no less urgent) desiderata of open circulation and common ownership amongst members of tape networks. Napster provided a central server which users could access in order to locate and obtain digital copies of specific pieces of music. If Fanning was motivated more by the technical challenges such a service could bring, its users brought to it an ideological fervour that established P2P file sharing of music on a massive scale: 'your biggest problem . . . is that instead of a business, you created a movement. And it's impossible to convert it' (Hilary Rosen, chief executive of the Recording Industry Association of America, cited in Walker 2003: 34). Despite successful prosecution by the RIAA for copyright infringements, Rosen's assertion has proved to be inaccurate: Napster has remained a business. In 2003 it was bought by the CD-burning company Roxio as part of its expanding portfolio of commercially driven download sites, with copyright clearance carefully negotiated with the major record and many independent record labels. It has been joined by other music downloading services such as Listen.com, OD2 and Apple's iTunes Music Store which all employ a central server model. iTunes also uses antifilesharing technology but some companies, such as the Internet service provider Playlouder and Wippit offer legal file-sharing services by subscription, with royalties paid to the rights holder by the companies. Yet, whilst some commentators see such services as evidence of 'the majors [relaxing] their attitude to digital-rights management' (Gibson 2003: 23), the continuing threat of legal action against Internet service providers and individual users suspected of illegal file sharing (Harmon 2003) demonstrates that the 'movement', as Rosen asserts, remains a significant one, as it contests legal definitions of ownership and distribution. In the case of Wippit, which has staked a claim as the world's first legal file sharing service, it is estimated that less than 10 per cent of its '165,000 regular users are paying subscribers' (Terazono 2003: 9).

The 'Napster movement' differed from the tape networks preceding it to the degree that it was not based on the principle of a gift economy based on cultural capital. This contrasts with the more closed communities of P2P Internet networks examined by Cooper and Harrison (2001), who found socially significant relations based on friendship, trust and cultural capital that were simply not found in the Napster community, which was a much more functional one. To join the Napster network, unlike the networks analysed by Cooper and Harrison, one merely had to make one's digital 'library' available to all. Whilst this requires some level of commitment, it can be argued that the exchanges that took place were motivated more simply by a selfish desire to obtain, rather than to share. When compared to the gift relationship, a relationship that is 'driven by social relations' (Kollock 1999: 222) or the social relations founded on cultural capital enacted through more specialised P2P networks (whether digital or analogue), Napster appears socially attenuated. The development of the P2P networks Gnutella and Freenet in 2000 signalled a far more ideologically driven and anti-propertarian approach to music file sharing on the Internet. Gnutella was developed using open source software and both it and Freenet dispensed with a central server, instead establishing a distributed network that drew explicitly on the ideological position of the Electronic Frontier Foundation, aiming to realise a digital commons for music based on non-propertarianism. These networks were more properly P2P. They enabled individual fans to make direct contact with each other, to establish the social relations that we have already seen at work in tape networks. Moreover, these networks were explicitly designed to contest the established bases of copyright and intellectual property; they had their 'roots in the hacking subculture, the open-software world and indie-music critics of the big record labels' (Walker 203: 34). Yet they do differ from each other in important ways. Gnutella may be considered as a 'searching and discovery network [that] promotes free interpretation and response to queries. Freenet is optimized for computerized access to those files rather than human inter-action' (Merriden 2001: 131). Freenet operates in similar fashion to the World Wide Web, providing a network through which any publications (including music) may circulate freely. On the other hand, Gnutella emphasises the transactions between users. Whilst both may develop the social relations we have been discussing, Gnutella is predicated upon them; on Freenet those relations may or may not develop. Together, though, taken as differing approaches to the set of issues around circulation, social relations, copyright and property rights and the development of a digital commons, both networks present socially focused ways of distributing information. The ways in which they do so, the ideologies from which they have developed and the consequences of their success in maximising circulation without restricting access (Toynbee 2001: 26) all point towards a normative set of social practices that represent the latest attempts to radically shift the practices of creativity and consumption away from capital-driven, scarcity-based models of production and distribution.

BACK TO THE SOURCE: CREATIVITY AND COPYRIGHT

It seems that the dominant regimes of copyright and intellectual property relations are unlikely to be replaced by a new model based on social authorship. At best, these practices of file sharing on the Internet appear as marginal interventions that can do little more than chip away at the enduring and limiting logic of capital. As if to recognise this, there have emerged interventions that exist quite separately from these restraints. Instead of struggling within the heart of the beast, so to speak, a small but growing number of independent musicians are establishing models of social creativity that do not directly challenge existing regimes, but seek to create spaces on the Internet from within which they might practise music sharing without interference from the legal or moral weight of the record industry. Like Freenet and Gnutella, they take their inspiration from the co-operative and communitarian ventures of the open source and free software movements. For musicians, though, the point is not to release and distribute software, but the music itself, using radical copyright licences. The Free Music Movement (www.free-music.org) explicitly draws on the rhetoric of the Free Software movement in its desire to 'free' music for personal copying, distribution and modification through sampling or remixing. The movement suggests a variety of strategies for the realisation of this project. Whilst it rehearses many of the arguments regarding already commercially available recordings that we have already encountered from the Electronic Frontier Foundation, Negativland and John Oswald, the Free Music Movement is primarily interested in encouraging musicians to step outside the existing legal regimes of copyright and to make their music available to others for their personal use on a non-commercial basis. Listeners (including other musicians) would then be free to use that music in any way (whether simply for further distribution or for creative reworking), providing that they too abide by the terms of a similar licence which permits reproduction only for personal, non-commercial use. The manifesto presented as Free Music Philosophy (www.ram.org/ramblings/philosophy/fmp.html) appears to be the work of a single author, which suggests a movement in its infancy (arguably, a movement in potential only). A 'provisional' draft of a Free Music Public License dated 15 April 2001 (www.fmpl.org/fmpl.html) summarises this personal, non-commercial application of free music sharing, but also makes tentative statements about how this model might also be applied to financially remunerative practices. These are to be arranged on the basis of trust, where potential users are expected to negotiate with the original musician for permission to sell the work (or a version of it). Laudable though this proposal may be, there is surely scope here for protracted and perhaps insoluble negotiations, particularly where, as in the case of sampled work, many original contributors may be involved. Dated only five days after the Free Music Public License, the Electronic Frontier Foundation's Open Audio License (www.eff.org/IP/Open_licenses/eff_oal.php) avoids this problem, emphasising instead two aims: to 'allow artists to grant the public permission to copy, distribute, adapt and publicly perform their works royalty-free as long as credit is given to the creator as the Original Author'; and to allow 'musicians to collaborate in creating a pool of "open audio" that can be freely modified, exchanged, and utilized in new ways' (ibid.). Interestingly, the licence makes use of existing copyright legislation to emphasise that ownership of the original work still remains with the original author. Anyone making use of the original work must undertake not only to credit the original author but to make any new version of the work also available under the terms of the same licence.

The open source record label Opsound (www.opsound.org) has applied the EFF's notion of 'open audio' to develop its vision of a digital music commons. Opsound uses a 'copyleft' licence produced by the Creative Commons organisation (www.creativecommons.org). Creative Commons was set up in 2001 to encourage what it calls 'reasonable copyright'. This seeks to replace the draconian music industry dictum of 'all rights reserved' with a copyleft licence that is more flexible, preferring 'some rights reserved'. Opsound invites musicians to contribute their sounds to an 'open pool', the contents of which may then be remixed, sampled – or simply listened to. The copyleft licence allows anyone to copy or distribute the work or, indeed, to 'make derivative works' from it through sampling or remixing. Works may also be sold commercially by others. Only two rights are reserved: the original author must be given credit and, crucially, any distribution, sale or reuse of the work must also be under the same copyleft licence. This should result in a community of musicians who share their creative work in a libertarian culture working on the principles of a gift economy and stimulating creative collaboration.

The EFF licence places great store by the potential of this practice to increase the visibility of the original author and their work through what it terms 'super distribution' and 'viral marketing'. And whilst it has little to say about commercial applications of the licence, it does suggest that musicians might wish to consider experimenting with new business models for financial remuneration. Whereas Opsound releases its music online only, Loca Records (www.locarecords.com) has gone further, releasing its music on vinyl and CD under the same Creative Commons licence (which also extends to cover art). By taking the work out of the virtual, Loca demonstrates that open source is not simply a marketplace of ideas, it can be an actual marketplace. Its open source artists operate commercially, releasing records that are indistinguishable from those next to them in the racks – save for the copyleft licence that comes with every disc. Loca releases recordings that are sold in the same way as non-open source releases, with profits going to both artists and the company. Significantly, though, anyone else is free to release these recordings on a commercial basis, providing they credit the original artist and the label, and release them under the same open source licence as the original. Loca currently releases recordings as music CDs and vinyl only, which offer only limited opportunity for reworking. Whilst such recordings may be sampled directly from the disc, any intending remixer or sampler does not have access to the original source files which would enable radical or large-scale reworking. Loca is currently working on releasing music/data CDs which do contain the original, computer-readable source files and which will enable other musicians to rework completely the original material.

These approaches to open source/free music licensing are in keeping with the libertarian impulse that underlies the philosophy of a digital commons. Always under development and open to various solutions to the problems of copyright, ownership, distribution and creativity, the Free Music movement, the EFF, Creative Commons, Opsound and Loca demonstrate that there need be no single way of encouraging creativity, collaboration and social authorship. Nor need such practices be entirely divorced from existing commercial and legal practices. Concerned less with confronting capital's limits head on and more modest in finding solutions to the public/commercial impasse to which the case of Napster has arguably brought us, the philosophy and practices of open source music production and distribution suggest that, though they may not be in a position to tear down John Oswald's fence of copyright once and for all, they do at least suggest nimble ways of negotiating it, the better to enjoy the field of creativity.

CHAPTER 5

Alternative Radio and the Internet

INTRODUCTION

Radio as a contemporary public medium tends to be considered primarily in terms of its industrial and cultural arrangements. We may identify five broad types of radio broadcasting: public service broadcasting, commercial radio, state radio, community (or micro) radio, and pirate radio. The first of these, perhaps best known in the West through long-established services such as the BBC, is predicated on providing services that, whilst funded largely by government, are independent of direct state control and are ideally free from commercial imperatives. The ideal of public service broadcasting, in the classic Reithian formulation, is to educate, inform and entertain, aims which are legally enshrined. By contrast, the commercial sector is under no such legal and social obligations; instead its aim is the maximisation of profit through the maximisation of audiences and the generation of advertising revenues. Radio under the direct control of the state is largely unknown in the West and tends to be associated with dirigiste regimes (whether secular or religious) which seek to standardise and limit content and formats to produce programmes that function as essentialised, arguably propagandist, attempts at national social control through the delimiting of debate and discussion. By contrast, community or micro radio operates at a hyper-local level, often as a result of the low power of transmitters, broadcasting (or better, 'narrowcasting') to specific, local geographic communities (whether cultural or social), determined by location or the interests of communities or both. Community radio might be considered as explicitly political but, where state radio is concerned with political control from the centre, the content and format of community radio ideally will be negotiated from the bottom up, involving the local community in its determination of needs and desires. Pirate radio also works at the local level, once more as a result of the low power of transmitters, but here the very act of broadcasting is seen as a political act. Pirate radio may be localised technologically, yet its content is not necessarily developed from a connection with the grassroots of society. Instead it may often be 'protest radio', using the act of broadcasting to make political statements about the regulation of the airwaves or restrictions about, say, political content.

These five types of radio may be divided into two 'sectors', according to how they accommodate or contest three broad features. These are the technological, the legal and the professional. Public broadcasting, commercial and state radio are typically the technologically most sophisticated, with their access to funding (whether via the state or the market) enabling them to purchase powerful transmitters, studio space and other equipment necessary to sustain large institutions capable of broadcasting (at least) nationally. Such organisations operate within the legal framework of their home nation-state and, though space on the airwaves may have to be competed for, they operate within the relative security of neoliberal market economies or the direct and assured support of the state. By contrast, community and pirate radio stations operate on the fringes of such support. Pirate radio, by its very definition, is illegal and thus highly volatile – few pirate stations have any longevity or consistency. When a pirate station is shut down through legal enforcement, broadcasting equipment is usually confiscated and the station will be unable to resume operations until new equipment is obtained. The voluntary and poorly funded nature of such operations makes resumption difficult. Community radio stations also tend to be run largely (if not entirely) by voluntary labour, funded through donations (of money or equipment), and they may likewise have short transmission lives. For their duration, they will operate legally, often competing for the limited frequency space assigned by government for community radio.

Taken together, community/micro-radio and pirate radio best demonstrate the notions of alternative media. They are based on the production and dissemination of material for specific communities (whether geographic or communities of interest, or both) that is located and created within those communities. In what we may now consider as a classic formulation of alternative media, they involve amateur, activist producers whose positioning within the communities prompts the creation of content that seeks to explore issues and perspectives (cultural, political, social) that are of direct relevance to those communities. They are not about producing content or replicating forms that, as is the case with commercial broadcasters, are concerned with 'deliver[ing] to advertisers a measured and defined group of consumers' (Fornatale and Mills 1980: 61, cited in Crisell 2002: 131). Arguably, they are not about consumption at all; instead, they are about participation, development and mobilisation. These aims are most clearly at work in the radical community radio stations examined, for example, by Howley (2000) or in the 'development radio' across Latin America, Africa and India (Gumucio Dagron 2001), but we might also see them realised in radio broadcasting that is less explicitly socio-political. As we know from studies of fans and fanzines (for example, Atton 2001b; Jenkins 1992; Triggs 1995) and as we shall see in Chapter 6, we might also think of development and mobilisation as encouraging consumers of artistic products (records, films, books) to become critics and even creators themselves, developing critical approaches to creativity that are avant-garde or experimental in their relation to dominant forms of criticism and creation. This is not to say that it is only through such activist or 'amateur' media that such developments arise. The history of avant-garde approaches in twentieth-century art has been shown to arise in the main from artistic institutions (Born 1995; Harrison 1991). Rather, these studies show the capacity of alternative media formations to nurture and sustain what I have called a 'demotic avant-garde' (Atton 2002a: 30) which is more or less free from institutional and bureaucratic pressures and ambitions (though that is not to say that it will be unaware of those other histories). The case study of Resonance FM in this chapter suggests a number of ways in which radical artistic production may be developed through alternative radio.

The community/micro radio experiments in the US discussed by Howley and the history of pirate radio (Chapman 1992; Harris 1970) share other features. In common with many other forms of alternative media, their anti-commercial ethos leads to underfunding and the use of 'self-exploited', volunteer labour. Consequently such stations are often short-lived. Low capital means that stations will not have access to high-quality, powerful transmitters; these low-power stations will have a very narrow reach. Whilst narrowcasting might well accord with a station's aim to serve a specific, geographic community, it might also act as a brake on the development of the station, not least in terms of attracting new recruits as operators, presenters and programme-makers. Both types of radio also find themselves on the wrong side of law. Unable (for financial reasons) or unwilling (for ideological reasons) to apply for licences – assuming that the government of a particular territory has made a part of the frequency spectrum available for such experiments – stations run the risks of having their equipment confiscated, of fines being levied, even of the staff being imprisoned. Whilst in countries such as the US and the UK commercial radio has been increasing at both national and local levels, the opportunities for alternative radio have remained limited. Crisell (2002: 121) notes that there were only forty-eight independent (that is, commercial) radio stations in the UK in 1984; by 2000 there were 248, 'outnumbering the BBC's by more than six to one'.

Opportunities have arisen, however. In the UK the Restricted Service Licence system (RSL) was established to promote local community and specialist radio stations. Operating under legal frameworks brings its own limits for such stations. Licences are typically issued on an annual basis, with renewal dependent on proven success. There are also limits on the content of broadcasts – direct political campaigning is outlawed by the RSL system, for example. This is not to say that there exists an unbridgeable professional divide between public/commercial/state on the one hand and community/micro/pirate on the other. Many UK stations operating under RSLs have adopted a community radio format that has more in common with local, commercial broadcasters. With support from local businesses, such stations become able to professionalise their output, that is, to make programmes that accord more closely with formats and styles familiar to us from public service and commercial radio. Furthermore, the low entry costs of radio (when compared to those of television, which also requires higher levels of technical knowledge) continue to attract new players in the radio game. The RSL scheme has also seen the emergence of a more radical broadcaster, London's Resonance FM, which has taken advantage of the scheme to produce what are surely some of the most challenging programmes on British radio – challenging in terms of content, experiments with form and the use of non-professional programme-makers and presenters (as we shall see later). The focus of this chapter is, however, radio on the Internet. Resonance FM, in common with many radio stations (commercial, public service, state and alternative), has begun to employ the Internet to supplement its analogue or digital transmissions. Later we will explore the implication of the Internet for an analogue-based station such as Resonance. First, thought we need to ask a broader question: what happens to radio when it is transmitted through the Internet?

INTERNET RADIO: FEATURES AND CHARACTERISTICS

The new players making use of the Internet are not limited to the voluntary or community sector alone. Returning to our five types of radio, we already find the first three (public broadcasting, state and commercial) using the Internet to enhance or replace existing services. The first of these we might call the 'replica-plus' model, where a radio station's web site broadcasts an audio stream identical to that broadcast through existing analogue means (or through digital audio broadcasting). In addition, a site such as the BBC's BBCi ('interactive') also provides a limited range of archived programmes through its 'Listen again' service. Such sites also typically provide programme information (playlists, addresses for further information, longer or unedited versions of broadcast interviews and performances) as well as discussion spaces and message boards for particular programmes, programme strands, genres and stations. Sites may also incorporate visual material in the form of still or moving images. These 'replica-plus' sites are especially popular with mainstream radio stations in the public broadcasting and commercial sectors. State radio broadcasters also make use of them, though the more determined nature of such services will tend towards more attenuated forms of presentation and interaction (the parallel here is with the global broadcasting services that have long been a feature of state radio broadcasting on the shortwave radio bands, where in pre-Internet days listeners were encouraged to contact stations by post, a valuable auditing mechanism for monitoring both the audience reach and the technological reach of the station). These forms of 'added value' through expanded services and the promotion of interactivity are also clearly valuable to community stations, in particular to those whose cultural reach may suggest the extension of a station's local reach to a wide, globalised community of interest (ethnic, religious, political, cultural). Some newer stations may even adopt this model as an Internet-only form of broadcasting, entirely abandoning analogue transmission. This is common in the commercial sector and leads to our second dominant form of Internet radio: computerised, format radio. This is prevalent amongst the thousands of commercial 'stations' that have arisen to broadcast via the Internet alone. Computerised format radio is already well established in analogue commercial radio. Presenters of format music radio (hit radio, Top 40 radio, AOR, and so on) have for many years used computerised systems to generate playlists from a database of music pre-selected to accord with the criteria of a particular show or format. At times even a DJ's announcements and jingles may be computerised. There are now many fully automated, commercial Internet radio stations (predominantly in the US) serving specialist audiences for genres as diverse as hip-hop, country and western, electronica and progressive rock. Musical selections are generated randomly, interspersed with advertisements and station identification messages.

Such specialist format stations are not restricted to commercial broadcasters. As Hendy (2000: 192) points out, the combination of low entry costs and volunteer labour, when taken with new channels of distribution (such as the Internet) and greater opportunities for an 'individualised production process' than is the case with television, continues to present significant creative possibilities for radio. Some of these have been realised by enthusiasts who produce specialist, format radio stations that reveal their own musical preferences rather than those of market researchers and advertisers; as Crisell points out, 'the history of radio formats is closely linked to the history of market research' (Crisell 2002: 131). The network of Internet radio stations managed by live365 (www.live365.com) enables enthusiasts or DJs to set up their own radio stations without the need for expensive studio equipment, offices or institutional arrangements. Neither is there, of course, any problem of legality or spectrum scarcity – such stations need no licence and do not need to compete for a frequency. The bulk of the stations available through live365 do, however, share the dominant feature of commercial Internet broadcasting: playlists are computerised, generated randomly from a largely unchanging stock of recordings. What we have is a set of specialist jukeboxes which, though they might on occasion result in serendipitous encounters with unfamiliar material (one of the guiding principles of Reithian-style public service broadcasting), they are most likely to cater for an audience whose tastes are predictable and who desire a selection of music that is similarly 'safe'. Whilst the formats thus presented may well be unusual in terms of commercial format radio, they seem to cater for a specific, more or less static notion of an audience. Such stations are only weakly 'alternative': far from creating new forms of programmes, they simply replicate existing, dominant models; they do not invite participation (most of these stations are single-person operations); and they do not seek creative or critical responses. The music is all there is; there is no commentary, no criticism, no progress, no experimentation with the medium. The curiously named Internet radio station rand()% (www.r4nd.org) offers a more creative application of computerised, specialist broadcasting. In the 1990s the composer and producer Brian Eno experimented with the notion of 'generative music', a non-repetitive form of music generated from a computerised algorithm. rand()% uses his notion to broadcast self-generated music continuously. The continuous stream at times resembles Eno's own ambient music, unhurried, ever-changing, yet largely static. At others it is more hard-edged, atonal electronica. Whilst this experiment in broadcasting goes well beyond format radio in its creativity and its scale (there are no discrete 'songs'; no performers as such), the station exists in isolation – one may 'tune in' but the opportunity to interact with it is very limited, in common with other, more conventional, computerised Internet radio stations.

After all, when a station contains no actual DJ presence there is little opportunity to develop any intimate relationship with an audience and that relationship, as we shall see, has long been argued as one of the distinctive features of radio listening. Interaction, though, remains a priority with radio broadcasters; it might be argued that the Internet offers richer forms of interactivity for broadcasters. But interactivity is a weasel word in many studies of the Internet. It is often considered as the *ne plus ultra* of a digital age, as if the mere capacity of a communication system to enable two-way communication is enough to lionise it as 'interactive'. Of course there are many ways of understanding interactivity, not all of them by any means new. A consumer affairs programme produced by a public service broadcaster might have long practised the publication of a 'factsheet' and the announcement of telephone 'helplines' and addresses for advice in its format. Internet 'interactivity' in this case may mean little more than publishing such information on the programme's web site, providing an email address and setting up a discussion list for its audience. Some stations have extended the phone-in or 'question time' formats to include off-air interviews with public figures, who are questioned by audience members online. Or, as we saw in Chapter 2, online journalists may well take soundings and develop stories through close attention to the discussions and opinion-formation that take place within an online discussion forum set up by their news organisation.

In the field of 'development' radio OneWorld Radio (www.one world.net/radio) offers a more radical form of interaction. OneWorld Radio is part of the global social-justice network OneWorld, which brings together over 1,000 organisations (NGOs, community groups, alternative media organisations). Its radio portal offers these organisations, along with individuals, the facility to listen to and exchange radio programmes produced by activists working in the areas of human rights, social change and sustainable development. These programmes are produced and broadcast by a mix of analogue and Internet radio stations. Programmes uploaded to the OneWorld Radio site may be freely broadcast by any member of the network. For reasons of bandwidth and connection time, programmes are limited in their length to a maximum of ten minutes, yet the resource makes it possible for small, alternative radio stations to broadcast programming cheaply and to offer programmes from across the world to their own more localised audiences. Programmes available at the time of writing include features on the criminal justice system in Russia, disabled women in Japan, sex education in South Africa and a 'mini-drama' about children and public health in a Senegalese village. OneWorld Radio's portal suggests an application of the Internet that is meaningfully globalised, egalitarian and creative. Yet its presence on the Internet is only part of its network; it does not exist solely in cyberspace. This should not be taken as a shortcoming. Indymedia has a number of radio projects available through its IMC radio network (radio.indymedia.org). The Global IMC Audio Newswire syndicates audio files uploaded from IMC sites around the world and is updated several times a day. As we have seen repeatedly throughout this book (and as was argued in the Introduction), to consider Internet practice as historically and culturally distinct from previous media technologies and practices is to essentialise the Internet. It is to fail to see its connectedness with other mediatised practices and with social practices at large. If, in all our examples so far, the applications of the Internet to radio appear largely as an adjunct to existing broadcast services (or as an Internet-only, but radio-like model), this is not to see such applications as deficient. Nor need an Internet-only example be considered iconoclastic in some way. What is more important – and more relevant – is to consider the use of Internet as radio in terms of an emphasis on its 'radiogenic' qualities, to emphasise connection not uniqueness.

Jo Tacchi (2000: 192) has used the term 'radiobility' to refer to the 'technical ability [of the Internet] to be radio, or to be radio-like or "radiogenic" '. This is a useful way to go beyond our historically and culturally limited notions of radio practice and at the same time to consider the Internet not as a distinct medium presenting entirely new and ahistorical opportunities for broadcasting. In Chapter 4 we saw how the practices of P2P file sharing and the debates over intellectual property rights and creativity are hardly explained simply in terms of a new medium; they have their histories in historical practices and cultural practices that in some cases pre-date electronic media. In the case of radio, P2P technology has also been employed to create what has been termed 'peercasting'. The Peercast (www.peercast.org) program is based on the same protocol as the file-sharing program Gnutella. Users produce their own radio programmes and distribute them through a P2P system using MP3-formatted music and sound files and an online broadcasting package such as Shoutcast. This is not only cheap (all the software is freely available), it does not rely on wide bandwidth for a high transmission speed. The distribution of the programmes through a network of online users reduces the need for expensive bandwidth technology, minimising the need for advertising or other large capital flows. And as with Gnutella, the P2P nature of the operation makes it hard to regulate against, since there is no central server to identify and shut down. In radio terms, we might think of these as the pirates of a digital age (Rojas 2002). And like the pirates before them, there are attempts to regulate the output of Internet radio stations. Whilst a regulatory body such as the US Federal Com-munications Commission (FCC) is unable to limit the number of radio stations using the Internet on the historico-legal grounds of spectrum scarcity, other bodies are attempting to do so. The Digital Millennium Copyright Act (DMCA) was passed by the US Congress in 1998. One of its provisions was to secure the right for record companies to collect royalties for works played on digital broadcasting systems (this includes Internet radio). These were to be calculated according to the number of songs broadcast and the size of a station's audience. In 2002 the Copyright Arbitration Royalty Panel (CARP) set a royalty rate of $0.0007 per song per listener. The amount may appear small, but when multiplied by the number of songs a station might play during a year multiplied by the number of listeners, an Internet radio station might easily find itself liable for a bill of tens of thousands of dollars, regardless of the size of the enterprise or its turnover. Such a decision favours the large, commercial broadcasters and is likely to push smaller stations off the air or force them underground. Peercasting, in the US at least, might become that under-ground.

The radiogenic qualities of the Internet can only be understood by reference to established practices of radio broadcasting in all its forms. It therefore makes sense to consider the practices and philosophies of Internet radio and, in particular, what we might call 'progressive' radio applications on the Internet, in the light of existing, dominant analogue practices. In some cases the Internet as a technological determinant of creativity is hardly significant at all; it is simply its appearance as low-cost channel that has encouraged creative use. This has little or nothing to do with the specific technological features of the Internet in terms of suggesting creative uses. In this way it resembles a technology such as CD-burning software. Whilst this method of production has resulted in a vast number of micro-labels being set up (almost all musician-run) for the distribution of original music in small print runs, the technology hardly determines the content of the CD. Yet without the vehicle being made available cheaply, we would have most likely seen a consolidation of independent record production around a smaller number of labels, with new entrants restricted to those with greatest financial security.

CASE STUDY: RESONANCE FM

To bring such considerations into close focus, the bulk of this chapter examines a single radio station, Resonance FM, a UK station broadcasting to central London. Resonance FM began broadcasting in 1998 under the British government's Restricted Service Licence scheme (RSL). This scheme aims to promote and encourage small-scale, community radio stations through a competitive framework which grants licences for a limited period (typically for one year) to stations broadcasting on the FM waveband. The crowdedness of the FM waveband offers only limited bandwidths for broadcast. Stations broadcasting under the RSL scheme are therefore restricted to the upper limits of the waveband (around 100–110 KHz), a segment reserved for local broadcasting (the lower, majority portion of the waveband being reserved for local and national commercial and public service broadcasting services). Resonance FM is permitted to broadcast only to listeners in central London. However, it also streams its broadcast on the Internet in RealAudio and MP3 formats. In one respect, then, it is simply an analogue community radio station with potentially global digital reach. The question arises: to what extent is this Internet radio, and not merely analogue radio employing digital technology? A bald answer would be that this is 'all' it is. Yet Resonance FM's rationale suggests a more complex answer. Established as London's 'first art radio station', its general remit is to present music and sonic art operating from the creative fringes. It presents contemporary 'serious' music, free improvised music, electronic music, sound poetry, 'avant rock' and a wide range of sonic art projects that exist even beyond these specialist genres. It seeks to present music from across the globe and to this extent might be thought of as a global radio station in terms of its sources. Moreover, despite the wide range of creative activity covered by the station, the ambit of its output is largely defined by terms such as 'experimental' or 'avant-garde' (there are exceptions, as we shall see later). Its audience reach in the central London area, despite that capital city being an internationally recognised centre for such activities, is therefore tiny, its specialist programming in these fields unlikely to win over new audiences of any size. By twinning its local analogue output with an Internet stream it is able to reach the globally fragmented, minority audience for such music. By so doing it also sidesteps the restriction on transmission range placed on it by the UK government's RSL scheme. Operating within the legal framework of its host country the station is able to reach a global audience. To this degree it is Internet radio, if by that we understand the use of a medium to 'radiogenically' reach its global audience. This is, though, to complicate the notion of radio and its audiences. Tacchi (2000: 293) points out that 'radio in one country or locality is not the same as it is elsewhere . . . there is no such place as "radiospace" in general, or in the abstract.' What sense are we to make, then, of a local radio station with global potential? Does this point to the notion of a specialist station being able to erase or, at least, to attenuate, local cultural differences in the experience of listening in different places at different times? After all, with the exception of a few hours of broadcasting for some of London's diasporic and ethnic communities, Resonance FM broadcasts in English. Does the combination of dominant language and a focus on what have been generally regarded as elite art practices result in a new species of media imperialism? In what follows I shall argue that it does not. This is due to a number of transformations and ruptures that Resonance has made within the conventions of mainstream broadcasting. As we shall see, its schedules and programmes, and its values and practices all exhibit a hybridity of approaches to the business of broadcasting. Just as we have already found hybridity in the transformation of news values and practices within alternative news services

such as Indymedia, Resonance's programming similarly displays transgressive approaches to broadcasting at the same time as it deploys
transformed notions of programme-making and scheduling based on
mainstream models. In so doing it also displays a resolutely postmodern
attitude to both its form and its content – and it is this that encourages
us to see the station as a form of resistance to Othering, rather than an
elitist coloniser of the airwaves (which has parallels to the project of
postmodern journalism suggested by Fursich (2002), which we met in
Chapter 2).

Resonance FM has dispensed with, or disregarded, a number of
scheduling features common to both commercial and public service
broadcasters. On the macro level it largely ignores the temporal
divisions of daytime, evening and late evening scheduling. These
divisions, along with their subdivisions such as breakfast and drivetime
slots, are typically used by broadcasters to organise a station's output
according to their audience reach; 'broadcasters position and sequence
programmes in ways which might help attract certain audiences at
certain times of the day, and keep them listening for longer periods'
(Hendy 2000: 104). As Hendy points out, scheduling tends to be based
on an existing knowledge of what kinds of audience are available at
particular times of day. Programmes will then be commissioned to fit
with this knowledge. Programmes that are considered more challenging
whether in terms of content or form, or for which audience research
suggests a minority audience, will typically be broadcast (if commissioned at all) in the evening, with late evening slots occupied by
programmes with the smallest audience reach. In the UK, the BBC's
'serious music' station Radio 3 provides a useful example. Whilst it does
on occasion present live or recorded broadcasts of concerts of contemporary music in its prime evening slot (roughly 19.30–21.30), its
regular programme strands for contemporary music (whether contemporary classical, jazz, 'roots' music or 'avant-rock') are scheduled in the
closing hours of the day, some not finishing until the early hours of the
next day. By comparison, Resonance FM broadcasts such content
throughout its day's programming.

Mainstream radio uses scheduling to establish 'patterns and
rhythms . . . mood, energy and tempo' (Hendy 2000: 173–4) that
unfold over a day's programming and which, through their standardisation and predictability, become familiar to audiences who become
equipped to choose from the programmes made available to them. At
other times, the audience may find themselves staying with a station, for

the transitions between such patterns and rhythms will tend to be formulated in ways which do not disrupt the larger, diurnal shape of the schedule (save for those minority programmes towards the end of a day's schedule). Resonance FM disrupts such patterning. It broadcasts no news bulletins; there are few inter-presenter links (in part this is due to the pre-recorded nature of much of its programming); there are no weather forecasts, traffic bulletins or news flashes and few programme trails. There are hardly any time-checks – those there are occur at the beginning of programmes, never within them. Programmes are typically framed by in-house idents for the station, though again these never appear within a programme (presenters do on occasion remind the listener of the station's name). The 'radiospace' thus produced is one that is far less bounded by internal temporal and rhythmic signifiers that are familiar to us from mainstream radio. Of course, mainstream radio also includes programmes that are similarly free of such markers. These tend to be either pre-recorded programmes (where time-checks are clearly impossible) or programmes which require a dramatic unity. These tend to occur on public broadcasting services, where much of the output suggests an aesthetic or educational imperative that seeks 'immunity' from interpolations which might be considered as distractions from the material being broadcast, such as documentaries, plays and 'serious' studio discussions. A station such as Resonance FM, dispensing largely with such conventions across its range of programming, establishes – whether deliberately or not – discrete programme spaces within which the listener becomes immersed on the programme's own terms. This is not unique to Resonance FM, nor is the positioning of the listener unusual in this respect. As Hendy (2000: 116) reminds us, the listening experience is produced by two sets of positions in tension. First, radio works at both a mass and an individual level: at the same time as broadcasters seek a mass audience the act of listening may be seen as a personal, individual experience. Programming that is aimed at a mass audience is able to invite particular, individual responses: the listener is part of a wider community of listeners whilst remaining separate from that community. Second, and relatedly, whilst the listener is exposed passively to the choices made by programmers, listeners are able actively to create their own 'images', interpretations and understanding from broadcasts, involving themselves in the 'imaginative potential of the aural domain' (2000: 118) to a far greater degree than is possible with a visually oriented medium like television. The listener comes to be engaged in active participation to construct meaning: radio to this extent offers an unfinished, partial experience, to be completed (interpretatively speaking) through the act of listening. It is this imaginative activity that is able to produce in the listener both an inward motion – where the broadcast encourages cognitive-affective responses particular to each listener – and an outward motion, where the act of listening becomes a social act, connecting individual listeners to a wider, ideal audience made up of those individual responses. Whilst this may in part be achieved through the 'liveness' of radio, that is not to say that only live radio may result in this: the output of many stations combines live and pre-recorded output, after all. It is rather that the imaginative potential of the medium, when taken with its mass/individual and active/passive dimensions, 'encourages a concentration of the present' (2000: 120) through its temporariness. It is fixed only in this present, a present which Hendy terms 'fleeting, perishable, immediate' (ibid.). It may be no more fleeting than television, yet the imaginative work of the listener involved in completing and constructing what is heard invests the act of listening with more attentive urgency than that required for the act of viewing.

Is this to place too high a premium on the individual listener's creative attachment to the medium? After all, however engaged listeners might be, they are only able to respond to the range of programmes, formats and content selected by the broadcaster. Yet this very choice, taken out of the listeners' hands, can paradoxically contribute to their sense of 'ownership', to their emotional attachment to a particular station, programme or broadcaster (Crisell's 'paradox of choice'). Here lies the difference between, say, listening to recorded music on compact disc and listening to the same performance on the radio. To do the latter is to connect oneself with a wider community (which includes the station itself and the particular presenter playing the music as well as other listeners). This is particularly important for a specialist station such as Resonance FM which, through presenting musical genres that are generally ignored by other stations (or, at best, marginalised on those stations), is able to create amongst its listeners a 'conspiratorial sense of *difference*' (Hendy 2000: 121, original emphasis). And here we find another paradox. The bulk of Resonance FM's programming is concerned with music that is out of the ordinary, avant-garde and experimental, popularly considered 'difficult'; for many lovers of music, it may not even be heard as music. Such musics – contemporary 'art' music, experimental electronic music, free jazz and improvised musics, musique concrète as well as 'pure', untampered field recordings – have popularly been considered as having the status of elite, 'high' art, at least with regard to their minority audience reach. If part of the appeal of radio is that, as Hendy argues (2000: 120), it fosters a social attachment based on the listeners' need for the ' "new-yet-reassuringly-familiar" [and] cravings for predictability', then how can a station such as Resonance, with so much of its output – and, indeed, a large part of its broadcasting philosophy – based on the unfamiliar and the unpredictable, offer a reassuring space in which to create a community of listeners that will return to it, who will consider it 'theirs'? We might argue that the strangeness of the musics presented on the station is chimeric; that they are only strange to those who do not know them (just as the music of a heavy rock station might be strange to a classical music audience, and vice-versa) and that the predictability and security of such broadcasts for an audience resides in catering for the tastes of that audience. It is, quite simply, a niche station broadcasting to a niche audience. Within that framework surprises there may be, but they are not radically different from the type of surprises a heavy rock audience might encounter in listening to its niche station (a heavy rock station is not about to play Stockhausen, though it may play music from a new and unsigned heavy metal group, for example). Without denying this aspect of a niche station, it is possible to find in Resonance's programming suggestions of a more complex approach to audiences which, far from resting on fulfilling the needs of a minority audience, seeks both to challenge even that audience's notions of the 'familiar' and to offer ways into the station's output for audiences that we would not expect to be attracted to such musics. Resonance does, however, retain a schedule that is largely unchanged from week to week: listeners tuning in at a particular time on the same day of the week will, in the main, hear the same show. But during the week its day-to-day schedules demonstrate little of the programming 'logic' familiar to us from commercial or public broadcast stations. There is neither the daily slot for the same presenter found in music or talk radio, nor the daily slot for a programme strand (as in BBC Radio 4's lunchtime quiz programmes – different every day, but always a quiz).

The types of programming on Resonance differ in two broad ways. First, most of the programmes are created, produced and hosted by non-professional broadcasters. For many programme-makers and presenters the station offers a first opportunity to work in radio. In some cases, people come from long-standing backgrounds in other fields – Mike Barnes and Ed Pouncey, who both present contemporary music shows, have been contributing to the contemporary music magazine the *Wire* for a number of years. The *Wire*'s strapline 'Adventures in Modern Music' has become the title for the magazine's own weekly show, presented in rotation by its contributors. The emphasis on the *Wire* for a pool of presenters across the station suggests not favouritism, nor even lack of imagination – as the only British monthly magazine to specialise in experimental and avant-garde musics across the spectrum (including rock, hip-hop, jazz and contemporary classical), it provides not only expertise but ready access (through review copies) of music that is distributed and retailed largely beyond the high-street music store. Such programmes generally cleave to the conventions of record shows, with presenters playing records and commenting on them. Whilst there do exist spaces for programming on public service broadcasting that deals with minority or specialist audiences (BBC Radio 3, for example, airs *Mixing It*, devoted to a similar range of music covered by the *Wire*), such output is not normalised – as we have seen, it is most often broadcast late at night. Resonance uses the full range of its broadcasting schedule to present such programmes – its 'serious' contemporary music programme (*New Music on Mondays*) is broadcast at lunchtime; *Adventures in Modern Music* in a mid-evening slot. There is a distinct attempt to normalise such programming, both to attract new audiences and to demonstrate to afficionados of these genres that the station is taking their needs seriously – after all, if the station were to marginalise the very activities it claims to support, it would be failing in its aims. In some respects the station appears to cleave to aspects of mainstream scheduling, if only to subvert or at least challenge the conventions. The station's arts discussion programme, *Lewisham Arthouse Presents*, takes a format familiar to listeners of mainstream arts programming but replaces professional, 'expert' commentators with expert practitioners from the avant-garde and experimental music scenes. To encounter these unprofessionalised voices is to eavesdrop on a largely unstructured conversation – though the presenter raises questions, his role is more that of a participant – and there is little evidence of the conventional presenter-as-director who shapes discussion, determines the length of contributions and ensures turn-taking. Instead a critical discourse emerges from less formalised, more everyday talk that is rooted in and through experience.

We have already noted that Resonance departs from the general practices of news bulletins and news magazine programmes, just as it has no use for weather reports or traffic updates. It broadcasts its weekly news programme in a lunchtime slot, evidently mimicking the broadcast conventions but its news output is run by members of Indymedia Radio London (IRL). Unlike the web-based, open publishing model of Indymedia we have already encountered, the programme is produced and presented by a small number of activist-journalists. Yet something of the flavour of Indymedia's collective approach to news remains. The hour-long programme broadcasts excerpts from other English-language Indymedia radio stations across the world (Indymedia Radio London is part of the international IMC Radio Network). This weekly programme is the only broadcast output of IRL; its programmes are also available on the collective's archive (http://www.indymedia.org.uk/en/static/radio.html). Whilst presenters read from scripts, the broadcast result is far from the values of professional news radio. Scripts might be mis-read, proper names and acronyms stumbled over (the result of under-rehearsal or enthusiasm?); cues from other presenters might be missed. Whilst the programme manages to retain coherence and clarity in its content, at times the format of the show resembles the DJ 'posse' format popularised by BBC Radio DJ Steve Wright, who filled his studio with enthusiastic friends, acquaintances and hangers-on, creating a chaotic spontaneity of multiple voices, punctuating news reports with whoops, cheers and raspberries. Given Indymedia's interest in challenging hierarchies of media access and encouraging a range of voices as reporters, this is not an inappropriate model.

The use of a format more familiar from music radio to present news takes us to the second broad difference between Resonance and mainstream radio: its use of radical formats coupled with radical content. Once again, we find many of these programmes inhabiting parts of the schedule we would expect – from our experiences of commercial or public radio – to find filled by far less demanding productions. And whilst there is undoubtedly a place for experimental radio in some public service broadcasting, such events are rare and usually one-offs. The New York-based radio producer Martin Spinelli has had his work broadcast on the BBC, but Resonance is the only British station to have broadcast his extensive, sixteen-part series *Radio Radio*, a set of interviews and performances by artists working with the experimental and avant-garde potential of sound. *Radio Radio* makes use of an innovative structuring device that Spinelli terms 'voice bumpers'. These are radical reformulations of the 'music bumper' used by mainstream radio to separate items in magazine programmes; his voice bumpers both separate and link items, by providing collaged and 'treated' voices that comment both formally and through their content on the works presented. The overall structure of Spinelli's series is largely familiar, though, employing lengthy interviews interspersed with illustrative performances by the sound artists themselves. Other programmes, however, present formats quite unknown to commercial or public radio, presented by programme-makers who, unlike Spinelli, have previously had little experience of radio production. Yet, rather than these being broadcast as experimental one-offs, all are weekly programmes, often as part of an open-ended series. These experiment at the same time with presenting unusual music and with employing radical formats. Many of these – such as the *Hellebore Shew*, *Xollob Park* and *Life and Living* – are broadcast in daytime slots. The *Hellebore Shew* resembles a radio version of what in the 1980s was termed 'cassette culture' – that is, the use of audio cassette by amateur musicians recording at home to distribute their music. The *Hellebore Shew* exists for the sole purpose of presenting the latest home recordings by its presenter (one Dan Wilson), curious, lop-sided songs written and played at home. A variant of this format, the *Memorex Hour*, is a review programme that plays only such home recordings from a global range of musicians. *Xollob Park* is surely the first radio show where 'everything runs backwards', as its publicity states. For thirty minutes each week its presenter plays commercial recordings and sound collages backwards – ranging from ambient soundscapes to hit songs by the Carpenters. The aim of the programme is obscure – the presenter's comic East European accent (clearly fake) is redolent of the caricature of the 'mad professor' and thwarts any attempt to consider the programme as a serious exploration of sonic creativity. Mick Hobbs's lunchtime show *Life and Living*, despite its anodyne title, does appear to have more serious intent, though it too dispenses with any conventional format, collaging field recordings, poetic musings on the mundane and fragments of recorded songs into a unfocused kaleidoscope that seems to capture both the banalities and the surprises of everyday life. In their different ways programmes such as these may be placed in the history of avant-garde radio, a history as long as the history of radio broadcasting itself. As Shingler (2000: 198) argues, we may think of such experiments as avant-garde to the extent in which they 'reject traditional and conventional sound broadcasting practices . . . are iconoclastic and set out to challenge, disturb, shock, and unsettle their audience.'

It is too simplistic, though, to evaluate a station such as Resonance as one which has broken all the rules of broadcasting. Judged from the safe, predictable perspective of mainstream radio this is tempting, yet a closer examination of Resonance FM's output suggests more subtle transformations and at times a style of scheduling that is not as radically removed from the mainstream as might first appear. Listeners tuning into the station for the first time during the daytime might well hear music, poetry or discussion that is quite unfamiliar to them. The differences between these 'unknown' patterns of programming and those broadcast late at night might appear negligible. The station does, however, seem to negotiate its scheduling with a much finer focus than the tyro listener might hear. The conditions of its licence bring a duty to the station to produce programmes not only for the 'taste communities' that make up its London audience – it must also provide community radio programming. Its magazine programme for senior citizens (*Calling All Pensioners*) might be uncharitably thought of as a necessary sop to the regulatory authority – by commissioning a programme that is so out of character with the station's self-description as an 'art station', Resonance is able to demonstrate audience reach beyond the minority that is its primary target audience. With its blend of information, advice and light music the programme resembles a community radio version of a long-running BBC radio programme for older listeners. First hosted by Charlie Chester and more recently by Ed Stewart, the eponymous Radio 2 show is broadcast on Sunday afternoons, a slot long identified as appropriate to 'easy listening'. Interestingly, while two editions of *Calling All Pensioners* are broadcast on weekday afternoons, its omnibus edition is reserved for Sunday afternoons. Yet even here there is departure from its mainstream model. Each programme is punctuated by a 'rant' from an activist pensioner (Harry Haward of the Deptford Action Group for the Elderly) which, in its blend of populist rhetoric and radical politics, inhabits a territory never approached by Chester or Stewart. Other programmes are aimed at cultural diasporas and are broadcast in the native languages of those diasporas: *Middle East Forum* in Arabic, *Zerbian Radio Slot* in Serbian.

In Resonance we see two simultaneous movements: towards specialisation in its adventurous music programming and experiments with format; and towards inclusiveness through its various community programme strands. The station works to attract a number of specialist or special-interest audiences (its music programming is not only concerned with the avant-garde and the experimental: it airs programmes of reggae, hip-hop and 'indie' music). Nevertheless, it is the station's approach to music and sound art that dominates its programming and which needs to be considered its most significant contribution to radio practice. This is due in large part to the paucity of such programming on mainstream radio, but it is also importantly due to the formats and modes of presentation employed by the station. An audience for this set of minority tastes had already been established to some extent through specialist mainstream radio programmes, yet these have typically and unsurprisingly been produced and presented by professional production companies. The *Wire* has, since its founding in 1982, established itself as the leading English-language monthly (with international distribution) for such musics. Yet the opportunity to hear more than a tiny fraction of the music reviewed in its pages before purchase remains remote; releases are on small, independent labels, distributed mostly through mail-order specialists. A small number of specialist shops exist, but these are few and far between. Audiences will be unwilling to take endless risks on purchasing decisions, however passionate they might be. Resonance provides the opportunity for listeners to hear such releases in advance, listeners who constitute a global, if small, audience. Resonance as a global Internet radio station offers this possibility and is functional in this respect; it also normalises such musics through addressing a global taste community.

RESONANCE AND THE INTERNET

We have already encountered one dimension of Internet radio that suggests uniqueness: the globalising possibilities of a local broadcaster. But there is surely another, one that we have already encountered in our discussion of the position of the audience, the listener as imaginatively attending to a discrete, private experience at the same time as being part of a wider, 'imagined community'. It is this 'wireless imagination' to which Gregory Whitehead (1992: 254) surely refers when he writes of 'a double infinity, the dreamland infinity of the human nervous system oscillating with (and against) the vast ghostland of deep space'. Whitehead speaks here of a notion of radio that is intimate, hermetically closed off from public display, yet connected with a 'ghostland' of other listeners who most likely will never be known to our private listener through experience, only ever to be imagined. For Whitehead, radio's defining technological characteristic – the ability to diffuse sound through electrical signals – is no longer enough to define, even less to explain, its uniqueness: 'the material of radio art is not just sound. Radio *happens* in sound, but sound is not really what matters about radio' (Whitehead 1992: 254, original emphasis). It is the imaginative situatedness of the body in space, of the individual body in relation to countless imagined bodies: 'the bisected heart of the infinite dreamland/ ghostland . . . the radio signal as intimate but untouchable, sensually charged but technically remote' (ibid.).

Before we dismiss such claims as nothing more than romantic flights of cod psychoanalysis, let us try to ground them in the radio practices we have already met. Commercial radio is, in the end, about maximising audiences for profit. Increasingly this is effected through the segmentation of audiences, through detailed audience research that seeks to optimise the relationship between a particular audience and a particular radio format or set of programme genres or content. Audience interactivity in these cases tends to the attenuated, limited to contributions to talk radio (discussion phone-ins, advice programmes and the like); it is not interested in the development of community through the involvement of audiences as active participants in the creative or productive processes of broadcasting. By comparison, the community or micro-radio stations examined, for example, by Howley (2000) privilege this close productive relationship of audience and broadcaster, an active relationship which typifies many forms of alternative media (Atton 2002a). Public service broadcasting lies somewhere between the two, though its accountability to government to justify its funding necessitates its occupying a position closer to the commercial than the community, at least to the degree that, notwithstanding its role as an occasional broadcaster of minority programming, it is concerned with maximising audiences (the BBC's adoption of digital audio broadcasting has seen it develop in ways similar to commercial models, establishing stations that deliver programmes aimed at highly specific audiences). The potential of the Internet to maximise audiences for public service or commercial broadcasting is largely achieved through the globalisation and standardisation of established formats, resulting in predictable programming. For the micro-radio movement the Internet remains problematic; the community radio experiments described by Howley are resolutely local – the application of low-power transmitters to the desire to serve proximate, geographically situated communities. Their global reach through the Internet is therefore of limited value. A station such as Resonance FM, at least in terms of its arts programming (which does, after all, comprise the bulk of its output), appears to offers new ways of thinking about audiences.

We have become so used to our mass media as one-way channels of communication that it is hard to recall that the medium's origins were as a two-way channel of communication. Today these origins persist popularly only in specialist, point-to-point applications, both of which have their roots in military hardware: the mobile phone and the far more specialised practices of hobby or 'ham' radio. Yet in the early days of radio the German playwright Bertolt Brecht (1979/1980) saw the potential of radio as a two-way, *mass* medium. Whilst we can see Brecht's notion of two-way, public radio enacted in the political discussion programme or the radio phone-in format, these are surely much more limited realisations than those he was idealising. If it is hard to recall the two-way origins of radio, it is almost impossible to conceive a radio for the twenty-first century that could be two-way and still be a mass medium of some kind. Kahn and Whitehead (1992) have shown how around this time there were many other notions, some wildly utopian, of imagining the potential of radio (such as those in the Futurist manifesto *La Radia* of 1933). What these share is a focus on what Whitehead (1992: 252) has termed 'the *problem* of the listener' (original emphasis), that is, the problem of how to establish 'a vital relationship to an audience'. Commercial radio has failed to do this because of its focus on considering audiences as profit margins; public service broadcasting has failed to do so in its occasional experimental programming since, as Whitehead argues, it is under little pressure to deepen audience relationships (or even audience reach) by such output. It may be argued that it is in 'art radio' broadcasting 'radio art' that the potential for the deepening of such a relationship might be attempted. This form of radio is able to abandon the 'intensified commodity circulation' (Whitehead 1992: 262) that has so limited the dominant practices of radio broadcasting since the 1920s. It is also better placed to develop radio as an imaginative space than radical community radio for, however radical the latter might be in terms of audience involvement in its creation and production, its fundamentally local relevance (if not its reach) obscures the formation of a space for a wireless imagination that exists beyond the binary of local/global. Such radio art has the capacity to make the unfamiliar familiar through demotic, non-professional approaches to programme-making, as well as making the 'predictably unusual' (that is, the unusual minority taste of an existing audience who have come to expect the unexpected) even more unusual through radically upsetting the expected formats in which such experiences might take place.

The artistic avant-garde has been historically regarded as part of the modernist project, typified by an emphasis on theoreticism and rationalism. Musical modernism has been located within a cerebral, scientistic culture that is institutionally based in universities and with state backing (Born 1995: 63). By comparison, the postmodernism of experimental music, Born argues, is practice-centred and presents a small-systems approach that is largely deinstitutionalised, and politically and socially engaged. Whilst Born's concerns are with exploring the distinctions and fractures within the professional 'high art' composers and performers of the twentieth century, her analysis might be applied to a 'demotic avant-garde' of cultural production. Whilst some of Resonance's musical output is interested in an avant-garde that has its roots in modernism, the bulk of its programming deals with the postmodern experimentalism that is practised not by what we think of as contemporary classical composers, but by musicians whose histories and influences combine from a range of genres (jazz, pop music, punk, 'noise', as well as 'high art' forms). These practices exhibit an aesthetic eclecticism as well as emphasising small scale, 'amateur' approaches to technologies (such as home recording, the use of self-built or relatively cheap, mass-produced equipment, small-scale methods of production and distribution). Such methods of production are not peculiar to these forms of creativity. The short-run recording with distribution to match is neither new nor confined to post-punk 'indie' record labels – the music of composers such as John Cage was originally released on private labels with minimal distribution (arguably, though, this strategy has more in common with the limited-edition art print than with practices of popular music production). Neither are these creative methods necessarily obvious to an audience.

Through the realisation and dissemination of an unprofessionalised and normalised demotic avant-garde, Resonance's music programming reveals aspects of an unpopular, 'difficult' set of art forms as imagined and created by 'ordinary people'. Its creators are thus situated not as expert in an elitist sense; their practices are shown to be part of their everyday lives. The presentation of their work, their processes and the critical-historical bases of their creativity and production are located explicitly within their habitus. We have already encountered Bourdieu's concept of habitus in our examination of creativity (Chapter 4). In terms of artistic practice, the field of cultural production is in part determined, as we have seen, by the personal history and situation of the artists, their values, training, educational and social background, and so on. We might consider the methods of programming on Resonance as revealing this habitus, as making explicit the cultural and social backgrounds and forces that contribute to the artistic practices of the groups and individuals who present their work and their critical discourses through their programmes. (Again, there are similarities here with the approaches to postmodern journalism proposed by Fursich that we met in Chapter 2.) Translated into the realm of artistic production, we see similar strategies of revealing production processes through an emphasis on the constructedness of discourses which present multi-voiced texts. These are unfinished in two ways. First, in the sense that they provide not definitive, expert commentaries or narratives that encourage closure on a particular practice (whether artistic or critical, or both). Second, in the sense that such accounts are 'unpolished' in the way that they displace professional conventions and values in favour of liminoid interventions that highlight popular rather than elitist perspectives on artistic practice through embedding them in a demotic setting that speaks as much about the artists' or presenters' social backgrounds and cultural contexts as they do about the practices and products themselves. This is to simultaneously upset our received, dominant notions of broadcasting for both specialist and general audiences, revealing aspects of practice (technical, social, cultural, political) in ways which are at once new and unexpected, and entirely 'normal'. The globalised reach of such programming in its formats, modes of presentation and its content offers new way of communicating about radical artistic practices to existing and potential audiences. This is hardly to return to us to Brecht's original vision for radio as a politicised, two-way medium, but these radical notions of radio bear some comparison with his ideals. For, as Hartley (2000b) has pointed out, the early days of radio were densely populated by amateurs – radio hams – who were turning the technology toward their own, demotic ends. This contemporary construction of a demotic, experimental radio once again places it in the hands of amateurs who not only broadcast the object of their enthusiasms, but demonstrate through their broadcasts the social and cultural processes that underlie those enthusiasms. In the following chapter we shall explore further aspects of amateur production as we examine how fans of the marginal musics that make up this field of cultural production have constructed themselves as critics, and in so doing have the potential to re-imagine even further the two-way possibilities of communication through the Internet.

CHAPTER 6

Fan Culture and the Internet

INTRODUCTION

In Chapter 4 we explored how the Internet has been employed by musicians and fans to shift the emphasis of musical production away from corporate control towards more libertarian and collectivist ways of production and circulation. The use of open source licensing is one such attempt to encourage radical ways of making music. The discussion of Internet radio in Chapter 5 developed these issues further, demonstrating the ways in which the application of new technology to a traditional medium might prompt audiences to create their own forms of creative communication. The present chapter focuses on these audiences as fans and examines how the online fanzine has developed as a means of building and maintaining taste communities across geographic boundaries. It will develop some of the arguments made in the previous chapter through its continued emphasis on avant-garde and experimental forms of contemporary popular music. Its aim is to identify particular fanzine projects that have emerged on the Internet and to examine them in terms of their historical connections with the printed fanzine, and to assess the extent to which the online fanzine is presenting new opportunities for fan production. It will also explore the creative potential of such publications and the opportunities they offer for fans to become creative artists themselves. The shifts in attitudes towards creativity we identified at the close of Chapter 4 are not only played out in the creativity of artists and the gift economies of fans. Fans have an additional creative role themselves to play, one which is increasingly played out on the Internet through their establishment of ezines and related fan-operated sites for information and criticism. Broadly we may think of fanzines as 'cultural fora for the exchange and circulation of knowledge and the building of a cultural community' (Fiske 1992a: 44–5). They are distinguished by the amateur nature of the contributions. Editors and writers are autodidacts, obtaining and developing their knowledge through informal, non-institutional means. As we shall see, though, specialist roles may arise with fans displaying their knowledge in different domains of expertise.

THE NATURE AND PURPOSE OF FANZINES

The ezine is the electronic, Internet-based manifestation of the fanzine. The term 'fanzine' ('fan magazine') has its origins in the American science fiction magazines of the 1930s. According to Teal Triggs, the term 'fanzine' was coined by Russ Chauvenet in 1941 'to describe a mimeographed publication devoted primarily to science fiction and superhero comic enthusiasts' (Triggs 1995: 77). The early science fiction magazines brought together professional writers and fans of their writing to create and sustain a cultural community for a literary genre that was at that time largely disregarded or dismissed by elite literary groups (critics, academics and readers). As such the early science fiction magazines sustained a contemporary cultural form that was marginalised by mainstream cultural agents. This is a significant function of the fanzine that persists to the present. We see its continuation through fanzines devoted to horror films, 'B' movies, science fiction television series and in avant-garde and experimental forms of popular music. In many of these cases, however, most notably in film and television culture, the cultural forms and their products gain a wider audience. As they move to the centre of mainstream culture, for example, or as they become the focus of professional critical attention or academic study, fanzines take on a different role. Fanzines begin to celebrate aspects of the form, genre or product that are less attended to by the mainstream. As if resisting the incorporation and assimilation of their objects of desire, fanzines engage in two complementary activities. First, they focus on the accumulation and display of detailed information about a topic. Fanzines become repositories and directories. In the case of a science fiction television series, for example, this will entail the assembling of programme details: dates of transmission, plot summaries, character development, actors' names and back-

grounds, production locations, background music. In turn, such information can be transformed into knowledge about character motiva-
tion, the development of characters across episodes and series, the
relationships between characters. In effect, fans come to perform their
own detailed critiques of their chosen subjects. Such displays of
specialised knowledge are common across the range of fanzines and
conspicuously set them apart from the bulk of any mainstream critical
attention. Second, and as an extension of such activities, fans become
involved in the creative process of their favoured subject matter. Of
course, they are already creators of a kind: after all, to write, edit and
publish a fanzine is to establish oneself as media producer. But fans will
also produce their own literary texts, applying their knowledge of their
subject to write their own fictions about the characters in a series. The
'slash' fiction produced by some *Star Trek* fans goes further, writing
against the grain of the dominant character and story types of the series.
Slash fiction takes its name from the 'slash' mark in the symbol 'K/S',
which abbreviates Kirk/Spock, respectively captain and first officer in
the original *Star Trek* series. Writing against the explicitly hetero-
sexual, masculinised world of the series, the fan authors of slash fiction
imagine a *Star Trek* where Kirk and Spock are homosexual lovers,
though still engaged in the deep space adventuring familiar to viewers of
the series. Henry Jenkins's (1992) study of *Star Trek* fans identifies
another creative fan activity, that of 'filking', or the writing, performing
and recording of songs about characters and themes from the series.

This second type of fan activity is not restricted to productions that
refer only to other cultural objects. The punk fanzines of the mid to late
1970s encouraged the 'DIY' nature of music-making; if punk was to
retain its subcultural value as a music that resisted assimilation and that
could develop independently of the corporate music industry, the
argument seemed to run, then it was necessary for musicians to write,
perform, record and distribute their own work. Fanzines would run
features on recording, record pressing, printing labels and covers, and
distribution. Such information and advice would also appear on record
sleeves (the early recordings of the British group Scritti Politti listed
where recording, pressing and printing took place, with addresses and a
breakdown of costs). The aim was to popularise the music through
encouraging and enabling creativity as well as through critical engagement.

The importance of the fanzine is not exhausted by these features. For
while, as Simon Frith has noted, the fanzine may be 'the most effective

way of putting together new taste and ideological musical [or other marginal cultural] communities' (Frith 2002: 240), some fanzines are 'less concerned to create or critique a scene than to celebrate its history' (ibid.). Frith terms these 'collectors' magazines', a form of fanzine that exists primarily to preserve a past musical history. Presently, as Frith argues and my own work shows (Atton 2001b), some of the most active fanzines of this type are devoted to the progressive rock groups of the 1970s, a genre that has shown itself to be remarkably resistant to critical recuperation. (Thomas 1998, is typical of the dismissive mainstream critical response to the genre that has persisted since, as rock mythology has it, progressive rock was ousted by punk. It has, for example, enjoyed little of the favourable critical and academic attention that disco – a contemporary genre – has seen.)

It is these dimensions of fanzine activity that we will explore in a contemporary setting on the Internet. We shall look at how ezines and fan-run web sites offer opportunities for the creation, maintenance and development of taste communities for marginalised musics; how they act as locations for the celebration of specific musical histories; and how they encourage and enable the creative activities of the fans themselves in specific musical genres. It has been claimed that the use of the Internet by fans 'allows greater access to information and association for fans than was ever possible with print fanzines' (Smith 1999: 96–7). In previous chapters we have seen how, in the application of P2P and 'radiogenic' technologies fans might reorganise, redistribute and create their own independent media. Dunaway's notion of relocalisation is useful here (Dunaway 1999: 24). We might extend his notion to consider such activities not so much as the globalisation of a localised medium but as a process of translocalisation. This is especially vivid for an analysis of fan communities where taste cuts across geographic boundaries: 'such constructions of the relationship between music and place are no longer confined to the mind of the individual listener or localized groups of music enthusiasts' (Bennett 2002: 89). Bennett himself alludes to this when he refers to 'a small network of globally dispersed fans' that generates 'transnational discourses' through 'trans-local phenomena' (p. 90). These processes are especially important for 'unpopular' popular culture, for cultural forms that are marginalised historically (as is the case with progressive rock) or currently (avant-garde and experimental forms of rock music). Despite the occasional essays into such musical genres and formations by academics, such musics are distant from both the critical mainstream and from media and cultural research (only a few academic studies exist, for example, on progressive rock, primarily Macan 1997; Martin 1998; Holm-Hudson 2002). This chapter will therefore focus on these musics. It will centre on the classic exemplar of fan productivity – the fanzine – and explore how it has been transformed on the Internet, before looking at other fan-created activities in this medium.

A THEORETICAL PERSPECTIVE

We have drawn on Bourdieu's (1993) theory of the field of cultural production in previous chapters and here too we find it a useful entry into our study of fan culture and fanzines. In delineating fields of cultural production, Bourdieu identifies two poles between which agents and their activities may be positioned. Fields are to be primarily distinguished oppositionally by economy and aesthetics. At one pole, cultural activity may be considered heteronomous. In other words, cultural production takes place in a 'mixed' context that brings together a variety of cultural determinants, namely an emphasis on large-scale means of production and economics and cultural worth judged by public success: in short, a commercial, professionalised pole of activity. In opposition, there is what Bourdieu terms an autonomous pole of production, focused on small-scale, artisanal methods and populated largely by autodidacts. Success here is gauged by the aesthetic con-sensus of a compact set of artists and critics, not by large-scale, public acclaim. The cultural production of fans can generally be seen to constitute a 'semi-autonomous' field between these two poles. At one level, its authors and creators are autonomous in Bourdieu's sense. They exhibit non-professionalised characteristics in their media activ-ities: they will tend to have no formal education or training in media production, nor formal education in the subject matter of their produc-tion, unlike, say, the art critic with a degree in art history. They will be largely self-taught and interested in producing a fanzine not for commercial gain or for wide public recognition, but in order to participate in a specialised community of like-minded individuals. Some fans and their fanzines will inhabit this pole exclusively, as is the case with specialised, minority musical genres such as free im-provisation or 'avant-rock'. Such genres also tend to establish close relations between fan and artist: here we find most music of these genres released on musician-run or fan-run record labels, distributed by fans and reviewed by fans in specialist publications. Where fanzines deal with artists who enjoy far greater popularity (at least in terms of their fan base, if not of mainstream critical acclaim), we can consider the field as 'semi-autonomous'. For example, to produce a fanzine about an artist who records for a major label is to engage with the large-scale economic activities of the record industry. In this case, fans and their fanzines might be thought of as working in a field that is similar to what Gudmundsson et al. (2002: 42) have termed the 'semi-autonomous field of rock journalism'. But there are differences. Gudmundsson et al.'s focus is on the professional rock journalists who, despite their status as autodidacts, are professionally implicated in the activities of the music industry, its public relations mechanisms and their own contracts of employment. Yet similarities remain, not only in the self-taught status of fans and rock journalists, but in their similar habitus, and in a continuing desire to resist legitimation by the musical orthodoxy (a difficult proposition for the rock journalist who must work within economic orthodoxies at least, to have any likelihood of professional success). Progressive rock fanzines complicate this bi-polar formation. Whilst they deal with large-scale, commercially produced products (and we should remember that in its heyday in the first half of the 1970s, progressive rock albums regularly reached the top ten in album charts in the US and across Europe), the scale of production presently enjoyed by such artists is often much smaller-scale. A group that was signed to a major label in the 1970s might well now release its music on its own label or, in some cases, on labels run by fans (Atton 2001b). We must bear these differences in mind when we turn to specific cases. Bourdieu's field of production offers us ways to structure these cases and to analyse them in terms of cultural agents (fans), their creative acts (fanzines and so on) and their relation to other cultural and economic forces at work.

PROGRESSIVE ROCK ON THE WEB

My earlier study of progressive rock fanzines has shown the extent to which they are used to celebrate and to revalidate a musical genre that once enjoyed great critical and popular acclaim, but which is currently largely ignored by the mass audience for rock music and by its critics (Atton 2001b). Our first example of a web-based fanzine, however, demonstrates that contemporary fan activities need not only look to the past. Elephant Talk is a web site dedicated to the music of the rock group King Crimson, its leader Robert Fripp and his musical associates. Whilst Fripp himself would cavil at King Crimson being considered a progressive rock group (to be placed alongside such groups as Emerson, Lake and Palmer (ELP), Genesis and Yes), fans, critics and academics have all placed the group's music in that category. Elephant Talk, though, does not simply deal with a defunct group, since King Crimson has had an interrupted but continuing performing and recording career from its founding in 1969 to the present. Additionally, the site does not simply celebrate the group's music through commentary and critique, it also offers fans the opportunity to recreate the group's music for themselves. Already, then, we see how the distinct characteristics of fanzine activity (as historical record, as promoting a marginalised present, as encouraging musical creativity) are combined in a single fan site. This is not a unique feature of web fanzines; print fanzines too have often blended these three features. The punk fanzine might just as comfortably have published articles on current groups, offered advice for aspiring musicians and addressed history, at least to the extent that it might feature artists considered as precursors of punk (such as Iggy and the Stooges and the Velvet Underground). What the web fanzine (or ezine) is able to do is present these strands as distinct endeavours that occupy discrete spaces on a website and to present each one cumulatively and integratedly.

One such feature concerns the practical, musical opportunities presented by sites for fans who want to perform the music of their favoured artists. Elephant Talk, in common with many fan sites, collects together such musical materials provided by the fans themselves. These are in the form of guitar tablature versions of the music recorded by King Crimson. Guitar tablature is an extension of the 'chord box' system of guitar notation. In place of the conventional five-line stave, tablature is written on six parallel lines, each line representing a string of a six-string guitar. A note is represented by a number, indicating which fret to finger. Guitar tablature is an important element in amateur music-making, particularly for rock musicians who wish to learn recorded music. Rock culture is largely populated by musicians (both amateur and professional) who have little or no formal musical training and for whom conventional, stave-based musical notation has little meaning. Guitar tablature presents the music as a representation of the physical act of music-making. It does not require an ability to translate the abstract system of conventional notation; instead, it is used in conjunction with the listening experience to construct the guitar parts. This is especially valuable for fans of progressive rock, where the complexity of the musical form would, even were it to exist in standard notation, be forbiddingly difficult. Phrasing, tempo dynamics and timbre may be learned from the recording and combined with the mechanical instructions in the tablature. Thus does the use of tablature bring together the oral, demotic approach to rock music and the complex, 'art music' basis of the composition. In this case the fan acts as both musical scribe and musical interpreter. Again, though, such methods are not unique to the Internet; the circulation of fan-produced tablature was already established in print fanzines. What is different, though, is the ease with which these transcriptions may be circulated amongst an international taste community. Further, the archiving of all submitted transcripts offers fan musicians the opportunity to compare their various attempts – where the printed fanzine would offer only restricted space to such transcriptions (after all, the fanzine has many other functions), the online database encourages comparison and critique – there may be a number of versions of a song presented, and their relative merits discussed. Rather than these disrupting what some fanzine editors might see as their 'core business' (discographies, reviews, comments and criticism of artists' work), a dedicated 'department' for transcriptions in an online fanzine does not prevent the non-musician fan from conducting their 'business'. Interestingly, in the case of Elephant Talk, this business does not extend to formal musical criticism, indeed, it is explicitly discouraged on the site. The site's FAQ section lists types of posts that are unlikely to be published in the site's newsletter, amongst which are 'posts drenched heavily in music theory' (www.elephant-talk.com; follow link to FAQ). This points to an inclusivity that appears at odds with the dominant critical reception of progressive rock in the rock press, namely, that it is an inauthentic, elitist form of music-making only enjoyed by a white, middle-class, well-educated section of Western society for intellectual rather than sensual/corporeal purposes. By contrast, discussions of the music on Elephant Talk, as is common in other progressive rock fanzines, are largely conducted using an affective discourse similar to that of its proximate 'parent' form, rock music, whereas the bulk of academic writing on the music of progressive rock still seeks to legitimate the music through the application of formal musical analysis (for example, in the studies presented in Holm-Hudson 2002 and Macan 1997). Such studies have their parallels in some progressive rock fan writing, such as the presentation and analysis of the music of Gentle Giant in the fanzine *Proclamation*, where standard musical notation is used to demonstrate the intricacy and complexity – and thus the artistic merit – of the group's use of medieval and renaissance musical forms. Elephant Talk's prohibition of this type of analysis, along with its promotion of guitar tablature, suggests the establishment of a community that privileges the autodidact, the demotic and the amateur rooted in a culture of rock music that, for all its musical differences (and there are many, not least of which is subcultural significance), is closer in outlook to the fan activity of, say, punk than to that of 'serious', high-art music.

This strain of self-taught, amateur music-making also appears in web sites devoted to more experimental forms of music-making. Experimental Musical Instruments (www.windworld.com/emi/home.htm) continues the work of a now-defunct magazine of the same name and is dedicated to the amateur activity of the design and construction of new musical instruments, employing unusual or unique forms of tuning and sound production (acoustic and electronic). The site contains advice, ideas and guidance for tools, materials and plans for building such instruments. Other sites emphasise the use of commercially produced equipment for the creation of music in experimental or avant-garde genres such as 'noise'. This term signifies a type of music that has its roots in the 'industrial' rock music scene of the 1980s, deriving from the music of groups such as Einsturzende Neubaten and Throbbing Gristle. Despite their various approaches, groups such as these privileged sound over song, in which the use of noise (unpitched, timbrally complex sounds) was integrated into the fabric of the composition or performance, rather than used for colouristic effect. In both recording and performance improvisation plays a substantial part, though this is often related to a repetitive and forceful rhythmic pattern and/or large-scale developmental structure. Perhaps in part because of its apparent abandonment of conventional musical skill, 'noise' music has become a popular genre for amateur music-making – perhaps the most popular genre out of all those we might characterise as avant-garde and experimental rock. On the Internet we find a very different approach to fan-based music-making from that of Elephant Talk's tablature archive. This is due to the unrepeatability of the recorded music; since it is improvised with ad hoc assemblages of electronic equipment that is unspecified on record sleeves or in interviews, the fan-musician will be unable to reproduce the piece as heard. Nor is this the point: amateur 'noise' music is not about reproduction, it is about original creation within a set of genre rules. These rules focus not on the note-to-note or event-to-event development of a piece, but simultaneously on broader, structural concerns (what the piece 'does' as a whole) and narrower concerns about sound sources (how to make sounds that 'fit' the rules). The former may be learned orally, the latter only through practical experimentation. The aspiring amateur musician must therefore attempt to open the 'black box' of sound processing technology in order to identify the function of various electronic devices, what they are and how they perform. A site such as Harshnoise.com is dedicated to reviews of the electronic equipment used in such musics. The reviews emphasise technical details and, importantly, the suitability of the equipment for 'noisicians'. Technical details are crucial; after all, these instruments are not used to play melodies and some are not even instruments in the conventional sense (such as guitar effects pedals used as sound generators and processors). Similarly, the ezine Pinknoises (pinknoises.com) provides 'gear reviews' as part of its wider remit as an information resource for women working in electronic music. Superficially such sites resemble the equipment reviews that abound in news stand magazines devoted to home recording and DJ-ing or, much earlier, the technical reviews that once made up a significant part of the British music weekly *Melody Maker*. In both cases we see a blurring of amateur and semi-professional musicians as audiences for such writing, though the commercial magazines will always be written by professional journalists/users. In the case of Harshnoise, not only are the reviews all written by musicians firmly outside the profession (largely a function of the unpopularity of the genre itself), the make-up of the site encourages and establishes multiple reviews of the same product. This provides a valuable comparative service to readers, all of whom are free to add their own reviews and comments. When choosing equipment for purchase the availability of multiple assessments is an evident advantage, but it is not the only form of multiple perspective to emerge from fanzines on the web. Some forms are of less obvious value, such as the multiple reviews of the same concert which is a particular feature of progressive rock sites (though not restricted to them). Groups such as ELP, King Crimson and Yes tour only rarely; it is as if the opportunity to write about one's favoured group in live performance is so constrained that the webzine editor is content to offer unlimited scope for reviews. Such reviews quickly lead to redundancy and repetition, however. The typical fan review focuses on the informational (what songs were played in what order with what changes) and the critical (mostly affective rather than argumentative). The function of such multiple 'scene writing' (as Andy Bennett has usefully labelled these activities; Bennett 2002: 93) appears less as a set of critical essays, more as a valorisation of the individual fan's taste and their place in the translocal community devoted to their taste. Elsewhere, multiple scene writing is more comparable to the production and development of a distinct body of knowledge around that taste.

THE FANZINE AS ENCYCLOPAEDIA

It is through the production of encyclopaedia-like bodies of knowledge that fans most conspicuously situate themselves as collectors and experts. The discographical function of fans and their publications is crucial for genres that are generally under-represented in the standard, commercially produced works. Even in the semi-autonomous fields of contemporary jazz and rock criticism, the commercial pressures for success in the marketplace will prevent the appearance of specialist works such as these. The discography is a key aspect of the historical work of the fanzine. This will include both official and unofficial (bootleg) releases. It might also include releases beyond the primary territories of the UK and the US, particularly where these releases differ from the 'originals' (perhaps in track listings or cover design). The discography is not a once-and-for-all task, nor, in the case of fan-produced discographies, is it the work of a single hand. As a continuing archaeological exercise, then, the electronic database housed on a web site has distinct advantages over the printed, serial form. Information may be updated and corrected easily – additional features such as cover illustrations, music samples and links to lyrics may be added without disturbing the integrity of the core discography. The periodicity of the printed discography – just like that of the printed fanzine – is overcome and with it economic decisions about the frequency of reprints and the efforts of distribution and sales. Such considerations are particularly important for publications working in an autonomous field of cultural production; the money may simply not be there for a subsequent edition of a discography in print. The investigative work of fans can be as careful and as detailed as that of a professional historian, with a consequent increase in the information coming to light. Philippe Renaud's independently published *Discographie du Jazz Anglais* (Renaud 1985) more than doubled its length for its second edition (Renaud

1995). By this time it was focusing as much on free improvisation as on jazz, which had seen a great explosion of releases since the first edition. Whilst the music continues to be produced in large quantities, there has been no third edition. Instead, Peter Stubley, a librarian at Sheffield University, England and a long-time fan of free improvisation, has developed one aspect of Renaud's discographies on his European Free Improvisation Home Page (www.shef.ac.uk/misc/rec/ps/efi/efhome. html). Stubley also draws explicitly on the work of other fan discographers; he thanks Richard Shapiro for 'allowing me to mount his marvellous Derek Bailey discography on this site'. It appears that much of the material that comprises this detailed site – artist and record company discographies, news about tours and new releases – comes from both the specialist press in Europe and significantly from the musicians and their record companies (which are very often run by the musicians themselves). The discography is not merely a matter of archaeology, but of laying down the present for the future.

Fan sites like Elephant Talk and the European Free Improvisation Home Page can be thought of as encyclopaedias. They bring together the range of 'departments' familiar to us from the printed fanzine – record and concert reviews, analysis and discussion, discographies and other information, musical materials and so on – but are able to arrange them in parallel and update them as necessary, whilst preserving their original arrangement. Some fan web sites operate explicitly as encyclopaedias. The Gibraltar Encyclopedia of Progressive Rock (www.gepr.net) does include an occasional webzine (produced roughly once a year) but its major function is as a multi-authored encyclopedia. All entries are written by fans and each is prefaced with a discography. Whilst the site does include articles on the better-known progressive rock groups, its general editor (Fred Trafton) stresses that its aim is to act as a guide to those fans who 'are looking for new territory to explore'. Its hundreds of entries organise groups and individual musicians alphabetically into short articles that cover the genre from its earliest days to the present. The site's home page lists over 100 contributors, and the collective nature of the enterprise is emphasised by the multiple entries that appear for many artists. Based in the US, Gibraltar draws on the scene writing of fans across the Americas and Europe. The result is an ever-growing and self-reflexive set of commentaries and critiques which goes well beyond the coverage accorded such artists in commercially available rock encyclopaedias; in the majority of cases we will find no entries for these groups in any 'standard' reference work – Gibraltar thus becomes the standard work.

MUSICIANS AND FANZINES

Musical styles and genres that do not enjoy mass popular or commercial success are not supported by fans alone. We also find musicians involved in the production and writing of fanzines, or fanzine-like publications. These can be seen as developments of the musician-run record labels we find in a range of genres, including avant-garde jazz (the American composer and band leader Sun Ra's Saturn label), improvised music (Incus, Matchless) and electronic music (Discus, Metamkine). The compact cultural communities that form around such specialist genres encourage close links between musicians and fans. In part, this is to do with identifying and retaining audiences. The minority status of such musicians makes it impossible for them to obtain recording contracts with major labels. Most often, ideological positions are taken about production and circulation of the music that finds musicians deliberately eschewing such relationships with the commercial record industry (even if such relationships were possible). The alternative is to set up their own record labels. The difficulties in distributing their music through mainstream channels that would place their recordings in the high street compel them to establish links with specialist forms of distribution, for example, through fan-run specialist shops and mail-order outlets and, significantly, through stalls at concerts. Such strategies establish close working relationships between fans and musicians, both of whom come to work in the record industry on a small-scale, amateur basis. It is therefore no surprise that some musicians will also come to take an active part in the production of publications dedicated to their field of music-making.

Fans and musicians sharing the cultural space of a marginal musical genre such as free improvisation provides fans with access to discographical and other information that would otherwise be difficult to obtain. This shared interest in maintaining a specific musical scene can also lead to fanzines gaining access to musicians as interviewees that might often be more fruitful than the access obtained by professional rock journalists through an artist's record label or public relations company. The long interviews that appear in a webzine such as Opprobium (www.info.net.nz/opprobium/html/online/) are made possible by such close relationships and by the open-ended nature of web space, enabling interviews to be conducted and published that would be impossible in a printed publication. The British fanzine Rubberneck (www.btinternet.com/~rubberneck/) moved to web-only publishing after fourteen years as a printed publication. Its broad remit (like the *Wire*, it encompasses improvised musics, avant-rock and contemporary classical composition) enables it to give much more detailed coverage than its print predecessor. Furthermore, its frequency as a print publication was constrained by economics: the magazine was funded through advertising obtained from some of the specialist labels releasing the music it reviewed. Given the generally small-scale nature of these labels, advertising revenue was neither lucrative nor regular; as a print publication *Rubberneck* averaged two issues each year. Distribution was a further restricting factor. The editor (Chris Blackford) was committed to making the magazine available free of charge which, along with its specialist nature, limited its attractiveness to retailers. Consequently it tended to be found only in a handful of specialist record shops and at concerts, mostly in the UK (despite its international coverage). To move to the web was for Blackford a way of addressing these problems of funding, distribution and frequency. It is now even more engaged in what is one of the classic strategies of alternative publishing, that of 'self-exploited' labour (Comedia 1984). As with most, and probably all, fanzines, Rubberneck continues to rely on the unpaid work of its reviewers who write out of commitment and enthusiasm to their chosen musics, with only the promise of free review copies of records as material reward. The web-based Rubberneck also exploits the editor's own access to the Internet and his ability and willingness to pay for its commercially obtained web space. Such access to technical resources is increasingly a given in ezine publication and goes some way to explain the dominance of affluent, middle-class editors and writers across a range of ezines.

Rubberneck also displays a further co-dependence between fans and musicians, here translated into the active participation of musicians as writers themselves, through a desire to comment on – and thereby promote – the music they practise. This has a history that predates the Internet – magazines like the *Wire* and *Resonance* (the house publication of the London Musicians' Collective) in the UK, both specialising in a wide range of avant-garde and experimental musics, continue to employ musicians as well as fans as freelance reviewers. The appearance of musicians as reviewers is most conspicuous in these genres, whereas in the case of progressive rock they hardly appear at all except as interviewees. Here the boundaries between musician and fan are more tightly drawn, a function of the status of the artist as expert in a distinct field, that of music-making. It is within the music that the artist will essay ideological claims about the importance of that music, where the aesthetic, political or social values of the music are displayed. This has as much to do with the established history and contemporary cultural invisibility of the music as it has to do with the musicians' judgement of their music to express those values in its performance. Despite the dominant historical assessment of progressive rock as a genre displaying 'inauthentic' or aberrant features that set it apart from 'rock 'n' roll' (as argued, for example, in the critical writings of Lester Bangs and Robert Christgau), its musical vocabulary and syntax are firmly enough based in rock to need no cultural explanation from the musicians themselves. Neither do fans appear to engage in such claims. As such, the scene writing of progressive rock fans tends to inhabit the sub-category of fanzines that Simon Frith identifies, in his typology of fanzines, as collectors' magazines (Frith 2002: 240–1). By contrast, freely improvised music has developed from a much broader range of musical genres (such as jazz, electronic music, rock and contemporary classical music) and, as some commentators have argued, might also be seen as forming a genre of its own that is distinct from other forms of improvisation, what free-improvising guitarist Derek Bailey has termed 'non-idiomatic improvisation' (Bailey 1980: 4). In addition, many free improvising musicians argue for the social and political significance of this practice, emphasising aspects such as the collectivity and spontaneity, and finding in such creative practices analogues with radically democratic forms of social and political organisation (for example, many musicians interviewed for Atton 1988/1989).These concerns result in publications written and produced by fans and musicians who are primarily prompted by the ideological value of the music – what Frith terms 'ideological magazines', which 'champion a particular sort of music in terms of its supposed political or social meaning' (Frith 2002: 240). Such ideological magazines are rare on the web. They are greatly outnumbered by the profusion of collectors' magazines, those publications which, as Frith has it, 'are less concerned to create or critique a scene than to celebrate its history' (p. 241). This is an important distinction. The two types of fanzines (the collectors' and the ideological) do share certain characteristics. They are both, inevitably, focused on the fan as producer and reader; across the genres discussed in this chapter they both emphasise the culturally and commercially marginal; they also share some common materials (discography, reviews, interviews). They differ, though, on how these relationships and materials are used. The collective work of the collectors' fanzines focuses on the informational and is interested in building up specialist knowledge for its own sake; we might think of the virtuosic display of the knowledge of the progressive rock fan as a parallel to the musical virtuosity of the progressive rock musician. The ideological fanzine puts such information at the service of broader claims for the music, as is the case with the improvised music fanzine.

Though not strictly a fanzine, we may find in the musician-run web site a coming together of the concerns of the collectors' magazine and those of the ideological, along with an attempt to create a commercial space outside the mainstream record markets. Discipline Global Mobile (DGM) is a record label set up by Robert Fripp initially to release recordings made by him and his colleagues which they were unable to release through major record labels. But DGM very soon became more than simply a record label – it offered a 'fan club' of sorts, in the shape of the King Crimson Collectors' Club, which offered to its members 'exclusive' recordings of unreleased studio and live performance by the group. It promotes these releases at invitation-only events in the US and the UK, as well as acting as an information point for news about forthcoming tours and releases. Most significantly, perhaps, DGM presented itself as a radical way of doing business, 'to be a model of ethical business in an industry founded on exploitation, oiled by deceit, riven with theft and fueled by greed' (Discipline Global Mobile 1997: 60). It also broke with the conventions of major record labels by offering distribution-only contracts to its artists – artists retained copyright in their work as well as responsibility for promoting their work through tours and interviews. For a number of years the site featured a regular personal diary written by Robert Fripp, which engaged in his life as a professional musician and offered insights into the operations and development of DGM and its relationship to the wider, commercial musical world. The DGM site shares many of the functions of the fan site – detailed information on an artist's activities, the establishment of a specialist cultural community through participation in a 'club' – though in the end the site emphasises consumption over participation. Fripp himself is careful to separate the site from fanzine sites, at the same time as he recognises the value of both in the cultural community of fans and musicians.

CONCLUSION

As we have seen, we do not find in the use of the Internet by fans an entirely novel form of cultural production. It is not accurate to talk of 'virtual scenes' as if what preceded them was a physical, geographic community. Audiences for all the specialist genres discussed in this chapter have always been spatially fragmented and (save for the progressive rock audience in the 1970s heyday of the genre) small minorities in specific geographic areas. The task of the fanzine – before and after the arrival of the Internet – has always been to sustain these minority taste communities. The problem for both audience and publication has been to identify each other through whatever means were available. Fan networks based on written correspondence, tape swapping and occasional meetings at concerts were able to sustain small-scale, national and international fanzine publishing. The use of the Internet by fans whose privileged social status enables them to develop and maintain these networks electronically brings with it two counterposing forces. The first is the opportunity that the Internet offers for collaboration on a far wider scale (geographically and numerically) than was previously possible – the Gibraltar Encyclopedia of Progressive Rock would have been impossible before the Internet, if only conceived as a serial publication. The second works against this. The facility of the Internet as a self-publishing mechanism fragments the efforts of individuals and groups into more numerous projects, potentially not only diluting the pool of available contributors for large-scale projects but also complicating fans' access to information and knowledge through a profusion of sites and links. At times this fragmentation is resisted or even turned to an advantage by the stratification of fan activities within a chosen genre. Pete Stubley's European Free Improvisation site is primarily a directory; its secondary function as a selected archive of interviews with musicians generates no new material, instead it collects together previously published work. Opprobrium's long interviews feature musicians familiar to readers of the *Wire*, but Opprobrium places the interviewee at the centre by reducing the interviewers' role to question formulator and stenographer (rather than critic) and presenting the interview as a complete transcript of the encounter.

Whatever the specific focus of a fanzine, whatever its aims or strategies, the primary characteristic of this form of self-publishing is its ability to bring together an ideally unrestricted range and number of voices in conversation, 'a democratic conversation between music lovers, a social celebration of a particular kind of musical attention and commitment' (Frith 2002: 241). These various fan voices share a common root in that they are autodidacts; they build knowledge not through formal educational structures but through direct and personal engagement with the objects of their desire. Expertise and cultural capital are further developed through the circulation of that knowledge within a like-minded community. As we have seen, however, it is possible to distinguish particular kinds of 'attention and commitment' across even the limited range of specialist fanzines discussed in this chapter. Our examples have shown how stratified the nature of the fanzine can be and how discrete the various forms of knowledge appear whether concerned with collecting, ideological matters or musical practice. Yet there is hybridity here. As we have seen, a web site like Elephant Talk demonstrates its hybridity in two ways. First, it combines different kinds of fanzine, bringing together the typical concerns of the collectors' magazine at the same time as it presents materials to enable fans to reproduce an artist's music through their own performances. Second, its function as this hybrid 'super fanzine' makes use of particular web-based technologies such as hyperlinking and seamless updating to create a publication that is not determined by the periodicity of the printed fanzine and the limits that places on opportunities for integrated and cumulative comment, criticism and information. And, as in the case of Stubley's European Free Improvisation site and Gibraltar, this results in a regularly updated encyclopaedia-like publication. Arguably it is through the use of the web for focused projects such as those discussed here that fanzine publishing will not only continue to flourish, it will continue in complementary and creative ways.

Conclusion

In their study of online fanzines produced by women, Cresser, Gunn and Balme (2001: 470) state that ezines represent '[a] unique medium for communication'. The ezines examined in the previous chapter have shown us that to make such a bold statement is not only dangerously iconoclastic, it is far from accurate. We have seen the powerful historical links that persist between the printed fanzine and its electronic successor (though that is not to say that the latter has usurped the former – there remain large numbers of printed fanzines). Whilst, as we have seen, communication between fans may have been ameliorated through the Internet, it is mistaken to think that the formation of an international taste community was impossible or unsustainable before the Internet. As both the previous chapter and Chapter 4 have shown, international networks of fans have long histories. It is to some extent a matter of degree – the use of the Internet as an occasion for the construction and development of alternative media has multiple outcomes. Alternative media producers might simply seek to replicate the media forms and relationships abiding in print – for example, the fanzine or the radical journalism site as a space for the presentation and discussion of particular forms of knowledge. They might seek to extend those forms and employ the Internet's capacity for 'interaction' to accelerate political organising. Web space might be used as an occasion to challenge the limits of print periodical publishing, as we have seen in examples as diverse as the open publishing strategies of Indymedia and the Gibraltar Encyclopedia of Progressive Rock. In seeking to solve technical and economic problems such as these, however, we will find social ramifications. The opening up of media spaces to a wide range of voices – to minority or marginalised individuals and groups, to communities formed through political affiliation, geographic proximity or aesthetic preference – is the wellspring of alternative media. We have seen how social relationships might develop as a consequence of technical problem-solving. At the same time we have seen communities emerge that, whilst their activities must not be thought as determined by the Internet, have embedded radicalised notions of freedom, intellectual property rights and creativity into Internet practice. In the introduction to this book we focused on the necessity to avoid essentialising the Internet and, in particular, assuming novelty and progress within it. We saw that it was not enough simply to identify its features and characteristics as if they were unique; as we have seen, the Internet – and its application and development within alternative media projects – is a complex, hybrid and historically located medium of communication which must be examined in relation to the similarly complex, hybrid histories of alternative media practice.

The present book marks ten years of my research into alternative media and thus suggests reflections on how my thinking has developed. Reading back through this book perhaps we can see something like scepticism emerging. Or, at least, we might notice, as each chapter unfolds, an increasing movement towards normalising and incorporating the Internet into existing practices. I have felt this movement as my own work has developed. For me the present book is the conclusion to a trilogy, though it was never my intention to write such a thing. My earliest work in this field (Atton 1996b) sought to set apart alternative media, the better to distinguish and 'promote' them. The promotion of this area was necessary for two reasons. The first was practical: the audience for that work was professional librarians, to whom I hoped to introduce sources of information and knowledge perhaps unknown to them. The second was intellectual: whilst my work was hardly the first essay into this field, it was the first book-length study to have been written since John Downing's important first edition of his *Radical Media* (Downing 1984). If promotion was the prompt for this work, celebration was not. Downing's (2001) revised position did much to relocate alternative media. Rather than seeing alternative media in unproblematic, 'pure' opposition to the mainstream, Downing's revised, 'anti-binarist' approach enabled us to do two things. First, we could more carefully compare alternative media projects with each other, encouraging the development of more subtle typologies than we had seen before. At the same time this enabled us to identify and valorise projects that, for example, in Downing's earlier work, had themselves been marginalised to the point of invisibility, such as the popular cultural work of fanzines. Second, the problematicisation of this binary divide encouraged the critical analysis and presentation of methods of production and organisation that were hybrid in nature. It became possible to consider, for example, the deployment of professional values and skills in alternative media without concern for the 'ideological impurity' of the task. Indeed, it was this very impurity, the processes of contamination and confluence, that Downing's anti-binarism encouraged, and which I attempted to work through in my second book (Atton 2002a).

For some this approach might smack of relativism. There are those who seem to wish for more secure boundaries around their work. This is largely the province of scholars of 'radical media', by which I mean alternative media produced by political activists for specific political and change. Within this model, whilst cultural production might be considered, it will always be subservient to the political cause. From this position, to collapse the oppositional categories of 'radical' and 'mainstream' is to deny the oppositional nature of alternative media. But we must take care here. Some scholars, such as Clemencia Rodriguez (2000), prefer the term 'citizens' media' over 'alternative media'. Rodriguez finds in the term 'alternative' a relativising that weakens the social and political power that she hopes to find in these media. For her, 'alternative' argues for such media being subordinate to the dominant 'mainstream', in hegemonic thrall to that mainstream, but fatally compromised by its reliance on that media for its existence. Rather than setting up a counter-hegemonic set of structures and processes, 'alternative' media are structurally and culturally too enmeshed in dominant media cultures – at best they will be reactive, at worst irrelevant. By adopting the term 'citizens' media' Rodriguez hopes to gain an oppositional position for these media, one based on distinctive, independent media processes and formations. But is it possible to imagine media formations that are independent across all their features? Some may strive for commercial independence and find it in a non-profit-making organisation, but economics remain a concern. Even if labour is provided voluntarily, it is the rare media project that can obtain all its printing for free, or all its equipment. Is any media project, however radical (politically or culturally), ever independent of abiding power structures, whether manifested in the political order or in the micro-organisation of everyday life? Does the journalistic ethic of

Indymedia demonstrate a rupture with journalistic norms? We have seen that it does not, even as it suggests ways of going on within journalism.

To consider alternative media as part-response, part-iconoclast and yet as part of the mainstream (at least in terms of its shared cultural and social situation) is not to seek its co-option, recuperation, or absorption. It is, first, to avoid the ghettoisation of such media, which might just as easily lead to their fetishisation as to their marginalisation. Second it is to recognise, as I hope this book has done, that we cannot judge our place in the world according to an ideal of a set of media practices. We may want to valorise alternative media in an effort to draw attention to the creative, critical and political capacities of individuals and groups in specific cultural and historical circumstances. We must avoid, however, starting from the assumption that such media are valuable precisely because they are different or particular, or indeed because they appear to 'resist' in a way that might be appealing to our own political sensibilities. Arguably, this is the problem of OURMedia (www.our medianet.org), an international network of scholars, activists and practitioners working in alternative media. This network has adopted Rodriguez's notion of citizens' media as both banner and conceptual framework; consequently the project is already bounded by limits that exclude certain types of alternative media as 'non-political' or reactionary.

This is what I have tried increasingly to avoid as my own work has developed. My scepticism toward the remarkableness of the Internet is born from a search for analytical and historical clarity. Alternative media practices are hybrid practices that embody continuation as well as reform and rupture. Nor are they to be understood solely in relation to political activism. The movement towards normalisation I spoke of earlier is necessary if we are to grasp the actual, lived relations between alternative media practices and the world. The bridge between, of course, is made up of the media producers themselves. The cultural choices of fans most often appear to place them within the commercial, heteronomous field of popular cultural consumption. The activation of those choices through their own media production engages them for a time in actions that are autonomous. As we saw in the last chapter, fans inhabit an uneasy terrain, one which already comes with compromise and capitulation built in. It is necessary for fans to negotiate that terrain through self-produced cultural processes and artefacts that exist as a result of and alongside those produced on the fans' behalf. This strategy prevents any idealisation of fanzines as culturally 'pure'. Unfortunately, we seem to find it difficult to see the mistake in considering radical political media as pure. Perhaps through focusing more on the cultural activities of alternative media projects we can acknowledge the abiding relations and continuities across the media landscape, as well as recognising the productive value of those connections in enabling the emergence of transformed media cultures.

References

Achbar, Mark (1994), *Manufacturing Consent: Noam Chomsky and the Media*, Montreal: Black Rose Books.

Alasuutari, Pertti (1995), *Researching Culture: Qualitative Method and Cultural Studies*, London: Sage.

Alderman, John (2002), *Sonic Boom: Napster, MP3, and the New Pioneers of Music*, London: Fourth Estate.

Allan, Stuart (1999), *News Culture*, Buckingham: Open University Press.

Allen, Peter (1985), '*Socialist Worker* – paper with a purpose', *Media, Culture and Society*, 7(2): 205–32.

Ashley, Laura and Beth Olson (1998), 'Constructing reality: print media's framing of the Women's Movement, 1966–1986', *Journalism and Mass Communication Quarterly* 75(2), Summer: 263–77.

Atton, Chris (1988/89), 'Some answers to some questions about improvised music', *The Improvisor* 8, Winter 1988–9: 32–40.

Atton, Chris (1996a), 'Anarchy on the Internet: obstacles and opportunities for alternative electronic publishing', *Anarchist Studies* 4, October: 115–32.

Atton, Chris (1996b), *Alternative Literature: A Practical Guide for Librarians*, Aldershot: Gower.

Atton, Chris (2000), 'Are there alternative media after CMC?', *M/C Reviews*, 12 April; www.uq.edu.au/mc/reviews/features/politics/altmedia.html.

Atton, Chris (2001a), 'The mundane and its reproduction in alternative media', *Journal of Mundane Behavior*, 2.1, pp. 122–7, www.mundanebehavior.org/index.htm (viewed 20 November 2002).

Atton, Chris (2001b), ' "Living in the past"? Value discourses in progressive rock fanzines', *Popular Music* 20(1): 29–46.

Atton, Chris (2002a), *Alternative Media*, London: Sage.

Atton, Chris (2002b), 'News cultures and new social movements: radical journalism and the mainstream media', *Journalism Studies* 3(4): 491–505.

Atton, Chris (2003), 'Indymedia and "Enduring Freedom": an exploration of sources, perspectives and news in an alternative Internet project', in Naren Chitty, Ramona R. Rush and Mehdi Semati (eds), *Studies in Terrorism: Media Scholarship and the Enigma of Terror*, Penang: Southbound Press, pp. 147–64.

Back, Les (2002a), 'Aryans reading Adorno: cyber-culture and twenty-first century racism', *Ethnic and Racial Studies* 25(4), July: 628–51.

Back, Les, (2002b), 'When hate speaks the language of love', paper presented at Social Movement Studies Conference, London School of Economics, April 2002, unpaginated.

Bailey, Derek (1980), *Improvisation: Its Nature and Practice in Music*, Ashbourne: Moorland Publishing in association with Incus Records.

Barlow, John Perry (1993), 'The Economy of Ideas', excerpted in Negativland, *Fair Use: The Story of the Letter U and the Numeral 2*, Concord, CA: Seeland, 1995: 247–50.

Benjamin, Walter (1936/1982), 'The work of art in the age of mechanical reproduction', edited translation in Francis Frascina and Charles Harrison (eds), *Modern Art and Modernism: A Critical Anthology*, London: Paul Chapman in association with the Open University, pp. 217–20.

Bennett, Andy (2002), 'Music, media and urban mythscapes: a study of the "Canterbury Sound"', *Media, Culture and Society* 24: 87–100.

Bennett, Tony (1983), 'Texts, readers, reading formations', *The Bulletin of the Midwest Modern Language Association* 61(1): 3–17.

Bennett, Tony (1986), 'Popular culture and "the turn to Gramsci"', in Tony Bennett, Colin Mercer and Janet Woollacott (eds), *Popular Culture and Social Relations*, Milton Keynes: Open University Press, pp. xi–xix; reprinted in Oliver Boyd-Barrett and Chris Newbold (eds), *Approaches to Media*, London: Arnold, 1995, pp. 348–53. References are to the latter.

Bookchin, Murray (1986), 'A note on affinity groups', in Murray Bookchin, *Post-scarcity Anarchism*, 2nd edn, Montreal: Black Rose, pp. 243–4.

Born, Georgina (1995), *Rationalizing Culture: IRCAM, Boulez, and the Institutionalization of the Musical Avant-Garde*, Berkeley, CA: University of California Press.

Bourdieu, Pierre (1984), *Distinction: A Social Critique of the Judgement of Taste*, (trans. Richard Nice), London: Routledge & Kegan Paul.

Bourdieu, Pierre (1993), *The Field of Cultural Production: Essays on Art and Literature*, New York: Columbia University Press.

Braudel, Fernand (1980), *On History*, London: Weidenfeld and Nicolson.

Brecht, Bertolt (1979/1980), 'Radio as a means of communication: a talk on the function of radio', *Screen* 20(3/4): 24–8.

Brophy, Peter, Jenny Craven, and Shelagh Fisher, (1999), *Extremism and the Internet* (British Library Research and Innovation Report 145), Manchester: CERLIM, 1999.

Burkeman, Oliver (2002), 'Bloggers catch what *Washington Post* missed', *The Guardian*, 21 December, available at www.guardian.co.uk/usa/story/0,12271,864036,00.html (accessed May 2003).

Bybee, Carl R. (1982), 'Mobilizing information and reader involvement', *Journalism Quarterly*, 59(3): 399–405, 413.

Carey, James W. (1992), *Communication as Culture: Essays on Media and Society*, London: Routledge.

Carey, James W. (1998), 'The Internet and the end of the national communication system: uncertain predictions of an uncertain future', *Journalism and Mass Communication Quarterly*, 75.1: 28–34.

Carstensen, Jeanne (1998), 'Hey ho, we won't go: civil disobedience comes to the web',

SFGate.com, available at www.sfgate.com/technology/beat/; reproduced as part of *Electronic Disturbance Theater News* (1), 5 June, available at: amsterdam.nettime.org/Lists-Archives/nettime-l-9806/msg00012.html (accessed November 2003).

Cassel, David (2000), 'Virtual vandals: hacktivism taken to the cyberstreets', *MetroActive Cyberspace*, reproduced from *Sonoma County Independent*, 31 August–6 September, available at: www.metroactive.com/papers/sonoma/08.31.00/hackers-0035.html (accessed November 2003).

Castells, Manuel (1997), *The Information Age: Economy, Society and Culture. Volume II: The Power of Identity*, Oxford: Blackwell.

Chalaby, Jean K. (2000), 'Journalism studies in an era of transition in public communications', *Journalism: Theory, Practice and Criticism* 1(1) April: 33–9.

Chapman, Robert (1992), *Selling the Sixties: Pirates and Pop Music Radio*, London: Routledge.

Chase, Michael S. and James C. Mulvenon (2002), *You've Got Dissent! Chinese Use of the Internet and Beijing's Counter-Strategies*, Santa Monica, CA: RAND.

Chomsky, Noam (1989), *Necessary illusions: Thought Control in Democratic Societies*, London: Pluto Press.

Chomsky, Noam (1992), *Deterring Democracy*, London: Vintage.

Chomsky, Noam (1993), *Year 501: The Conquest Continues*, London: Verso.

'ChuckO' (2002), 'The sad decline of Indymedia', www.infoshop.org/inews/stories.php?story = 02/12/08/2553147.

Clement, Ellie and Charles Oppenheim (2002), 'Anarchism, alternative publishers and copyright', *Anarchist Studies* 10(1), Spring: 41–69.

Comedia (1984), 'The alternative press: The development of underdevelopment', *Media, Culture and Society*, 6: 95–102.

Cooper, Jon and Daniel M. Harrison (2001), 'The social organization of audio piracy on the Internet', *Media, Culture and Society* 23: 71–89.

Couldry, Nick (2000a), *Inside Culture*, London: Sage.

Couldry, Nick (2000b), *The Place of Media Power: Pilgrims and Witnesses of the Media Age*, London and New York: Routledge.

Couldry, Nick (2002), 'Alternative media and mediated community', paper presented at the International Association for Media and Communication Research, Barcelona, 23 July.

Couldry, Nick (2003), *Media Rituals: A Critical Approach*, London: Routledge.

Cresser, Frances, Lesley Gunn and Helen Balme (2001), 'Women's experiences of on-line e-zine publication', *Media, Culture and Society* 23: 457–73.

Crisell, Andrew (2002), 'Radio: public service, commercialism and the paradox of choice', in Adam Briggs and Paul Cobley (eds), *The Media: An Introduction*, Harlow: Longman, pp. 121–34.

Cult of the Dead Cow (2000), 'Hacktivismo', available at www.cultdeadcow.com/details.php3?listing_id = 410 (accessed November 2003).

Curran, James and Jean Seaton (1997), Power without Responsibility: The Press and Broadcasting in Britain, 5th edn, London: Routledge.

Cutler, Chris (1985), *File Under Popular: Theoretical and Critical Writings on Music*, London: November Books.

Cutler, Chris (1994), 'Plunderphonia', available at www.ccutler.com (unpaginated).

Dahlgren, Peter (1997), 'Cultural studies as a research perspective: themes and tensions', in John Corner, Philip Schlesinger and Roger Silverstone (eds), *International Media Research: A Critical Survey*, London: Routledge, pp. 48–64.

Davis, Steve (2000), 'Public journalism: The case against', *Journalism Studies* 1(4): 686–9.

Debord, Guy (1967/1983), *Society of the Spectacle*, Detroit, Michigan: Black and Red, 1983, originally published in French, Paris: Editions Buchet-Chastel, 1967.

Deleuze, Gilles and Félix Guattari (1988), *A Thousand Plateaus: Capitalism and Schizophrenia*, London: Continuum.

Denning, Dorothy (2001) 'Is cyber terror next?', New York: Social Science Research Council, available at www.ssrc.org/sept11/essays/denning.htm.

Deuze, Mark (2003), 'The Internet and its journalisms: considering the consequences of different types of newsmedia online', *New Media and Society* 5(2), June: 203–30.

Deuze, Mark and Christina Dimoudi (2002), 'Online journalists in the Netherlands: Towards a profile of a new profession', *Journalism: Theory, Practice and Criticism* 3(1): 85–100.

Discipline Global Mobile (1997), 'Business aims', reproduced in booklet accompanying King Crimson, *Epitaph* (Discipline Global Mobile compact disc DGM 9607): 60–1.

Dowmunt, Tony (1993), *Channels of Resistance: Global Television and Local Empowerment*, London: British Film Institute, in association with Channel Four.

Downing, John (1980), *The Media Machine*, London: Pluto Press.

Downing, John (1984), *Radical Media: The Political Experience of Alternative Communication*, Boston, MA: South End Press.

Downing, John (2001), *Radical Media: Rebellious Communication and Social Movements*, Thousand Oaks, CA: Sage.

Downing, John (2002), 'Independent Media Centres: A multi-local, multi-media challenge to global neo-liberalism', in Marc Raboy (ed.), *Global Media Policy in the New Millennium*, Luton: Luton University Press, pp. 215–32.

Downing, John (2003), 'Audiences and readers of alternative media: the absent lure of the virtually unknown', *Media, Culture and Society* 25(5): 625–45.

Dunaway, David King (1999), 'Digital radio production: towards an aesthetic', *New Media and Society* 1(2): 29–50.

Edgar, Andrew (1992), 'Objectivity, bias and truth', in Andrew Belsey and Ruth Chadwick (eds), *Ethical Issues in Journalism and the Media*, London: Routledge, pp. 112–219.

Eldridge, John (2000), 'The contribution of the Glasgow Media Group to the study of television and print journalism', *Journalism Studies* 1(1): 113–27.

Electrohippie Collective (2003), *Electrohippie Collective Archive: A Collection of the Information and Reports Produced by the electrohippie collective, 1999–2002*, available at www.fraw.org.uk/ehippies/index.shtml (accessed: November 2003).

Fairclough, Norman (1995), *Media Discourse*, London: Edward Arnold.

Fairclough, Norman (2001), *Language and Power*, 2nd edn, Harlow: Pearson.

Falk, Richard A. (1993), 'The making of global citizenship', in Jeremy Brecher, John Brown Childs and Jill Cutler (eds), *Global Visions: Beyond the New World Order*, Boston: South End Press, pp. 39–50.

Fiske, John (1992a), 'The cultural economy of fandom', in Lisa A. Lewis (ed.), *The Adoring Audience: Fan Culture and Popular Media*, London: Routledge, pp. 30–49.

Fiske, John (1992b), 'Cultural dtudies and the culture of everyday life', in Lawrence Grossberg, Cary Nelson, Paula A. Treichler (eds), *Cultural Studies*, New York and London: Routledge, pp. 154–73.

Fiske, John (1992c), 'British cultural studies and television', in Robert C. Allen (ed.), *Channels of Discourse, Reassembled*, 2nd edn, London: Routledge, pp. 284–326.

Ford, Tamar Villarreal and Gil Geneve (2001), 'Radical Internet use', in John Downing, *Radical Media: Rebellious Communication and Social Movements*, Thousand Oaks, CA: Sage, pp. 201–34.

Fornatale, Peter and Joshua E. Mills (1980), *Radio in the Television Age*, Woodstock, NY: Overlook.

Foucault, Michel (1980), *Power/Knowledge: Selected Interviews and Other Writings, 1972–1977*, ed. by Colin Gordon, New York: Pantheon.

Fraser, Nancy (1992), 'Rethinking the public sphere – a contribution to the critique of actually existing democracy', in Craig Calhoun (ed.), *Habermas and the Public Sphere*, Cambridge, MA and London: MIT Press, 1992, pp. 109–42.

Freeman, Jo (1972), 'The tyranny of structurelessness', *Berkeley Journal of Sociology*, 17: 151–64.

Frith, Simon (2002), 'Fragments of a sociology of rock criticism', in Steve Jones (ed.), *Pop Music and the Press*, Philadelphia, PA: Temple University Press, pp. 235–46.

Fursich, Elfriede (2002), 'How can global journalists represent the "Other"? A critical assessment of the cultural studies concept for media practice', *Journalism: Theory, Practice and Criticism* 3(1): 57–84.

Gibson, Owen (2003), 'Music industry wipes away tracks of its fears', *The Guardian Weekly* 12–18 June: 23.

Giddens, Anthony (1991/1997), 'The globalizing of modernity', in Annabelle Sreberny-Mohammadi et al. (eds), *Media in Global Context: A Reader*, London: Edward Arnold, pp. 19–26, originally published 1991.

Giordano, A. (2002), 'Ethics problems at Alternet: 'Alternative' media can be corrupted, too' (Narco News White Paper). Available at www.narconews.com/Issue21/hazenstory1.html. Unpaginated

Gitlin, Todd (1980), *The Whole World is Watching: Mass Media in the Making and Unmaking of the New Left*, Los Angeles, CA and London: University of California Press.

Glasgow University Media Group (1976), *Bad News*, London: Routledge and Kegan Paul.

Glasser, Theodore L. (2000), 'The politics of public journalism', *Journalism Studies* 1(4): 683–6.

GNU Project (1999), *What is Copyleft?*, available at www.fsf.org/copyleft/copyleft.html.

Golding, Peter (1999), 'The political and the popular: getting the measure of tabloidisation', in the Proceedings of the AMCCS Conference, Sheffield, UK, 1998, ed. by Tessa Perkins, Sheffield: Association of Media, Communication and Cultural Studies, pp. 2–18.

Gramsci, Antonio (1971), *Selections from the Prison Notebooks*, trans. Quintin Hoare and Geoffrey Nowell Smith, London: Lawrence and Wishart.

Gudmundsson, Gestur et al. (2002), 'Brit Crit: turning points in British rock criticism', in Steve Jones (ed), *Pop Music and the Press*, Philadelphia, PA: Temple University Press, pp. 41–64.

Gumucio Dagron, Alfonso (2001), *Making Waves: Stories of Participatory Communication for Social Change*, New York: Rockefeller Foundation.

Habermas, Jurgen (1992), 'Further reflections on the public sphere', in Craig Calhoun (ed.), *Habermas and the Public Sphere*, Cambridge, MA and London: MIT Press, 1992, pp. 421–61.

Hall, Stuart (1990), 'Cultural identity and diaspora', in Rutherford, J. (ed.), *Identity: Community, Culture, Difference*, London: Lawrence and Wishart, pp. 222–37.

Hamelink, Cees J. (2000), *The Ethics of Cyberspace*, London: Sage.

Hamilton, James (2003), 'Remaking media participation in early modern England', *Journalism: Theory, Practice and Criticism* 4(3): 293–313.

Hamilton, James and Chris Atton (2001), 'Theorizing Anglo-American alternative media: toward a contextual history and analysis of US and UK scholarship', *Media History* 7(2): 119–35.

Hamilton, James and Tonya Couch (2002), 'Complicating communication: revisiting and revising production/consumption', paper presented at the Association for Journalism and Mass Communication, Miami Beach, Florida, 7 August.

Harcup, Tony (2002), 'Journalists and ethics: the quest for a collective voice', *Journalism Studies* 3(1): 101–14.

Harding, Thomas (1997), *The Video Activist Handbook*, London: Pluto Press.

Harmon, Amy (2003), 'Subpoenas sent to file-sharers prompt anger and remorse', *New York Times*, 28 July, available at www.nytimes.com/auth/login?URI = http://www.nytimes.com/2003/07/28/technology/28TUNE.html.

Harris, Paul (1970), *When Pirates Ruled the Waves*, 4th edn, London and Aberdeen: Impulse.

Harrison, Charles (1991), *Essays on Art and Language*, Oxford: Basil Blackwell.

Hartley, John (2000a), 'Communicative democracy in a redactional society: the future of journalism studies', *Journalism: Theory, Practice and Criticism* 1(1) April: 39–48.

Hartley, John (2000b), 'Radiocracy: sound and citizenship', *International Journal of Cultural Studies* 3(2), August: 153–9.

Hebdige, Dick (1979), *Subculture: The Meaning of Style*, London: Routledge.

Hendy, David (2000), *Radio in the Global Age*, Cambridge: Polity Press.

Hennock, Mary (2002), 'The cost of China's Web censors', BBCi (BBC News World Edition), 23 September, available at news.bbc.co.uk/2/hi/business/2264508.stm.

Herman, Edward S. and Noam Chomsky (1994), *Manufacturing Consent: The Political Economy of the Mass Media*, London: Vintage, originally published New York: Pantheon, 1988.

Heylin, Clinton (1994), *The Great White Wonders: A History of Rock Bootlegs*, London: Viking.

Holm-Hudson, Kevin (ed.) (2002), *Progressive Rock Reconsidered*, New York and London: Routledge.

Holtzman, David (2003), 'Homeland security and you', 21 January, CNET News.com, available at news.com.com/2010-1071-981262.html.

Howley, Kevin (2000), 'Radiocracy rulz! Microradio as electronic activism', *International Journal of Cultural Studies* 3(2), August: 256–67.

Jenkins, Henry (1992), ' "Strangers no more, we sing": Filking and the construction of the science fiction fan community', in Lisa A. Lewis (ed.), *The Adoring Audience: Fan Culture and Popular Media*, London: Routledge, pp. 208–36

Jensen, Klaus Bruhn and Karl Erik Rosengren (1990), 'Five traditions in search of the audience', *European Journal of Communication*, 5.2–3: 207–38.

Jordan, John (2001), 'Zapatismo and the invisible icons of anti-capitalism', *Red Pepper*, September: 19–21.

Juhasz, Alexandra (1995), *AIDS TV: Identity, Community and Alternative Video*, London: Duke University Press.

Kahn, Douglas and Gregory Whitehead (eds), *Wireless Imagination: Sound, Radio and the Avant-garde*, Cambridge, MA and London: MIT Press.

Kahn, Richard and Douglas Kellner (2003), 'Internet subcultures and political activism', available at: www.gseis.ucla.edu/courses/ed253a/oppositionalinternet.htm (accessed May 2003).

Keeble, Richard (2001), *Ethics for Journalists*, London: Routledge.

Kellner, Douglas (1995), *Media Culture: Cultural Studies, Identity and Politics between the Modern and the Postmodern*, London: Routledge.

Kidd, Dorothy (2002), 'Which would you rather: Seattle or Porto Alegre?', paper presented at Our Media, Not Theirs II, a preconference at the International Association for Media and Communication Research, Barcelona, 20 July.

Kidd, Dorothy (2003), 'Carnival and commons: the global IMC network', paper prepared for Our Media III Conference, Barranquilla, Colombia, May (not delivered), copy in author's possession.

Kollock, Peter (1999), 'The economies of online cooperation: gifts and public goods in cyberspace', in Marc A. Smith and Peter Kollock (eds), *Communities in Cyberspace*, London: Routledge, pp. 220–39.

Korn, Alan (1992), 'Renaming that tune: audio collage, parody, and fair use', in Negativland (1995), *Fair Use: The Story of The Letter U and the Numeral 2*, Concord, CA: Seeland, pp. 221–34, reprinted from *22 Golden Gate University Law Review* 321, 1992.

Kurtz, Howard (2003), ' "Webloggers," signing on as war correspondents', *Washington Post*, 23 March: F04.

Langer, John (1998), *Tabloid Television: Popular Journalism and the 'Other News'*, London: Routledge.

Lemert, James B. and Marguerite Gemson Ashman (1983), 'Extent of mobilizing information in opinion and news magazines', *Journalism Quarterly*, 60(4): 657–62.

Library Association Record (1999a), 'The beginning of the end for filters?', *Library Association Record* 101(1), January: 7.

Library Association Record (1999b), 'Another Internet regulation bill struck down', *Library Association Record* 101(3), March: 139.

Library Association Record (1999c), 'Rapprochement over censorware?', *Library Association Record* 101(5), May: 262.

Library Association Record (2000), 'Look out – it's the Bill!', *Library Association Record* 102(5), May: 261.

McLachlan, Shelley and Peter Golding (2000), 'Tabloidization in the British press: a quantitative investigation into changes in British newspapers, 1952–1997', in Colin Sparks and John Tulloch (eds), *Tabloid Tales: Global Debates over Media Standards*, Lanham, MD and Oxford: Rowman and Littlefield, pp. 75–89.

Macan, Edward (1997), *Rocking the Classics: English Progressive Rock and the Counterculture*, New York: Oxford University Press.

Martin, Bill (1998), *Listening to the Future: The Time of Progressive Rock, 1968–1978*, Chicago and La Salle, IL: Open Court.

Matheson, Donald and Stuart Allan (2003), 'Weblogs and the war in Iraq: journalism for the network society?', paper presented at the Digital Dynamics conference, Loughborough, UK, 6–9 November.

Mattelart, Armand (2002), 'An archaeology of the global era: constructing a belief', *Media, Culture and Society* 24: 591–612.

Melucci, Alberto (1996), *Challenging Codes: Collective Action in the Information Age*, Cambridge: Cambridge University Press.

Merriden, Trevor (2001), *Irresistible Forces: The Business Legacy of Napster and the Growth of the Underground Internet*, Oxford: Capstone.

Metropolitan Police Service (1996), 'Letter from the Metropolitan Police to the UK ISPs, August 1996', available at www.cyber-rights.org/documents/themet.htm.

Morley, David (1980), The 'Nationwide' Audience: Structure and Decoding, London: British Film Institute.

Morley, Dave and Worpole, Ken (1982), The Republic of Letters: Working Class Writing and Local Publishing (Comedia/Minority Press Group Series no. 6), London: Comedia.

Morris, Meaghan (1988), 'Banality in cultural studies', Discourse: Journal for Theoretical Studies in Media and Culture, X.2, pp. 3–29, reprinted in John Storey (ed.) (1996), What is Cultural Studies? A Reader, London: Edward Arnold, pp. 147–67. References are to the latter.

Negativland (1995), Fair Use: The Story of the letter U and the Numeral 2, Concord, CA: Seeland.

Negroponte, Nicholas (1996), Being Digital, London: Hodder and Stoughton.

Oswald, John (1990), 'Taking sampling fifty times beyond the expected', in Negativland (1995), Fair Use: The Story of the Letter U and The Numeral 2, Concord, CA: Seeland, pp. 218–20.

Papacharissi, Zizi (2002), 'The virtual sphere: The Internet as a public sphere', New Media and Society 4(1): 9–27.

Platon, Sara (2002), 'Re: The sad decline of Indymedia', personal communication (email).

Platon, Sara and Mark Deuze (2003), 'Indymedia journalism: a radical way of making, selecting and sharing news?', Journalism: Theory, Practice and Criticism 4(3): 336–55.

Poster, Mark (1999), 'Underdetermination', New Media and Society 1(1): 12–17.

Preston, Paschal (2001), Reshaping Communications: Technology, Information and Social Change, London: Sage.

RAND (2002), Poor Connections: Trouble on the Internet Frontiers. Santa Monica, CA: RAND, available at www.rand.org/publications/randreview/issues/rr.12.02/connections.html.

Renaud, Philippe (1985), La Discographie du Jazz Anglais, Retonfey: Notes.

Renaud, Philippe (1995), Simply Not Cricket: Catalogue du jazz Britannique, 1964–1994, Blois: Improjazz.

Robertson, Roland (1992/1997), 'Mapping the global condition', in Annabelle Sreberny-Mohammadi et al. (eds), Media in Global Context: A Reader, London: Edward Arnold, pp. 2–10, originally published 1992.

Rodriguez, Clemencia (2001), Fissures in the Mediascape: An International Study of Citizens' Media, Cresskill, NJ: Hampton Press.

Rojas, Peter (2002), 'Pirates of peercasting', The Guardian (Online supplement), 25 July: 6.

Roscoe, Timothy (1999), 'The construction of the World Wide Web audience', Media, Culture and Society, 21: 673–84.

Said, Edward (1981), Covering Islam: How the Media and the Experts Determine How We See the Rest of the World, New York: Pantheon.

Schudson, Michael (1978), Discovering the News, New York, Basic Books.

Schudson, Michael (1978/1999), 'Discovering the news: a social history of American newspapers', in Howard Tumber (ed.), News: A Reader, Oxford: Oxford University Press, 1999, pp. 291–6.

Schudson, Michael (2001), 'The objectivity norm in American journalism', Journalism: Theory, Practice and Criticism 2(2): 149–70.

Schumacher, Thomas G. (1995), ' "This is a sampling sport": digital sampling, rap music, and the law in cultural production', *Media, Culture and Society* 17: 253–73.

Searchlight (1999), 'Griffin heads for victory', *Searchlight,* October, available at www.searchlightmagazine.com/stories/GriffinVictory.htm, unpaginated.

Searchlight (2003), 'Tyndall's last stand', *Searchlight*, August, available at www.searchlightmagazine.com/stories/082003_story03.htm, unpaginated.

Shingler, Martin (2000), 'Some recurring features of European avant-garde radio', *Journal of Radio Studies* 7(1): 196–212.

Silverstone, Roger (1999), 'What's new about new media? Introduction', *New Media and Society* 1(1): 10–12

Slater, Don and Jo Tacchi (2002), 'Modernity under construction: comparative ethnographies of Internet', paper presented at the second Study of IT workshop at the London School of Economics, 22–3 April, copy in author's possession.

Slevin, James (2000), *The Internet and Society*, Cambridge: Polity.

Smith, Matthew J. (1999), 'Strands on the Web: community-building strategies in online fanzines', *Journal of Popular Culture* 33(2), Fall: 87–99.

Sparks, Colin (1985), 'The working-class press: radical and revolutionary alternatives', *Media, Culture and Society*, 7(2), April: 133–46.

Stempel, Guido and Robert K. Stewart (2000), 'The Internet provides both opportunities and challenges for mass communication researchers', *Journalism and Mass Communication Quarterly* 77(3), Autumn: 541–8.

Sterne, Jonathan (1999), 'Thinking the Internet: cultural studies versus the millennium', in Steve Jones (ed.), *Doing Internet Research: Critical Issues and Methods for Examining the Net*, Thousand Oaks, CA and London: Sage.

Tacchi, Jo (2000), 'The need for radio theory in the digital age', *International Journal of Cultural Studies* 3(2), August: 289–98.

Terazono, Emiko (2003), 'Download sites proliferate . . .', *Financial Times* Creative Business supplement, 4 November: 9.

Terranova, Tiziana (2002), 'The degree zero of politics: virtual cultures and virtual social movements', paper presented at Our Media, Not Theirs II, a preconference at the International Association for Media and Communication Research, Barcelona, 20 July.

Thomas, David (1998), 'Oh no, it's Yes: where even irony fears to tread', *The Observer*, 9 March: 5.

Thompson, John (1984), *Studies in the Theory of Ideology*, Cambridge: Polity Press.

Toynbee, Jason (2001), *Creating Problems: Social Authorship, Copyright and the Production of Culture* (Pavis Papers in Social and Cultural Research, no. 3), Milton Keynes: Open University, Pavis Centre for Social and Cultural Research.

Traber, Michael (1985), *Alternative Journalism, Alternative Media* (Communication Resource, no. 7, October 1985), London: World Association for Christian Communication.

Triggs, Teal (1995), 'Alphabet Soup: reading British fanzines', *Visible Language* 29(1): 72–87.

Van Dijk, Teun A. (ed.) (1997), *Discourse as Structure and Process* (vol. 1), London: Sage.

van Zoonen, Elisabeth A. (1992), 'The Women's Movement and the media: constructing a public identity', *European Journal of Communication* 7: 453–76.

Walker, Jesse (2003), 'The company that spawned a movement', *Guardian Weekly* 17–23 July: 34.

Ware, Vron and Les Back (2002), *Out of Whiteness: Color, Politics and Culture*, Chicago, IL: University of Chicago Press.

Weigert, Andrew J. (1981), *Sociology of Everyday Life*, New York and London: Longman.

Wetherell, Margaret and Jonathan Potter (1992), *Mapping the Language of Racism: Discourse and the Legitimation of Exploitation*, New York and London: Harvester Wheatsheaf.

Whitehead, Gregory (1992), 'Out of the dark: notes on the nobodies of radio art', in Douglas Kahn and Gregory Whitehead (eds), *Wireless Imagination: Sound, Radio, and the Avant-garde*, Cambridge, MA and London: MIT Press.

Williams, Raymond (1980), 'Means of communication as means of production', in *Problems in Materialism and Culture: Selected Essays*, London: Verso, pp. 50–63.

Woodstock, Louise (2002), 'Public journalism's talking cure: an analysis of the movement's "Problem" and "Solution" narratives', *Journalism: Theory, Practice and Criticism* 3(1): 37–55.

Index

As the entire volume is about the Internet, the use of Internet as entry point has been minimised in this index. Titles of works are shown in *italics*.